KT-458-662

THE ENCYCLOPEDIA OF CREATIVE COOKERY

TREASURE PRESS

CONTENTS

'uddings and Desserts

'reads, Cakes and Biscuits

EFERENCE SECTION

The Authors

JACKIE BURROW
SOUPS
STARTERS
VEGETABLES AND SALADS
RICE, PASTA AND PULSES

MARY REYNOLDS
FISH
MEAT
POULTRY AND GAME
SAUCES, DRESSINGS AND SAVOURY BUTTERS

ELIZABETH SELDON
EGGS
PUDDINGS AND DESSERTS
BREADS, CAKES AND BISCUITS
PASTRIES

First published in 1980
by Sundial Books Limited
59 Grosvenor Street, London W1

Second impression, 1981

ISBN 0 906320 08 9

Printed in Hong Kong

INTRODUCTION

It is very satisfying to produce a delicious meal for the family or when entertaining friends, and ringing the changes with new recipes adds variety to meals, as well as adding to one's repertoire. There is a wide range of imaginative dishes in this book and each recipe has been thoroughly tested.

At the end of the book there is a reference section, which includes helpful hints and suggestions on each area of cooking. It serves as a useful summary of basic cooking methods, and enables you to expand or underline your culinary knowledge.

PLANNING MEALS

As food bills are always on the increase, and about a third of our income is spent on food, it is advisable to budget wisely and to plan meals at least three to four days or even a week in advance, as this will not only save on the housekeeping, but also simplify the shopping and cooking.

Planning a well-balanced meal is quite simple. The easiest way to begin is to decide on the protein of the main course, and then to choose the vegetables. The starter and/or pudding can then be chosen more easily, taking flavours, textures, and colour balance into consideration. For example, if a chicken casserole is chosen for the main course, lightly cooked broccoli, buttered carrots and jacket potatoes would add colour and texture to the meal. If a starter is to be served, a light vegetable dish such as baked stuffed tomatoes, leeks vinaigrette or a fish terrine would be most acceptable. A soup would not be a good choice for a starter as the chicken is served in a sauce.

A pastry sweet or a mousse would be a delicious end to the meal, or a cheese board ar fresh fruit could be served, which would be le fattening and more nutritious than a pudding.

If you choose to cook a grilled chop or steak you will have more time to prepare an unusua vegetable dish such as fennel in cider, courgettes provençale, fried broccoli, or Chinese stir-fried vegetables, and this would make a delicious meal.

SENSIBLE SHOPPING

Once the week's menus are planned it is alway the wisest policy to write out a shopping list. Shop in stores with a good turnover where food is fresh. The big supermarkets are probably the best value for money as they purchase in bulk and offer many items at reduced prices; beware of reductions on dent cans – the contents can easily become contaminated if not used immediately, so the are not good for long storage. Once bought, perishable foods must be stored, wrapped or covered, in the refrigerator. A cool larder is th next best storage place to the refrigerator. Mo modern homes have non-ventilated food cupboards which are of limited use.

Convenience foods tend to be expensive and is far better value nutritionally and economically to buy fresh foods in season instead. However, it is a good idea to buy some convenience foods, as a well-stocked store cupboard is useful for emergencies. Car of soup, meat, fish and fruit are good standby and a selection of sauces and dried herbs for flavouring can be stored. For freezer owners, frozen foods are usually bulk packed, so in th way there is a good stock in hand.

NTERTAINING

ntertaining at home is a pleasant way of
pending time with one's friends, and it needn't
e too expensive. It is far better to cook a
mple meal well, than cook an over-rich meal
hich is neither well-balanced nor easily
igested.

RESENTATION OF FOOD

resenting food to make it look as attractive as
ossible acts as an appetite stimulant. Both the
pe of dish which you choose and the look of
e finished food are relevant. There is a large
nge of attractive oven-to-table ware which is
ery versatile, and is well worth buying,
articularly at sale time or from 'seconds'
nges in stores. When buying such dishes, do
heck on their bases for the 'fireproof' mark if
ey are to be used on the hob. Otherwise they
n only be used in the oven. To complement
e food a simple garnish makes an otherwise
rdinary dish into something special.

ASIC EQUIPMENT

is advisable to have an electric hand mixer
d blender, a set of hard-wearing saucepans, a
nge of good quality French cook's knives,
fferent-sized basins and mixing bowls and
ooden spoons. Wooden chopping boards are
eferable to the melamine varieties, which
nd to blunt the knife edge. A grater and
mon squeezer should be included as well as a
lling pin, metal cutters and baking tins.

NOTE

1. All recipes serve four unless otherwise stated.

2. All spoon measurements are level.

3. All eggs are sizes 3, 4, 5 (standard) unless otherwise stated.

4. Preparation times given are an average calculated during recipe testing.

5. Metric and imperial measurements have been calculated separately. Use one set of measurements only as they are not exact equivalents.

6. Cooking times may vary slightly depending on the individual oven. Dishes should be placed in the centre of the oven unless otherwise specified.

7. Always preheat the oven or grill to the specified temperature.

8. Spoon measures can be bought in both imperial and metric sizes to give accurate measurement of small quantities. Use the 5 ml spoon in place of 1 teaspoon and the 15 ml spoon in place of 1 tablespoon.

MENU SUGGESTIONS

FAMILY MEALS

Winter

Asparagus and Lemon Quiche
Orange Glazed Corner of Gammon
Braised Red Cabbage
Creamed Potatoes
Pineapple Sponge Pudding and Sauce

Jerusalem Artichoke Soup
Steak, Kidney and Mushroom Pie
Carrots
Braised Leeks
Chocolate Surprise Pudding

Golden Fish Goujons
Flemish Beef in Beer
Brussels Sprouts
Potato and Leek Layer
Grapefruit Meringue Pie

Summer

Chilled Courgette and Yogurt Soup
Fish Kebabs
New Potatoes
French Beans with Almonds and Lemon
Spicy Raisin Tart

Fish Terrine
French Roast Chicken with Herb Baked Tomatoes
Mixed Vegetable Fritters
Plain Rice
Bramble Cream

General

Mushroom and Spinach Pancakes
Stifatho
French Braised Peas
Grilled Aubergines
Fresh Fruit Salad

Tuna Fish Mousse
Lamb Brodettato
Courgettes Niçoise
Tagliatelle
Barbados Bananas

ENTERTAINING

Winter

Eggs en Cocotte with Mushrooms

Stuffed Fillet of Pork en Croûte

Carrots with Yogurt and Parsley Sauce

Jerusalem Artichokes with Lemon and Herbs

Caramelized Pears with Brandy

Mushrooms and Leeks à la Grecque

Pigeons Braised with Peas

Fennel in Cider Sauce

Creamed Potatoes

Hot Orange Soufflé

Summer

Avocado Pâté

Chicken Breasts Italiana

Herb-baked Tomatoes

Spinach

Plain Rice

Glazed Cherry Flan

Consommé (chilled)

Guard of Honour with Apricot Rice

Fennel in Cider Sauce

French Beans

Strawberry Crème Caramel

Cheese and Thyme Soufflé

Turkey Portions Creole

Vegetable Pilaff

Chinese Salad

French Apple Flan

Special

Spinach and Mushroom Roulade

Duckling à l'Orange

French Braised Peas

Cauliflower Polonaise

New Potatoes

Gooseberry Soufflé

Scallops with Mushrooms and Parsley

Neopolitan Veal Rolls

Courgettes Niçoise

Broccoli

Tagliatelle

Fresh Raspberry Mousse

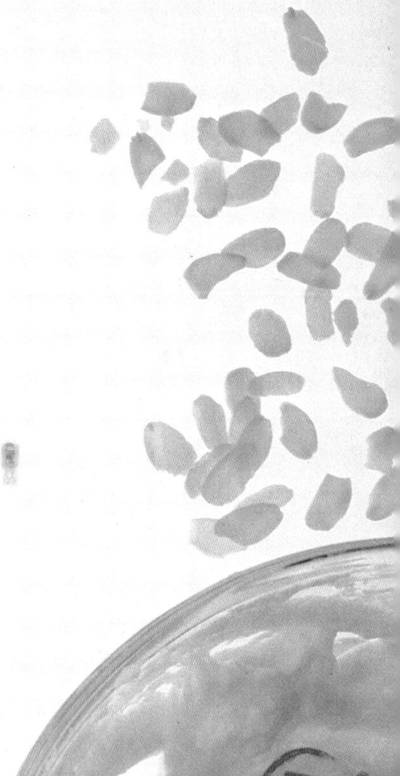

Soups

CLEAR AND SEMI-CLEAR SOUPS AND BROTHS

Consommé

Makes about 900 ml/1½ pints
Preparation time: 5 minutes
Cooking time: 40 minutes

1.2 litres/2 pints beef stock skimmed of all fat
100 g/4 oz lean beef steak, eg. chuck, trimmed of all fat, shredded
1 small onion, peeled and sliced
1 carrot, peeled and sliced
1 egg white and shell
1 bouquet garni, or bay leaf, sprig of parsley and thyme
salt
freshly ground black pepper
2 tablespoons dry sherry
To garnish:
lemon slices
chopped fresh herbs
shredded almonds

1. Pour the stock into a large saucepan and add the steak, onion and carrot. Put the egg white into a small basin, add the egg shell and crush it. Add the egg white and shell to the pan with the bouquet garni.
2. Bring to the boil, whisking all the time until a thick froth forms. As the liquid comes to the boil, stop whisking, reduce the heat and simmer gently for 30 minutes, without disturbing the froth.
3. Remove from the heat and strain through a scalded jelly bag or cloth into a bowl. If the consommé is not completely clear, strain again through the bag or cloth.
4. Adjust the seasoning and stir in the sherry.
5. Serve hot with finely shredded cooked vegetables and cooked rice or pasta, added just before serving.
6. To serve cold, chill in the refrigerator until very lightly set and garnish with slices of lemon, chopped herbs and shredded almonds.

Genoese Minestrone

Serves 4–6
Makes about 1.5 litres/2½ pints
Preparation time: 15 minutes
Cooking time: 15 minutes

1.2 litres/2 pints stock (white, chicken, or vegetable)
1 onion, peeled and chopped
1 carrot, scrubbed and diced
1 leek, sliced
1 celery stick, sliced
225 g/8 oz tomatoes, peeled and roughly chopped
50 g/2 oz pasta, broken
¼ small cabbage, shredded
50 g/2 oz shelled peas
50 g/2 oz green beans, sliced
salt
freshly ground black pepper
Garlic paste:
2 large garlic cloves, peeled and crushed
1 tablespoon chopped fresh basil or parsley
2 tablespoons grated Parmesan cheese
1 tablespoon olive oil

1. Pour the stock into a large saucepan and bring to the boil. Add the onion, carrot, leak, celery and tomatoes. Cover and simmer for 20 minutes.
2. Add the pasta, cabbage, peas and beans, salt and pepper and simmer for 15 minutes.
3. Mix together all the ingredients for the garlic paste, then stir into the soup. Simmer for 5 minutes. Serve hot.

Back: Genoese minestrone
Front: Consommé

French Onion Soup

akes about 1.2 litres / 2 pints
eparation time: 5 minutes
ooking time: 1–1¼ hours

) g / 2 oz butter or margarine
i0 g/1 lb onions, peeled and sliced
tablespoons plain flour
2 litres/2 pints stock (beef, chicken or vegetable)
bay leaf
lt
eshly ground black pepper
tablespoons brandy or sherry
slices French bread
) g/2 oz Gruyère cheese, grated

1. Melt the butter in a large saucepan and fry the onions gently for about 30 minutes, stirring frequently until evenly browned.
2. Stir in the flour and cook for 2 minutes. Add the stock, bay leaf, salt and pepper and bring to the boil. Cover and simmer for 30 minutes. Stir in the brandy or sherry and adjust the seasoning.
3. Place the bread in a soup tureen (or individual bowls) and add the soup. Sprinkle the top with grated cheese. If liked, brown the top in a hot oven or under the grill.

Scotch Broth

rves 6 as broth and 4 as a main urse and soup
akes 1.75 litres / 3 pints of broth
eparation time: 5 minutes
ooking time: 2¼ hours

0 g/1 lb scrag or middle neck of lamb
75 litres/3 pints water
lt
eshly ground black pepper
bay leaf
arge onion, peeled and chopped
arge carrot, peeled and diced
urnip, peeled and diced
eeks, sliced
g / 2 oz pearl barley
ablespoons chopped parsley, to garnish

1. Place the lamb in a large saucepan. Add the water, salt, pepper and the bay leaf. Cover, bring to the boil and simmer for 1 hour.
2. Add the vegetables and pearl barley, return to the boil and simmer, covered, for 1 hour. Skim off the fat from the surface.
3. Serve the meat with a little of the broth as a main course, and serve the remaining soup separately.
4. Alternatively, remove the meat from the broth, scrape the meat off the bones and return the shredded meat to the broth. Reheat and serve sprinkled with parsley.

Cock-a-leekie

ves: 4–6
akes: about 1.25 litres/2¼ pints
eparation time: 10 minutes
oking time: 1¼ hours

hicken quarters
litres/2 pints chicken stock or water
g/2 oz prunes, stoned and halved
ated rind and juice of ½ lemon
teaspoon ground nutmeg
ay leaf
t
shly ground black pepper
) g/12 oz leeks, sliced
ablespoons chopped fresh parsley

This is a variation on the traditional Scottish recipe in which a whole chicken is cooked with the soup and then served as a main course.

1. Place the chicken quarters in a saucepan and pour in the stock. Add the prunes, lemon rind and juice, nutmeg, bay leaf and salt and pepper. Cover the pan, bring to the boil and simmer for 1 hour.
2. Remove the chicken from the pan. Add the sliced leeks and continue to simmer, covered, for 10 minutes.
3. Meanwhile, discard the chicken skin and bones, and chop the chicken meat.
4. Add the chicken to the soup with the chopped parsley and simmer for 5 minutes until the leeks are cooked and the chicken is reheated. Serve hot.

k: French onion soup
nt left: Scotch broth
nt right: Cock-a-leekie

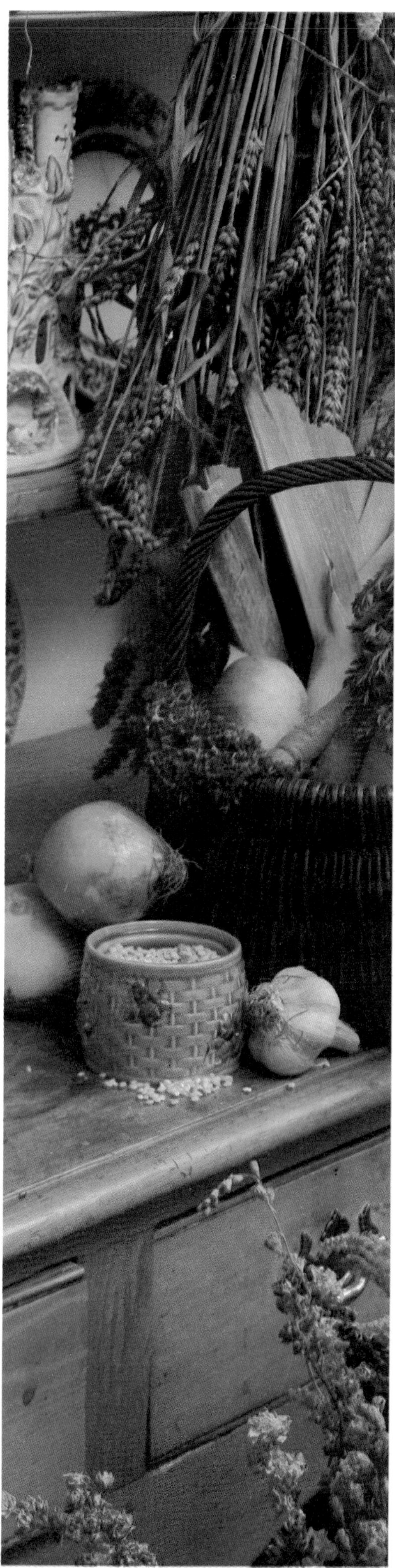

Fish Chowder

Makes 1.2 litres / 2 pints
Preparation time: 10 minutes
Cooking time: 40 minutes

1 tablespoon oil
2 rashers streaky bacon, rinded and chopped
1 onion, peeled and chopped
1 garlic clove, crushed (optional)
1 celery stick, sliced
1 small green pepper, cored, seeded and chopped
600 ml/1 pint Fish Stock (page 145)
grated rind of ½ lemon
2 teaspoons lemon juice
225 g/8 oz potatoes, peeled and diced
225 g/8 oz firm white fish fillets, skinned (eg. cod, haddock, coley)
1 bay leaf
150 ml/¼ pint milk
2 tablespoons chopped fresh parsley
salt
freshly ground black pepper

1. Heat the oil in a large saucepan and fry the bacon, onion, garlic, celery and pepper for 5 minutes, without browning.
2. Pour in the stock and stir in the lemon rind and juice. Add the potatoes and bring to the boil. Place the fish on top, in 1 or 2 pieces with the bay leaf. Cover and simmer for 20 minutes.
3. Remove the bay leaf, stir in the milk and chopped parsley. Reheat and taste and adjust the seasoning.

Chinese Chicken Broth

akes 1 litre/1¾ pints
eparation time: 10 minutes
ooking time: 15 minutes

0 ml/1½ pints chicken stock
5 g/8 oz boned chicken breast, skinned and thinly sliced
g/2 oz button mushrooms, thinly sliced
spring onions, chopped
g/2 oz bean-sprouts (optional)
nm/¼ inch slice root ginger, peeled and finely chopped or grated
easpoon soy sauce

1. Pour the stock into a saucepan and bring to the boil. Add the remaining ingredients and bring back to the boil. Cover and simmer for 10 minutes until the chicken is cooked.
2. Taste and adjust the seasoning and serve immediately.

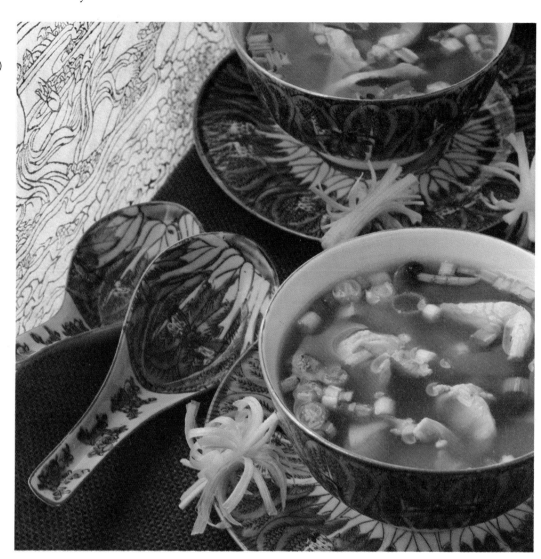

Mushroom and Sherry Soup

kes 1 litre/1¾ pints
paration time: 5 minutes
oking time: 20 minutes

g/1 oz butter
nion, peeled and chopped
g/8 oz button mushrooms, hinly sliced
) ml/1½ pints chicken or egetable stock
aspoon lemon juice
aspoon fresh thyme leaves, or ¼ teaspoon dried thyme

shly ground black pepper
ablespoons sherry (dry or nedium)
ablespoons chopped fresh parsley or thyme, to garnish

1. Heat the butter in a saucepan and fry the onion for 5 minutes until lightly browned. Add the mushrooms and fry for 2 minutes.
2. Pour in the stock and add the lemon juice, thyme, salt and pepper. Bring to the boil and simmer for 5 minutes. Stir in the sherry.
3. Serve hot, sprinkled with parsley.

Lentil and Ham Soup

Serves 4–6
Makes about 1.5 litres/2½ pints
Preparation time: 5 minutes
Cooking time: 1¼ hours

100 g/4 oz split red lentils
1 large onion, peeled and chopped
1 large carrot, peeled and diced
2 celery sticks, sliced
1.2 litres/2 pints stock (beef, white, chicken or vegetable)
salt
freshly ground black pepper
1 bay leaf
100 g/4 oz cooked ham, chopped
2 tablespoons chopped fresh parsley, to garnish

1. Place the lentils in a large saucepan and add the onion, carrot and celery. Pour in the stock and add the salt, pepper and bay leaf. Cover the pan and bring to the boil.
2. Reduce the heat and simmer for 1 hour until the lentils are soft and have thickened the soup. The soup may now be liquidized or pressed through a sieve to make a smooth consistency, if liked.
3. Add the chopped ham and reheat. Serve hot, sprinkled with parsley.

Jerusalem Artichoke Soup

Serves 4–6
Makes about 1.25 litres/2¼ pints
Preparation time: 10 minutes
Cooking time: 45 minutes

25 g/1 oz butter or margarine
1 large onion, peeled and chopped
500 g/1¼ lb Jerusalem artichokes
a little vinegar or lemon juice
600 ml/1 pint stock (white, chicken or vegetable)
300 ml/½ pint milk
salt
freshly ground black pepper
2 tablespoons chopped fresh parsley or a little cream, to garnish

1. Melt the butter in a saucepan and gently fry the onion for 5 minutes. Peel the artichokes, and place them immediately into a bowl of cold water, with a little vinegar or lemon juice added to prevent browning.
2. Drain the artichokes, roughly chop and add them to the onion in the pan. Cook gently without browning for 5 minutes. Add the stock, milk, salt and pepper and bring to the boil. Simmer, covered, for 30 minutes until the artichokes are soft.
3. Rub the soup through a sieve or mouli-légumes, or liquidize to a smooth purée. Return the soup to the pan, reheat and taste and adjust the seasoning.
4. Serve hot, garnished with chopped parsley or a swirl of cream.

Oxtail Soup

Serves 4 – 6
Makes about 1.2 litres / 2 pints
Preparation time : 5 minutes
Cooking time: 3½ – 4½ hours

25 g/1 oz lard or dripping
1 large oxtail, chopped and excess fat removed
1 large onion, peeled and chopped
1 large carrot, peeled and chopped
1.75 litres/3 pints water
1 bay leaf
salt
freshly ground black pepper
2 tablespoons cornflour
2 tablespoons water
2 tablespoons port
grated rind of 1 orange, to garnish

1. Melt the fat in a large saucepan, and add the oxtail, onion and carrot. Fry gently for 15 minutes until the oxtail and vegetables are browned.
2. Add the water, bay leaf, salt and pepper and bring to the boil. Cover and simmer for 3–4 hours until the oxtail is tender and falling away from the bones.
3. (Alternatively cook in a pressure cooker using only 1.2 litres / 2 pints water for 45 minutes at high pressure, following the manufacturer's instructions.)
4. Remove the oxtail, take the meat off the bones and shred it, discarding the bones. Skim the fat from the top of the stock (this can be done while still hot or leave to cool first).
5. Blend the cornflour with the water and stir into the stock . Bring to the boil, stirring until lightly thickened. Add the shredded meat with the port and simmer for 5 minutes.
6. Serve hot, garnished with the grated oran rind.

Above left: Oxtail soup
Above centre: Lentil and ham soup
Above right: Jerusalem artichoke soup

Tomato and Orange Soup

akes 1.2 litres/2 pints
eparation time: 10 minutes
oking time: 45 minutes

0 g/1 lb ripe tomatoes, quartered
arge onion, peeled and chopped
5 g/8 oz potato, peeled and diced
0 ml/1 pint chicken or vegetable stock
ated rind and juice of 1 orange
easpoon dried marjoram or oregano
t
shly ground black pepper
garnish:
ange slices, quartered
ûtons

1. Place the tomatoes in a saucepan with the onion and potato. Add the stock, orange rind and juice, herbs, and salt and pepper. Bring to the boil, cover and simmer for 30 minutes until the vegetables are very soft.
2. Sieve the soup, or liquidize and then sieve it to remove the seeds. Return the puréed soup to the pan and reheat.
3. Adjust the seasoning and the consistency if necessary by adding a little more stock. Serve hot garnished with orange and croûtons.

Goulash Dumpling Soup

Serves 4–6
Makes about 1.5 litres/2½ pints soup, plus dumplings
Preparation time: 20 minutes
Cooking time: 1 hour 20 minutes

2 tablespoons oil
50 g/2 oz streaky bacon, chopped
1 large onion, peeled and chopped
1 garlic clove, crushed (optional)
2 celery sticks, sliced
2 carrots, peeled and sliced
50 g/2 oz mushrooms, sliced
1 small green pepper, cored, seeded and sliced
1 tablespoon paprika pepper
1 tablespoon plain flour
1.5 litres/2½ pints stock (beef, chicken, vegetable)
1 tablespoon tomato purée
Dumplings:
100 g/4 oz self-raising flour
50 g/2 oz shredded suet
2 tablespoons chopped fresh parsley
salt
freshly ground black pepper
4 tablespoons water

1. Heat the oil in a large saucepan and fry the bacon, onion, garlic, celery, carrots, mushrooms and green pepper for 10 minutes until lightly browned.
2. Stir in the paprika and flour and cook for 1 minute. Add the stock and tomato purée and bring to the boil. Cover and simmer for 45 minutes until the vegetables are tender.
3. To make the dumplings, mix the flour, suet, parsley, salt and pepper in a bowl. Add the water to make a soft dough. Divide into 8 or 12 pieces and shape into balls. Add the dumplings to the soup, cover and simmer for 15 – 20 minutes until they have risen and plumped up.
4. Serve hot, allowing two parsley dumplings for each serving.

Spinach Soup

akes about 1.2 litres/2 pints
eparation time: 5 – 15 minutes
ooking time: 20 minutes

0 g/1 lb spinach or 225 g/8 oz packet frozen, chopped spinach
g/1½ oz butter or margarine
nion, peeled and chopped
g/1 oz plain flour
0 ml/1 pint stock (white, chicken or vegetable)
0 ml/¼ pint milk
ated rind of ½ lemon
easpoons lemon juice
teaspoon grated nutmeg
t
shly ground black pepper
pint single cream
oûtons, to garnish

1. If using fresh spinach, wash it and place it in a saucepan with only the water that clings to it. Cover the pan and cook gently for about 10 minutes until tender.
2. Drain the spinach, squeezing out all the water with a wooden spoon, then chop it finely.
3. Melt the butter in a saucepan and fry the onion gently for 5 minutes without browning. Stir in the flour, then add the stock and the milk. Bring to the boil, stirring all the time until the sauce thickens. Stir in the chopped spinach with the lemon rind and juice, nutmeg, and salt and pepper. Simmer for 5 minutes.
4. For a smoother and greener soup liquidize the mixture then return it to the pan. Stir in most of the cream and reheat without boiling. Serve hot garnished with a swirl of cream and croûtons.

VARIATION:
Serve the soup chilled, thinned down with 150 ml/¼ pint of milk or stock.

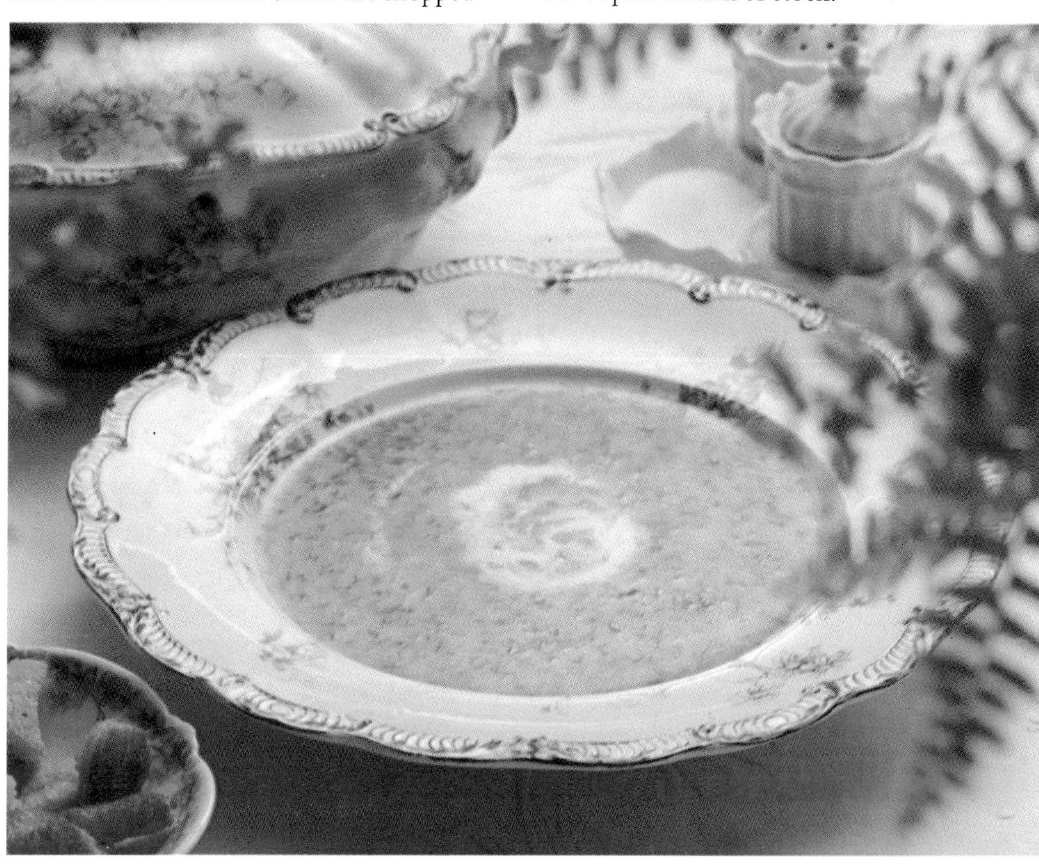

Dried Bean Soup

ves 4–6
kes about 1.5 litres / 2½ pints
paration time: 10 minutes, luding soaking time
oking time: 1¾ hours

g/8 oz dried white beans haricot and/or butter)
ml/1 pint water
ut 1 litre / 1¾ pints beef or egetable stock
rge onion, peeled and hopped
arlic clove, crushed (optional)
elery stick, sliced
g/8oz tomatoes, peeled and oughly chopped
rig rosemary or ½ teaspoon ried rosemary

hly ground black pepper
blespoons chopped fresh arsley, to garnish

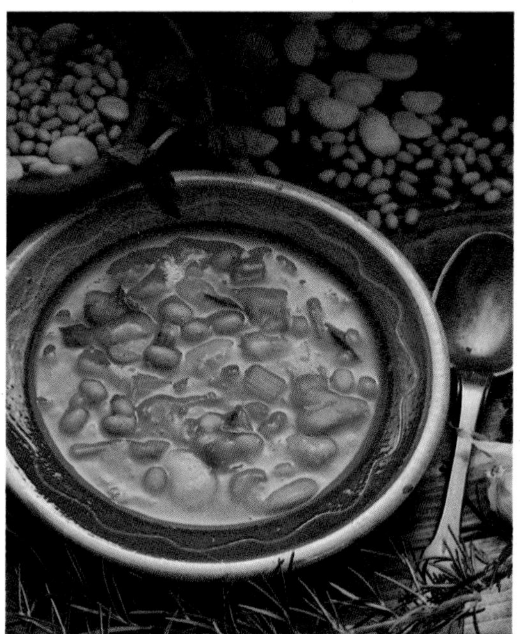

1. Soak the beans in the water overnight, or alternatively cover with boiling water and soak for several hours.
2. Drain the beans, reserving the liquid and make up to 1.2 litres/2 pints with the stock. Place the beans and the stock in a large saucepan and add all the remaining ingredients, except the parsley. Cover the pan, bring to the boil and simmer for about 1½ hours until the beans are soft.
3. Ladle about half of the beans , with some liquid, into a liquidizer and blend to a purée. Return the bean purée to the soup and bring to the boil, stirring. Adjust the seasoning and consistency if necessary by adding a little more stock.
4. Serve hot, sprinkled with chopped parsley.

Avgolemono

Serves 4–6
Makes about 1.2 litres / 2 pints
Preparation time: 5 minutes
Cooking time: 40 minutes

1.2 litres / 2 pints chicken stock
juice and grated rind of 1 large lemon
1 sprig each parsley and thyme
50 g/2 oz rice
2 eggs
lemon slices or sprigs of parsley, to garnish

1. Pour the stock into a saucepan and add the grated lemon rind and sprigs of parsley and thyme. Bring to the boil, add the rice and simmer for about 20 minutes until the rice is tender.
2. Beat the eggs and lemon juice together, then beat in a little of the hot stock, and pour the egg mixture into the soup. Reheat, stirring all the time until the soup thickens, but do not allow it to boil as the eggs may curdle.
3. Taste and adjust the seasoning and serve at once, garnished with slices of lemon or sprigs of parsley.

Left: Avgolemono
Right: Cream of root soup

Cream of Root Soup

Serves 4–6
Makes about 1.25 litres / 2¼ pints
Preparation time: 10 minutes
Cooking time: 1¼ hours

50 g/2 oz butter
450 g/1 lb mixed root vegetables (carrots, turnips, swedes and parsnips), peeled and chopped
1 large onion, peeled and chopped
1 litre/1¾ pints stock (white, chicken or vegetable)
1 bay leaf
salt
freshly ground black pepper
150 ml/¼ pint single cream
croûtons, to garnish

1. Melt the butter in a large saucepan and gently fry the root vegetables and the onion, without browning, for 5 minutes. Add the stock, bay leaf, salt and pepper and bring to the boil. Cover and simmer for about 1 hour until the vegetables are soft.
2. Remove from the heat and rub through a sieve or mouli-légumes, or liquidize to a purée. Return to the pan and reheat.
3. Stir in the cream and garnish with croûtons.

Chilled Watercress Vichyssoise

rves 4–6
akes about 1.5 litres/2½ pints
eparation time: 10 minutes
ooking time: 45 minutes

- g/1 oz butter or margarine
- arge onion, peeled and chopped
- 5 g/8 oz leeks, sliced
- 0 g/12 oz potatoes, peeled and diced
- itre/1¾ pints chicken or vegetable stock
- ated rind of ½ lemon
- lt
- eshly ground black pepper
- bunches watercress
- 0 ml/¼ pint milk or single cream

1. Melt the butter in a large saucepan and fry the onion and leeks gently for 5 minutes. Add the potatoes to the pan and pour in the stock with the lemon rind, and salt and pepper.
2. Cover the pan and bring to the boil. Simmer for 30 minutes until the vegetables are tender.
3. Wash the watercress, remove the coarse stalks, and reserve a few sprigs for garnish. Coarsely chop the watercress, add it to the pan and simmer for 2 minutes.
4. Liquidize to a smooth purée. Stir in the milk and taste and adjust the seasoning. Chill well before serving. Garnish with sprigs of watercress.

ck: Chilled watercress vichyssoise
nt: Chilled courgette and
gurt soup

Chilled Courgette and Yogurt Soup

ves 4–6
akes about 1.25 litres/2¼ pints
eparation time: 5 minutes
oking time: 35 minutes

- g/2 oz butter or margarine
- nion, peeled and chopped
- g/1 lb courgettes, cut into 5 mm/¼ inch slices
- ml/1½ pints stock (chicken, white or vegetable)
- prig mint
- t
- shly ground black pepper
- ml/¼ pint plain, unsweetened yogurt
- le extra yogurt, to garnish

1. Melt the butter in a large saucepan and gently fry the onion and courgettes for 5 minutes. Add the stock, mint, salt and pepper and bring to the boil. Simmer covered for 20–30 minutes until the courgettes are soft.
2. Reserve a few courgette slices for a garnish, and liquidize or sieve the soup to a smooth purée. Stir in the yogurt and chill in the refrigerator.
3. Serve chilled, garnished with reserved courgette slices and swirls of yogurt.

Starters

HOT AND COLD STARTERS

Salmon Roulade

Serves 6–8 as a starter or 4 as a main course
Preparation time: 30 minutes
Cooking time: 20 minutes

200 g / 7 oz can salmon
4 eggs, separated
1 tablespoon tomato purée
salt
freshly ground black pepper
2 tablespoons grated Parmesan cheese

Filling:
300 ml / ½ pint milk
1 small onion, peeled and quartered
2 parsley stalks, chopped finely
1 bay leaf
strip of lemon rind
25 g / 1 oz butter
25 g / 1 oz plain flour
4 hard-boiled eggs, chopped
2 tablespoons chopped fresh parsley or dill
2 teaspoons lemon juice
salt and pepper

To garnish:
slices of cucumber and lemon,
sprigs of fresh dill or parsley, or cress

1. Transfer the salmon and juices from the can to a mixing bowl. Remove the black skin and any bones. Mash the salmon to a purée with a fork. Beat in the egg yolks, tomato purée, salt and pepper.
2. Whisk the egg whites until stiff and fold them into the mixture.
3. Line a Swiss roll tin or shallow baking sheet, about 33 × 23 cm / 13 × 9 inches, with greaseproof paper to come above the sides of the tin and brush with oil.
4. Pour the roulade mixture into the prepared tin and level the surface. Bake near the top of a preheated moderately hot oven at 200°C, 400°F, Gas Mark 6 for 10–15 minutes until the roulade is well risen, firm and just beginning to brown.
5. Meanwhile prepare the filling. Pour the milk into a small saucepan and add the onion, parsley, bay leaf and lemon rind. Bring to the boil, remove from the heat and leave to infuse for at least 10 minutes, then strain into a jug.
6. Melt the butter in a saucepan, stir in the flour and then the flavoured milk over a low heat. Bring to the boil, stirring until the sauce thickens and simmer for 2 minutes. Stir in the chopped eggs, parsley or dill, lemon juice and salt and pepper to taste.
7. Just before removing the roulade from the oven, sprinkle a large sheet of greaseproof paper with the Parmesan cheese.
8. Turn the roulade on to the paper, remove the tin and peel off the lining paper.
9. Reheat the filling and spread the mixture over the roulade, leaving a 2.5 cm / 1 inch margin all the way round.
10. Roll up the roulade like a Swiss roll by gently lifting the paper so that the roulade falls over into a roll. Lift it on to a serving dish.
11. Serve immediately or cover and keep warm in the oven for a short time if necessary.
12. Garnish with lemon and cucumber slices and sprigs of dill or parsley and serve cut into slices. For a special occasion garnish with smoked salmon rolls.

VARIATION:
The roulade may also be served cold. To do' this turn out the roulade on to the greaseproof paper and roll up without the filling, but with greaseproof paper inside, and leave to cool. Cover and chill in the refrigerator until required or the next day.

For the filling, fold the chopped egg and parsley into 300 ml / ½ pint mixed mayonnaise and sour cream or yogurt.

Unroll the roulade, remove the paper and spread with the filling, re-roll and serve.

Savoury Choux Buns

Serves 8
Preparation time: 20 minutes
Cooking time: 40 minutes

150 ml/¼ pint water
50 g/2 oz butter or hard margarine
65 g/2½ oz plain flour
pinch of salt
2 eggs, beaten
50 g/2 oz Cheddar cheese, grated
Hot chicken filling:
50 g butter or margarine
2 rashers streaky bacon, chopped
1 onion, peeled and chopped
40 g/1½ oz plain flour
300 ml/½ pint milk
grated rind of ½ lemon
1 teaspoon lemon juice
½ teaspoon dried thyme
225 g/8 oz cooked chicken meat, shredded
salt
freshly ground black pepper
2 tablespoons single cream
Cold ham filling:
225 g/8 oz full fat soft cheese
150 ml/5 fl oz soured cream or yogurt
2 tablespoons chopped chives
2 tablespoons chopped fresh parsley
225 g/8 oz sliced cooked ham, chopped
salt
freshly ground black pepper
sprigs of fresh parsley, to garnish

The choux buns may be made the day before and stored in an airtight tin. If they become soft, return them to a hot oven to make the pastry crisper. Whether to be served hot or cold, do not fill the buns in advance as this will make the choux pastry soft.

1. To make choux pastry, pour the water into a saucepan and add the butter.
2. Heat gently until the butter is melted, then bring to the boil. Remove from the heat immediately and pour in all the flour and salt.
3. Beat well with a wooden spoon until the mixture is smooth and comes away from the sides of the pan.
4. Leave to cool slightly, then gradually beat in the eggs until they are absorbed and the mixture is smooth and shiny. Beat in the grated cheese.
5. Spoon the mixture on to a greased baking tray to make 8 buns. Bake near the top of a preheated moderately hot oven at 200°C, 400°F, Gas Mark 6 for 30 minutes until the buns have risen and are golden brown and crisp.
6. Remove them from the oven and make a slit across the top of each bun to allow the steam to escape. Return to the oven for 10 minutes until very crisp.
7. To make the hot chicken filling, melt the butter in a saucepan and fry the bacon and onion for 5 minutes. Stir in the flour and the the milk.
8. Bring to the boil, stirring until the sauce is thickened. Add the lemon rind and juice and the thyme and simmer for 2 minutes. Add th shredded chicken and simmer for 2–3 minut until heated through. Taste and add salt and pepper.
9. Remove the saucepan from the heat and st in the cream.
10. To serve, spoon the hot filling into the h buns, through the slit across the top.
11. Keep them warm in the oven for a short time, if necessary. Garnish with sprigs of parsley and serve.
12. To make the cold ham filling, mix the sof cheese with the soured cream or yogurt and st in the chives, parsley, ham and salt and peppe to taste. Spoon the mixture into the cold chou buns just before serving. Garnish with sprigs parsley.

Left: Savoury choux buns
Right: Asparagus and lemon quiche

Neapolitan Stuffed Peppers

eparation time: 15 minutes
ɔoking time: 45 minutes

ed or green peppers
uffing:
0 g/4 oz fresh breadcrumbs
g/2 oz can anchovies, chopped
ablespoon grated onion
garlic clove, crushed (optional)
omatoes, peeled and chopped
lack olives, stoned and chopped
ablespoon chopped fresh parsley
ablespoon chopped fresh basil, oregano or marjoram
shly ground black pepper

1. Cut the peppers in half, lengthways, keeping the stalks attached if possible, and remove the seeds.
2. To make the stuffing, place the breadcrumbs in a mixing bowl, add the anchovies with the oil from the can. Add the onion, garlic, tomatoes, olives, parsley, basil and ground pepper and stir until well mixed.
3. Pile the stuffing into the pepper halves. Place the peppers in a greased, ovenproof dish. Pour 6 tablespoons water round the peppers.
4. Bake in a preheated moderately hot oven at 190°C, 375°F, Gas Mark 5 for 45 minutes until the stuffing is crisp and golden brown and the peppers are just tender.
5. Serve hot or cold.

Fish Terrine

rves 8
eparation time: 30 minutes
ɔoking time: 40 minutes

0 g/1 lb white fish fillets, skinned and flaked (cod, haddock or whiting)
ggs
arge sorrel leaves or 8 sprigs watercress, chopped
t
shly ground black pepper
g/1 oz button mushrooms, thinly sliced
5 g/6 oz smoked haddock fillets, skinned
ce of 1 small lemon
ablespoon fresh thyme leaves chopped or 1 teaspoon dried thyme
ıard-boiled eggs
ɔay leaf
rigs of thyme or parsley, to garnish

1. Place the flaked fish, eggs, sorrel leaves, salt and pepper in a liquidizer and purée together until smooth.
2. Lightly grease a 450 g/1 lb loaf tin (19 × 9 × 6 cm/7½ × 3½ × 2½ inch) or a 1 litre/1¾ pint ovenproof dish.
3. Spread a thin layer of the fish purée in the bottom. Sprinkle half of the mushrooms, half the lemon juice and half the thyme on top of the purée, and then arrange half of the smoked haddock on top. Place the hard-boiled eggs, lengthways down the centre.
4. Spread some of the remaining fish purée round the eggs and scatter the remaining mushrooms, lemon juice and thyme over the top. Make another layer with the remaining smoked haddock and spread the last of the fish purée over the top. Press the bay leaf into the centre.
5. Cover with greased foil. Bake in a bain marie (a roasting tin filled with water) in a preheated oven at 180°C, 350°F, Gas Mark 4 for 40 minutes.
6. To serve hot, turn the tin out on to a serving dish, and serve at once, sliced and garnished with sprigs of thyme or parsley.
7. To serve cold, leave to cool in the tin, then turn out. If cooked in an ovenware dish, serve straight from the dish.

Asparagus and Lemon Quiche

rves 6
eparation time: 30 minutes
ɔoking time: 45 minutes

5 g/6 oz plain flour
ıch of salt
g/3 oz butter or hard margarine, cut into pieces
ablespoons grated Parmesan cheese
ablespoons beaten egg
ling:
5 g/8 oz thin asparagus spears (fresh or frozen)
ggs
0 ml/¼ pint single cream or milk
ated rind of ½ lemon
easpoon lemon juice
t
shly ground black pepper
non slices, to garnish

1. To make the pastry, place the flour and salt in a mixing bowl and rub in the butter or margarine until the mixture resembles fine breadcrumbs.
2. Stir in the Parmesan cheese, then add the beaten egg and mix to a firm dough. Turn out on to a lightly floured surface and knead gently.
3. Roll out and use to line a 20 cm/8 inch flan ring or dish. Place a circle of greaseproof paper in the base of the flan and weight with beans.
4. Bake blind near the top of a preheated moderately hot oven at 200°C, 400°F, Gas Mark 6 for 15 minutes. Remove the baking beans and paper and cook for a further 5 minutes.
5. To make the filling, pick out 24 good asparagus spears for the top and cut them into 7.5 cm/3 inch lengths. Chop the remaining stems and spears and cook in boiling water for 5 minutes if frozen, and a little longer if fresh, until just tender.
6. Remove the chopped asparagus with a perforated spoon, then cook the reserved asparagus spears and drain.
7. Place the chopped asparagus in the partially baked flan case.
8. Beat the eggs and cream together with the lemon rind and juice, and salt and pepper, then pour over the asparagus in the flan.
9. Bake in a moderate oven at 180°C, 350°F, Gas Mark 4 for 25–30 minutes or until the custard is set.
10. Arrange the reserved asparagus spears in 6 bundles of 4 spears and place the bundles on the quiche with the spears pointing towards the edge. Garnish the centre with twists of lemon slices. Serve hot or cold.

Sherried Kidney Vol-au-vents

Preparation time: 25 minutes
Cooking time: 30 minutes

375 g/13 oz packet frozen puff pastry, thawed
beaten egg, to glaze
Filling:
25 g/1 oz butter or margarine
1 rasher streaky bacon, rinded and chopped
1 small onion, peeled and chopped
50 g/2 oz mushrooms, sliced
225 g/8 oz lamb's kidneys, skinned, halved, cored and sliced
25 g/1 oz plain flour
200 ml/⅓ pint stock
1 tablespoon dry sherry
salt
freshly ground black pepper
watercress, to garnish

1. Roll out the pastry to make an approximate 35 × 28 cm/14 × 11 inch rectangle. Using a 9 cm/3½ inch, fluted cutter, stamp out 12 rounds. Place 6 of the pastry rounds on a baking sheet and brush the edges with the beaten egg.
2. Using a 5 cm/2 inch cutter, stamp out the centres of the remaining 6 pastry rounds. Lay these over the first 6, pressing the edges gently together. Place the centres, for lids, on the baking sheet and brush the tops of the vol-au-vents and the lids with beaten egg.
3. Bake in a preheated oven at 200°C, 400°F, Gas Mark 6 for 15 –20 minutes until they have risen and are golden brown and crisp.
4. To make the filling, melt the butter in a saucepan and fry the bacon, onion, mushrooms and kidney for 5 minutes until lightly browned. Stir in the flour and then the stock. Bring to the boil, stirring until the sauce is thickened.
5. Simmer for 5 minutes, then stir in the sherry and add salt and pepper to taste.
6. To serve, reheat the vol-au-vent cases in th oven. Place the vol-au-vents on a serving dish or individual dishes and spoon in the hot sauce. Top with the pastry lids.
7. Alternatively, spoon the filling into cold cases and reheat at 180°C, 350°F, Gas Mark 4 for 15 minutes.
8. Serve hot, garnished with watercress.

Croûte au Fromage

Preparation time: 5 minutes
Cooking time: 10 minutes

½ small, fat, French stick
25 g/1 oz butter
1 tablespoon olive oil
100 g/4 oz cooked ham, in 4 slices
4 slices Gruyère or Emmenthal cheese
150 ml/¼ pint dry white wine
To garnish:
2 tomatoes
watercress

1. Cut the bread diagonally into 2.5 cm/1 inch slices, so that each slice is about 15 cm/6 inches long.
2. Heat the butter and oil in a frying pan and fry the slices of bread until golden brown on both sides.
3. Fold the slices of ham and cheese in half so that they are approximately the shape of the bread slices. Place the ham, and then the cheese, on top of the fried bread.
4. Pour over the wine, cover the pan and cook for 3 – 5 minutes until the cheese is melted.
5. Serve at once, garnished with tomato slices or wedges and watercress.

Egg and Prawn au Gratin

Serves 6
Preparation time: 15 minutes
Cooking time: 20 minutes

5 hard-boiled eggs, chopped
175 g/6 oz peeled prawns
Cheese sauce:
25 g/1 oz butter
25 g/1 oz plain flour
300 ml/½ pint milk
100 g/4 oz grated cheese (Cheddar or Gruyère)
2 teaspoons lemon juice
salt
freshly ground black pepper
2 tablespoons grated Parmesan cheese
To garnish:
6 unpeeled prawns (optional)
sprigs of parsley

1. Divide the chopped, hard-boiled eggs between 6 × 150 ml/¼ pint ramekin dishes. Lay the peeled prawns on top.
2. To make the sauce, heat the butter in a saucepan, stir in the flour and then the milk over a low heat. Bring to the boil, stirring until thickened and smooth. Stir in the cheese and lemon juice and add salt and pepper to taste.
3. Pour the sauce over the eggs and prawns in the dishes. Sprinkle with Parmesan cheese.
4. Bake near the top of a preheated oven at 200°C, 400°F, Gas Mark 6 for 15–20 minutes until bubbling and golden brown, or chill until required and then bake.
5. Serve hot, garnished with unpeeled prawns and parsley.

Mushroom and Spinach Pancakes

rves 8 as a starter or 4 as a main
urse
eparation time: 45 minutes
oking time: 20 minutes

0 g/4 oz plain flour
teaspoon salt
gg
0 ml/½ pint milk (or milk and water mixed)
for frying
ling:
g/2 oz butter
arge onion, peeled and chopped
ashers streaky bacon, rinded and chopped
0 g/4 oz mushrooms, sliced
5 g/8 oz tomatoes, peeled and roughly chopped
t
shly ground black pepper
uce:
g/1 oz butter
ablespoon plain flour
0 ml/¼ pint milk
5 g /8 oz packet frozen, chopped spinach, thawed
easpoon lemon juice
ch of grated nutmeg
t
shly ground black pepper

The pancakes can be made in advance and will keep for up to two days wrapped in foil and stored in the refrigerator. When needed, spread the cold pancakes with filling, roll them up and place in an ovenproof serving dish. Pour over the sauce. Cover and reheat in a moderately hot oven at 200°C, 400°F, Gas Mark 6 for 20 minutes until heated through.

1. To make the pancakes, place the flour and salt in a mixing bowl, make a well in the centre and crack in the egg. Add half of the milk and stir with a wooden spoon until smooth. Beat well. Stir in the remaining milk.
2. Heat a little oil in a 20 cm / 8 inch frying pan, and when hot, pour in just enough pancake batter to coat the bottom of the pan. Tilt the pan to spread the batter evenly.
3. Cook until the top of the batter is set and the underneath is golden brown. Turn, or toss the pancake over and cook the other side.
4. Slide the pancakes on to a wire rack to cool, or, if serving immediately, turn on to a hot plate, cover with foil and keep warm. Repeat until the batter is used up, making 8 pancakes.
5. To make the filling, melt the butter in a saucepan and fry the onion and bacon for 3 minutes. Add the mushrooms and fry for 2 minutes. Add the tomatoes and salt and pepper, cover the pan and simmer for 15–20 minutes, stirring occasionally until the tomatoes are reduced to a pulp.
6. To make the sauce, melt the butter in a saucepan, stir in the flour and then the milk over a low heat. Bring to the boil, stirring until the sauce thickens.
7. Add the spinach, lemon juice, nutmeg and salt and pepper, return to the boil and simmer for 2 minutes.
8. Spread the hot pancakes with hot filling, roll up and place on a serving dish or individual dishes and pour over the hot sauce. Serve immediately.

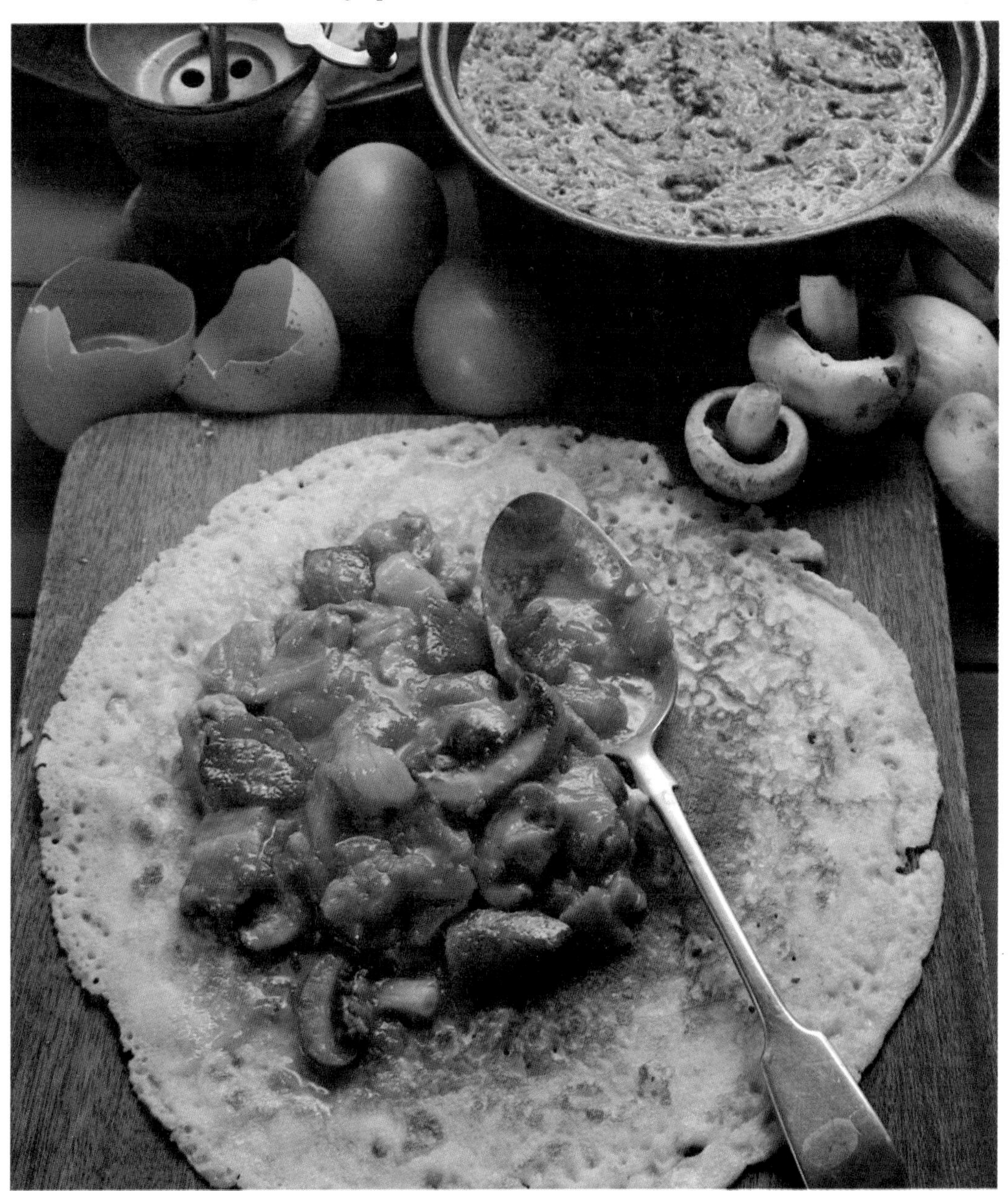

Cider Soused Mackerel

Preparation time: 15 minutes
Cooking time: 30–40 minutes

4 small mackerel
salt
freshly ground black pepper
1 onion, peeled and thinly sliced
1 eating apple, peeled, cored and sliced
1 tablespoon lemon juice
6 peppercorns
2 bay leaves
300 ml/½ pint cider

1. Remove the heads, fins and guts from the mackerel. Clean the fish and remove the backbones without removing the tails. Season the flesh with salt and pepper, then roll up each fish towards the tail. Place the rolled mackerel in a shallow ovenproof dish, with the tails pointing upwards.
2. Scatter the onion slices over and around the fish. Peel, core and slice the apple and toss in lemon juice. Add to the dish, with the peppercorns and bay leaves. Pour over the cider and cover the dish.
3. Bake in a preheated moderate oven at 180°C, 350°F, Gas Mark 4 for 30–40 minutes until the fish is tender.
4. Leave to cool before serving.

Tuna Fish Mousse

Serves 6–8
Preparation time: 15 minutes
Cooking time: 10 minutes

300 ml/½ pint milk
1 small onion, peeled and quartered
2 parsley stalks
1 bay leaf
strip of lemon rind
25 g/1 oz butter
25 g/1 oz plain flour
200 g/7 oz can tuna fish
150 ml/¼ pint mayonnaise
150 ml/¼ pint soured cream or yogurt
grated rind and juice of ½ small lemon
1 tablespoon tomato purée
2 teaspoons anchovy essence
salt
freshly ground black pepper
1 egg, separated
15 g/½ oz powdered gelatine
2 tablespoons water
To garnish:
slices of cucumber
100 g/4 oz prawns (optional)

1. To make the sauce, pour the milk into a small saucepan, and add the onion, parsley, bay leaf and lemon rind. Bring to the boil, remove from the heat and leave to infuse for at least 10 minutes, then strain.
2. Melt the butter in a saucepan, stir in the flour and then the flavoured milk over a low heat. Bring to the boil, stirring until the sauce is thickened and smooth. Simmer for 2 minutes.
3. Turn the tuna fish into a mixing bowl, with the juices from the can and mash well with a fork. Beat in the sauce, then the mayonnaise and soured cream or yogurt.
4. Stir in the lemon rind and juice, tomato purée, anchovy essence, and salt and pepper to taste. Beat in the egg yolk.
5. Dissolve the gelatine in the water and stir into the mixture. Whisk the egg white until stiff and fold in.
6. Turn into a 900 ml/1½ pint ring or fish mould, or soufflé dish, and chill in the refrigerator until set.
7. To serve, dip the mould in hot water for a few seconds, then turn it out on to a serving plate. Garnish with cucumber and prawns.

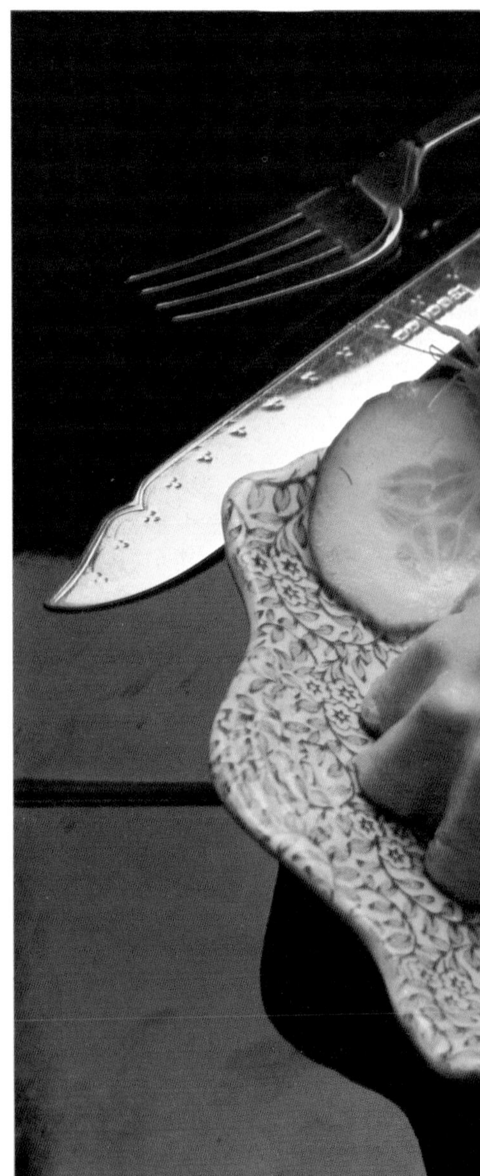

Avocado Pâté

eparation time: 15 minutes

arge ripe avocado pear
ated rind and juice of ½ lemon
) g/4 oz full fat soft cheese
ablespoon grated onion
arlic clove, crushed (optional)
v drops of Tabasco sauce
t
shly ground black pepper
arge tomatoes
sh parsley, to garnish

1. Cut the avocado pear in half and remove the stone. Scoop out the flesh into a mixing bowl and immediately pour over the lemon rind and juice to prevent the avocado from browning. Mash the avocado roughly with a fork, until fairly smooth.
2. Stir in the cheese, onion and garlic. Add the Tabasco sauce, and salt and pepper to taste.
3. Either serve at once, or place in a dish, cover immediately and chill until required. It will keep for several hours in the refrigerator without browning.
4. Cut the tops off the tomatoes and scoop out the seeds from the centre. Turn the tomatoes upside down for a minute to drain off the juice.
5. Place the tomatoes on a serving dish or on individual dishes.
6. Pile the avocado pâté into the centre of the tomatoes. Garnish with parsley, or, for a special occasion, sprinkle 1 tablespoon lumpfish roe on to the tops. If preferred the tomato tops can be replaced. Serve at once.

Mushrooms and Leeks à la Grecque

Preparation time: 15 minutes
Cooking time: 15 minutes

2 tablespoons oil, preferably olive oil
1 large onion, peeled and sliced
1 large garlic clove, crushed
1 celery stick, sliced
225 g/8 oz leeks, sliced
150 ml/¼ pint dry white wine
225 g/8 oz tomatoes, peeled, quartered, and seeds removed
salt
freshly ground black pepper
1 tablespoon chopped fresh parsley
1 tablespoon fresh thyme leaves or 1 teaspoon dried thyme
1 bay leaf
225 g/8 oz button mushrooms
2 tablespoons chopped fresh parsley, to garnish

1. Heat the oil in a large pan and add the onion, garlic, celery and leeks. Fry gently for 5 minutes without browning. Add the wine, tomatoes, salt and pepper and herbs, and bring to the boil. Add the mushrooms and simmer gently for 10 minutes.
2. Leave to cool, then pour into a serving dish and chill.
3. Serve cold, sprinkled with chopped parsley.

Left: Mushrooms and leeks à la Grecque
Centre: Chicken liver and mushroom pâté
Right: Minted melon and orange cocktail

Chicken Liver and Mushroom Pâté

Preparation time: 10 minutes
Cooking time: 10 minutes

100 g/4 oz butter
2 rashers streaky bacon, chopped
1 onion, peeled and chopped
1 garlic clove, crushed
100 g/4 oz mushrooms, sliced
225 g/8 oz chicken livers, cleaned and roughly chopped
sprig of fresh thyme or pinch dried thyme
1 bay leaf
1–2 tablespoons brandy
3 tablespoons green peppercorns (optional)
salt

1. Melt half of the butter in a frying pan and add the bacon, onion, garlic, mushrooms, livers, herbs and bay leaf. Fry for 10 minutes, stirring occasionally until cooked.
2. Spoon into a liquidizer with the pan juices and the brandy, discarding the bay leaf, and blend until smooth.
3. Stir in 2 tablespoons of the green peppercorns if using and add salt to taste.
4. Spoon into a small serving dish (about 450 ml/¾ pint) and smooth the top.
5. Clarify the remaining butter by heating it until it foams, then straining through muslin.
6. Sprinkle the remaining green peppercorns over the surface of the pâté and pour over the melted clarified butter. Extra small sprigs of fresh thyme may be arranged under the clarified butter, if liked.
7. Chill in the refrigerator until set.
8. Serve with toast or melba toast.

Minted Melon and Orange Cocktail

erves 4–6
reparation time: 15 minutes

small, ripe honeydew melon or 2 small ogen melons
large oranges
cm/2 inch piece cucumber, sliced and quartered
tablespoons chopped fresh mint
5 g/1 oz toasted almonds or hazelnuts
2 small lettuce, shredded
prigs of fresh mint, to garnish

1. Cut the melon into quarters and remove the seeds. Using a round vegetable baller, scoop out the flesh into balls, or cut into small cubes with a knife. Place the melon in a mixing bowl.
2. Cut the peel and pith from the oranges, and cut the flesh into segments between the membrane.
3. Add the orange segments to the melon with any juice left from the oranges. Add the cucumber, mint and nuts, and toss lightly. Chill in the refrigerator until required.
4. Divide the lettuce between 4–6 individual serving dishes or glasses. Spoon in the melon cocktail, pouring over the juice.
5. Serve chilled, garnished with sprigs of fresh mint.

VARIATION:

If using ogen melons, cut them in half and scoop out the seeds. Scoop out the flesh and mix with the other ingredients and serve the melon cocktail in the melon cases.

Cauliflower and Mustard Hors d'Oeuvre

eparation time: 10 minutes

mall cauliflower
0 g/4 oz cooked ham, shredded
ustard dressing:
ablespoons oil (olive or corn oil)
ablespoons wine vinegar
easpoons French mustard
easpoon sugar
t
shly ground black pepper
ablespoons chopped chives, to garnish

1. Divide the cauliflower into small florets. Remove the coarse stalk at the base but keep the small leaves.
2. Blanch the florets and the leaves in boiling salted water for 1 minute. Drain and refresh them by rinsing in cold water.
3. Mix all the dressing ingredients together. Place the drained cauliflower and the ham in a mixing bowl and pour over the dressing. Leave to marinate for at least 30 minutes, tossing occasionally.
4. Turn into a serving dish or individual dishes and pour over all the dressing. Garnish with chopped chives.

Eggs

SOUFFLÉS

Basic Hot Soufflé

Preparation time: 20 minutes
Cooking time: 35 minutes

40 g/1½ oz butter
25 g/1 oz plain flour
150 ml/¼ pint milk
4 eggs (sizes 1 or 2), separated
flavouring (see below)
salt
freshly ground black pepper

1. Grease an 18 cm/7 inch soufflé dish. Cut a strip of greaseproof paper with 5 cm / 2 inches folded up at the bottom, long enough to wrap around the outside of the soufflé dish with the ends overlapping, and to extend 7½ cm/3 inches above the rim of the dish. Secure with string or paper clips. Lightly grease the inside of the paper collar with oil.
2. Melt the butter in a large saucepan and stir in the flour. Cook for 2 minutes, then stir in the milk over a low heat.
3. Bring to the boil stirring all the time. Cool slightly and beat in the egg yolks one at a time. Add the flavouring (see below) and salt and pepper.
4. In a large bowl, whisk the egg whites until just holding their shape. Fold a small quantity of egg white into the sauce, using a large metal spoon. Fold in the rest of the beaten egg whites. Pour the mixture into the prepared soufflé dish and bake in the centre of a preheated oven at 190°C, 375°F, Gas Mark 5 for about 35 minutes, until well risen and firm to the touch. Remove the greaseproof paper and serve immediately.

FLAVOURINGS:

Cheese and Thyme Soufflé:
Add 75 g/3 oz grated Cheddar cheese and ½ teaspoon dried thyme to the sauce. Sprinkle 15 g/½ oz grated cheese and 1 tablespoon fresh breadcrumbs over the surface before baking.

Mushroom Soufflé:
Gently fry 100 g/4 oz chopped mushrooms in 15 g/½ oz butter until soft, then add to the sauce.

Ham and Onion Soufflé:
Gently fry 1 small chopped onion in 15 g/½ oz butter until soft. Add to the sauce with 75 g/3 oz finely chopped ham.

Spinach Soufflé:
Reheat a 225 g/8 oz packet frozen spinach with a knob of butter. Stir 2 tablespoons of the sauce into the spinach and spread over the base of the soufflé dish. Stir 1 teaspoon dried thyme and 25 g/1 oz grated Cheddar cheese into the rest of the sauce.

Smoked Haddock Soufflé:
Cook 2 tablespoons peeled and chopped shallots in the butter. Add the flour and make the sauce as above. Stir in 175 g/6 oz cooked flaked haddock.

Left: Ham and onion soufflés
Right: Cheese and thyme soufflé

Plain Omelette

Serves 2
Preparation time: 5 minutes
Cooking time: 2 minutes

3–4 eggs
1½ tablespoons water
salt
freshly ground black pepper
25 g/1 oz butter
chopped fresh parsley, to garnish

To increase the quantity of this recipe make two omelettes rather than one with a larger number of eggs.

1. Break the eggs into a bowl and beat them with a fork. Add the water, salt and pepper.
2. Heat an 18–20 cm/7–8 inch omelette pan over a medium heat. Add the butter and, when frothing, pour in the beaten eggs.
3. After 15 seconds stir gently with the back of a fork, drawing the mixture from the sides to the centre. As the egg begins to set, tilt the pan to let the liquid egg from the centre run t[o] the sides.
4. When the egg has set, stop stirring and cook for a further minute. Using a palette knife, fold over a third of the omelette in to the centre, then fold over the opposite third.
5. Turn the omelette out on to a warmed plate. Garnish with chopped parsley and serv[e] immediately.

Above left: Plain omelette
Above right: Cheese and chive omelette

VARIATIONS:

Omelette Fines Herbes:
Add 2 teaspoons chopped fresh mixed herbs or 1 teaspoon dried mixed herbs to the beaten egg mixture.

Cheese and Chive Omelette:
Grate 40 g/1½ oz cheese and put half of it into the egg mixture with 1 teaspoon chopped chives. Sprinkle the remaining cheese over the omelette.

Spinach Omelette:
Cook 100 g/4 oz fresh spinach, add salt an[d] pepper to taste and place in the centre of th[e] omelette before folding.

Mushroom and Bacon Omelette

erves 2
reparation time: 10 minutes
ooking time: 8 minutes

5 g/½ oz butter
0 g/2 oz mushrooms, sliced
rashers streaky bacon, rinded and chopped
tablespoon chopped fresh parsley
asic Omelette:
–4 eggs
½ tablespoons water
alt
eshly ground black pepper
5 g/1 oz butter

1. To prepare the stuffing, heat the butter in a pan and gently fry the mushrooms and bacon together for 3–4 minutes. Add salt, pepper and parsley.
2. Break the eggs into a bowl and beat with a fork. Add the water, salt and pepper.
3. Melt the butter in an omelette pan over a medium heat. Pour in the beaten eggs.
4. After 15 seconds stir gently with the back of a fork, drawing the mixture from the sides to the centre. As the egg begins to set, tilt the pan to let the liquid egg from the centre run to the sides.
5. Spoon the mushroom filling over the top of the omelette. Fold the omelette over and slide it out on to a hot serving plate.

VARIATIONS:

Kidney and Onion Omelette:
Skin, core and chop 1 lamb's kidney. Fry in 25 g/1 oz butter with 2 teaspoons chopped onion, until tender. Spread the filling over the omelette before folding.

Watercress and Parmesan Cheese Omelette:
Melt 15 g/½ oz butter and cook a washed and chopped bunch of watercress for a few minutes. Add salt, pepper and a dash of Tabasco sauce. Sprinkle 25 g/1 oz grated Parmesan cheese over the omelette in the pan and top with the watercress. Fold over and serve.

Omelette Arnold Bennett

Serves 2
Preparation time: 10 minutes
Cooking time: 6 minutes

25 g/1 oz butter
100 g/4 oz cooked smoked haddock, flaked
2 tablespoons single cream
Omelette:
3 eggs, separated
1 tablespoon milk
salt
freshly ground black pepper
2 tablespoons grated Parmesan or Cheddar cheese
25 g/1 oz butter
2 tablespoons single cream
watercress, to garnish

1. Heat the butter in an omelette pan and add the cooked flaked haddock and cream. Cook for 2–3 minutes and leave on one side.
2. Beat the egg yolks with the milk. Add salt and pepper.
3. Whisk the egg whites until just holding their shape. Using a large metal spoon, fold them into the yolks with the haddock mixture and half the cheese.
4. Reheat the omelette pan, add 25 g/1 oz butter and, when frothing, pour in the egg mixture. Cook until just setting, then slide th omelette on to a heatproof plate.
5. Sprinkle the rest of the cheese over the surface of the omelette and then pour over th cream. Flash under a hot grill and serve at onc garnished with watercress.

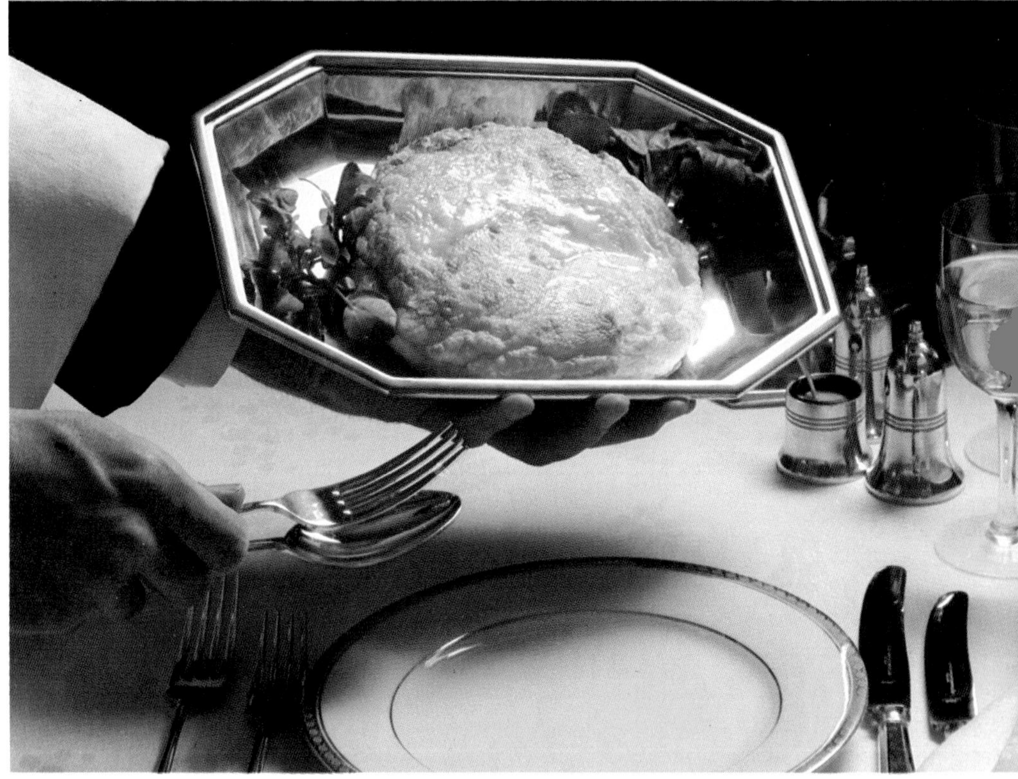

Spinach and Mushroom Roulade

Preparation time: 25 minutes
Cooking time: 10 minutes

225 g/8 oz frozen spinach or 450 g/1 lb fresh spinach
knob of butter
4 eggs, separated
salt
freshly ground black pepper
25 g/1 oz Parmesan cheese, grated
Filling:
15 g / ½ oz butter
175 g/6 oz mushrooms, sliced
1 tablespoon plain flour
150 ml / ¼ pint milk
pinch of nutmeg

1. Line a 30 × 20 cm/12 × 8 inch Swiss roll tin with greaseproof paper and oil lightly, or make a case of the same measurements with aluminium foil.
2. Cook the spinach with a knob of butter until completely softened. Drain the spinach well, chop if fresh and place in a large bowl. Add the egg yolks and beat them well into the spinach. Season with salt and pepper. Whisk the egg whites in a large bowl until just holding their shape. Using a metal spoon, quickly fold these into the spinach mixture. Turn the mixture into the prepared tin, sprinkle the Parmesan cheese over the surface, and bake in a preheated oven at 200°C, 400°F, Gas Mark 6 for 10 minutes.
3. Meanwhile make the filling. Heat the butter in a saucepan and gently fry the mushrooms until softened. Stir in the flour and cook for a further 1 minute. Slowly stir in the milk and cook until thickened. Stir in the nutmeg, salt and pepper to taste.
4. Remove the roulade from the oven and turn out on to a sheet of greaseproof paper. Spread the mushroom filling over the surface and gently roll the roulade up.
5. Serve immediately.

Peach and Rum Souffle´ Omelette

rves 1
eparation time: 10 minutes
oking time: 3 minutes

resh peach, peeled, stoned and sliced
ablespoons rum
easpoons sugar
ggs
ablespoon water
g/½ oz butter
ster sugar, to finish

1. Put the sliced peach in a saucepan with 1 tablespoon of the rum and cook over a low heat for 2 minutes. Stir in 2 teaspoons of the sugar, then remove the saucepan from the heat.
2. Separate the eggs into two bowls. Whisk the yolks and the rest of the sugar until creamy. Add the water and remaining rum and beat again.
3. Place the omelette pan over a low heat and melt the butter. Quickly whisk the egg whites and fold them into the yolk mixture using a large metal spoon.
4. Tilt the omelette pan in all directions to coat the sides with butter. Pour in the omelette mixture and cook over a moderate heat until the underside is golden brown.
5. Place the pan under a preheated hot grill to brown the top of the omelette. Spoon the peach and brandy mixture over one half of the omelette and flip the other half over with a palette knife. Carefully turn out on to a warm plate and sprinkle with the caster sugar.

VARIATIONS:

Jam Soufflé Omelette:
Spread the cooked omelette with jam of your choice, fold over and sprinkle with caster sugar.

Savoury Soufflé Omelette:
Omit the sugar from the basic mixture and see page 37 for fillings under Stuffed Omelettes.

Mexican eggs

Preparation time: 10 minutes
Cooking time: 20 minutes

25 g/1 oz butter
1 onion, peeled and chopped
1 red pepper, cored, seeded and diced
300 g/11 oz can sweetcorn kernels, drained or 175 g/6 oz frozen sweetcorn, cooked and drained
2 tablespoons chutney
salt
freshly ground black pepper
Sauce:
25 g/1 oz butter
25 g/1 oz plain flour
300 ml/½ pint milk
50 g/2 oz Cheddar cheese, grated
4 eggs

1. Melt the butter in a saucepan and fry the onion until just soft. Add the pepper, sweetcorn and chutney, salt and pepper, and cook, stirring all the time, for a further 5 minutes, then set aside.
2. To make the sauce, melt the butter in a saucepan, stir in the flour and cook for 2–3 minutes. Gradually stir in the milk over a low heat. Bring slowly to the boil and cook for a further 2 minutes. Stir in half the cheese and salt and pepper. Cover and leave on one side off the heat.
3. Poach the eggs in simmering water. Alternatively, soft boil them for 6 minutes, plunge them into cold water, then crack the surface gently by tapping all over with a spoon. Peel off a band across the middle of the egg. The shell can then be pulled off at each end. Dry the peeled eggs on kitchen paper.
4. Reheat the vegetable mixture and spread over the base of an ovenproof dish. Top with the eggs. Reheat the sauce and pour it over the eggs. Sprinkle on the remaining cheese and put under a preheated hot grill until lightly browned. Serve immediately.

Curried Eggs

Preparation time: 25 minutes
Cooking time: 20 minutes

25 g/1 oz butter
1 medium onion, peeled and sliced
1 eating apple, peeled and diced
½ green pepper, cored, seeded and diced
1½ teaspoons curry powder
1 tablespoon plain flour
450 ml/¾ pint water or chicken stock
1 tablespoon lemon juice
2 tablespoons mango chutney
½ teaspoon ground ginger
4 eggs

1. Heat the butter in a saucepan and cook the onions, apple and green pepper for 2 minutes. Stir in the curry powder and cook for a further 2 minutes. Add the flour and cook for 2 minutes, then add water or stock and bring to the boil, stirring all the time. Reduce the heat and add lemon juice, chutney and ginger. Simmer, covered, for 20 minutes.
2. Hard-boil the eggs for 12 minutes. Run them under cold water, then shell them. Cut the eggs in half lengthwise and arrange them on a serving dish. Pour over the sauce and serve with boiled long-grain rice.

Eggs Benedict

Above left: Curried eggs
Above right: Mexican eggs

Eggs Benedict

paration time: 15 minutes
oking time: 15 minutes

g/1½ oz butter
g/1½ oz plain flour
ml/½ pint milk and 150
nl/¼ pint double cream, or
50 ml/¾ pint milk

hly ground black pepper
g/1 lb cooked cod, flaked
arlic clove, crushed
blespoon chopped fresh
arsley
blespoons cooking oil
ices white bread, crusts
emoved and cut into triangles
gs
ly chopped fresh parsley, to
arnish

1. Melt the butter in a pan, stir in the flour and cook for 2 minutes. Gradually stir in the milk and cream over a low heat. Bring to the boil, stirring continuously. Add salt and pepper.
2. Put 5 tablespoons of the sauce in a bowl with the flaked fish and stir in the crushed garlic and parsley.
3. Heat the oil and fry the triangles of bread. Drain them well on kitchen paper.
4. Poach the eggs until just set and dry them on absorbent paper. Gently reheat the fish mixture and the remaining sauce in 2 separate saucepans. Spoon the fish mixture over the base of a serving dish. Top with the poached eggs and pour over the remaining sauce.
5. Garnish with the croûtes and chopped parsley. Serve immediately.

Eggs Florentine

Preparation time: 25 minutes
Cooking time: 15–20 minutes

225 g/8 oz packet frozen spinach
knob of butter
Sauce:
25 g/1 oz butter
25 g/1 oz plain flour
300 ml/½ pint milk
pinch of dry English mustard
50 g/2 oz Cheddar cheese, grated
salt
freshly ground black pepper
4 eggs

1. Cook the spinach with a knob of butter until completely thawed and heated through. Drain the spinach, and spoon it over the base of a serving dish.
2. To make the sauce, melt the butter in a pan, stir in the flour and cook for 2 minutes. Gradually stir in the milk over a low heat. Bring to the boil, stirring, then add the mustard, half the cheese and salt and pepper. Remove from the heat.
3. Poach the eggs until just set. Arrange the drained poached eggs over the spinach.
4. Reheat the sauce and pour it over the eggs. Sprinkle the remaining cheese over the top and reheat in a preheated oven at 180°C, 350°F, Gas Mark 4 for 10–15 minutes.

Left: Eggs Florentine
Right: Eggs Greek-style

Eggs Milton

Preparation time: 10 minutes
Cooking time: 6 minutes

50 g/2 oz butter
225 g/8 oz tomatoes, skinned and sliced
2 slices white bread, crusts removed, and cut into triangles
2 spring onions, chopped
100 g/4 oz button mushrooms, sliced
½ green pepper, cored, seeded and diced
4 eggs
4 tablespoons milk
salt
freshly ground black pepper
1 teaspoon dried thyme

1. Heat 15 g/½ oz of the butter in a frying pan and fry the tomato slices for a few minutes.
2. Place the fried tomatoes in the base of a heatproof serving dish, and keep warm.
3. Wipe out the pan with kitchen paper and melt a further 15 g/½ oz butter in it. Fry the croûtes of bread on both sides, and drain well. Put them aside.
4. Heat another 15 g/½ oz butter in the pan and gently fry the onion, mushrooms and green pepper until soft. Take off the heat.
5. In a basin, beat together the eggs and milk. Add the salt, pepper and herbs.
6. Melt the remaining butter in a saucepan ar cook the eggs gently, stirring from time to time, until they become creamy and thickened. Do not overheat.
7. Stir the cooked vegetables into the scrambled eggs and spoon this mixture over the tomatoes.
8. Arrange the croûtes down each side of the dish and serve immediately.

VARIATIONS:

Substitute 2 rashers bacon, rinded and chopped for the green pepper.
Substitute 100 g/4 oz flaked, cooked smokec haddock for the green pepper.

Eggs en Cocotte with Mushrooms

Preparation time: 15 minutes
Cooking time: 10 minutes

salt
freshly ground black pepper
25 g/1 oz butter
50 g/2 oz mushrooms, chopped
4 eggs
150 ml/¼ pint single cream
chopped fresh parsley, to garnish

The eggs will continue cooking after the dish has been removed from the oven, so be careful not to overcook them.

1. Lightly butter 4 cocotte or ramekin dishes, or a shallow ovenproof dish and sprinkle with salt and pepper.
2. Melt the butter in a saucepan and fry the mushrooms until softened. Divide the mushrooms between the cocotte dishes. Break an egg into each dish and place the dishes in a roasting tin half-filled with water.
3. Bake in the centre of a preheated oven at 180°C, 350°F, Gas Mark 4 for about 10 minutes until the whites are barely set, and the yolks still soft.
4. Meanwhile heat the cream in a saucepan, but do not boil it. Add salt and pepper.
5. Remove the dishes from the oven and spoon the cream over each egg. Garnish with chopped parsley. Serve with hot toast.

VARIATIONS:

Use 100 g/4 oz chopped ham or chicken instead of mushrooms, or simply bake the eggs without a filling.

Eggs Greek-style

eparation time: 30 minutes
ooking time: 15 minutes

nedium aubergine
t
ablespoons oil
nedium onion, peeled and diced
green pepper, cored, seeded and diced
5 g/8 oz tomatoes, skinned and sliced
shly ground black pepper
ggs
ashers back bacon, rinded and chopped

This is a simple but delicious fried egg dish.

1. Slice the aubergine thinly and sprinkle salt over the slices. Leave them to stand in a colander for 30 minutes. Drain off the liquid and rinse them under cold running water. Dry the slices well with kitchen paper.
2. Heat 1 tablespoon of the oil in a frying pan, and cook the onion and pepper until softened. Remove and set aside.
3. Using 4 tablespoons of the oil, fry the aubergine slices in batches until browned and drain them on kitchen paper.
4. Return all the cooked aubergines to the pan with the onion and pepper and stir in the tomatoes. Add salt and pepper and cook for a further 5 minutes. Spoon the aubergine mixture over the base of a serving dish and keep warm.
5. Meanwhile fry the eggs in the remaining oil and then the bacon. Arrange the eggs over the vegetable mixture and sprinkle chopped bacon over the top. Serve immediately.

Left to right: Eggs Milton;
Eggs en cocotte with mushrooms

Stuffed Eggs

Preparation time: 15 minutes
Cooking time: 12 minutes

4 hard-boiled eggs
25 g/1 oz butter
1 tablespoon Mayonnaise (page 149)
1 teaspoon curry powder
salt
To garnish:
watercress
cayenne pepper

1. Shell the eggs and, when cold, cut each in half lengthwise. Remove the yolks using the handle of a teaspoon, being careful not to break the whites.
2. With a fork, mash the yolks in a bowl and beat in the butter and mayonnaise. Stir in the curry powder, and a little salt. Mix until smooth and put the mixture into a forcing bag fitted with a 1 cm/½ inch star pipe.
3. Pipe the mixture back into the egg whites. Arrange the eggs on a bed of watercress and sprinkle over a little cayenne pepper.

VARIATIONS:

Add a small can of drained, mashed sardines or anchovies to the yolk mixture.

Add a little minced ham or grated cheese to the yolk mixture.

Eggs Mimosa

Preparation time: 25 minutes

4 hard-boiled eggs
100 g/4 oz peeled shrimps or prawns, chopped, or 100 g/4 oz can shrimps or prawns, drained and chopped
250 ml/8 fl oz Mayonnaise (page 149)
1 tablespoon hot water
watercress, to garnish

This dish is suitable as a first course.

1. Cool the eggs in cold water and shell them. Cut each egg in half lengthwise. Using a teaspoon, scoop out the yolks of all the eggs but one.
2. Rub the yolks through a sieve into a bowl. Stir in the shrimps or prawns and add 1 tablespoon of the mayonnaise.
3. Scoop out the remaining egg yolk and reserve.
4. Rinse the egg whites carefully in cold water and dry them on kitchen paper.
5. Arrange them on a serving dish and fill each white with the egg mixture.
6. Add the hot water to the remaining mayonnaise, stirring until it is of a coating consistency. Coat the eggs with the mayonnaise.
7. Rub the remaining yolk through the sieve and sprinkle over the eggs. Garnish with watercress and serve with thin slices of brown bread and butter.

Pipérade Loaf

Preparation time: 30 minutes
Cooking time: 10 minutes

50 g/2 oz softened butter
1 garlic clove, crushed
1 small French loaf
Filling:
50 g/2 oz butter
1 shallot, peeled and chopped
1 garlic clove, crushed
350 g/12 oz tomatoes, skinned and chopped
2 red peppers, cored, seeded and diced
salt
freshly ground black pepper
4 eggs

This is very suitable to take on a picnic. Alternatively, the pipérade filling may be served hot garnished with croûtes of bread.

1. With a fork, mash the softened butter and garlic in a bowl until well blended.
2. Cut off the top of the small French loaf and scoop out most of the crumbs. Spread the garlic butter inside and outside the loaf, including the lid. Wrap in foil and bake in a preheated oven at 180°C, 350°F, Gas Mark 4, for 10 minutes until crisp.
3. Melt half the butter in a frying pan and add the shallot, garlic, tomatoes and peppers. Cook slowly, stirring occasionally, until the mixture is reduced to a thick pulp, about 10 minutes. Add salt and pepper.
4. Beat the eggs together in a bowl with a fork, add the rest of the butter and pour the eggs into the tomato mixture. Stir with a metal spoon over a gentle heat until the eggs begin to thicken.
5. Allow the mixture to cool completely, then fill the French loaf with it. Replace the lid and serve sliced.

Salami Scotch Eggs

'reparation time: 15 minutes
;ooking time: 8 minutes per egg

hard-boiled eggs
tablespoon seasoned flour
) g/2 oz salami, finely chopped
00 g/4 oz pork sausagemeat
egg, beaten
ry breadcrumbs for coating
il or fat for deep frying

1. Shell the eggs and dust them with seasoned flour.
2. Mix the chopped salami with the sausagemeat until thoroughly blended. Divide the sausage mixture into four portions. Shape or roll each piece into a round and work it around an egg, making it as even as possible and without cracks. Brush the prepared eggs with the beaten egg, and toss them in the breadcrumbs.
3. Heat the oil or fat in a deep frying pan, to a temperature of 170°C, 340°F. If you do not have a thermometer, test the oil or fat by adding a cube of bread to the oil. It should take 1 minute to brown.
4. Fry the eggs for 7–8 minutes until they are cooked through and golden brown. Remove the eggs from the pan with a perforated spoon and drain them on kitchen paper.
5. Cut the eggs in half lengthwise and either serve hot with a Tomato Sauce (page 151), or cold with a green salad.

Back, left to right: Eggs mimosa; Pipérade loaf; Salami Scotch eggs
Front centre: Stuffed eggs

Vegetables and Salads

SALADS

Courgette Salad with Mint and Lemon

Preparation time: 5 minutes
Cooking time: 5 minutes

450 ml/¾ pint water
salt
450 g/1 lb courgettes, thickly sliced
sprig of mint
2 tablespoons oil
grated rind and juice of ½ small lemon
½ teaspoon caster sugar
freshly ground black pepper
1 tablespoon chopped mint

1. Bring the salted water to the boil in a saucepan. Add the courgettes and sprig of mint, simmer for 3–5 minutes until just tender and still crisp.
2. Drain and leave to cool in a serving dish.
3. To make the dressing, mix together the oil, lemon rind and juice, sugar, salt and pepper and chopped mint. Pour the dressing over the courgettes when they are completely cold.

Leaf Salad

Serves 4 – 6
Preparation time: 10 minutes

½ small lettuce, separated into leaves
1 head of chicory, separated into leaves
1 small head of radicchio, if available, separated into leaves
100 g/4 oz small spinach leaves
small bunch watercress, coarse stalks removed
4 tablespoons French Dressing (page 152)

1. Wash and dry all the leaves and place them together in a salad bowl.
2. Pour over the dressing before serving and toss well.

Greek Salad

Serves 4 – 6
Preparation time: 10 minutes

½ cucumber, thickly sliced and quartered
225 g/8 oz tomatoes, thickly sliced and halved
1 onion, peeled and sliced into rings
12 black olives, stoned
Dressing:
150 ml/¼ pint plain unsweetened yogurt
1 tablespoon olive oil
1 garlic clove, crushed (optional)
1 tablespoon chopped fresh oregano or 1 teaspoon dried oregano
salt
freshly ground black pepper

1. Place the cucumber, tomatoes, onion and olives in a salad bowl.
2. Mix all the dressing ingredients together in a jug and pour over the salad. Toss well and leave for 10 minutes before serving.

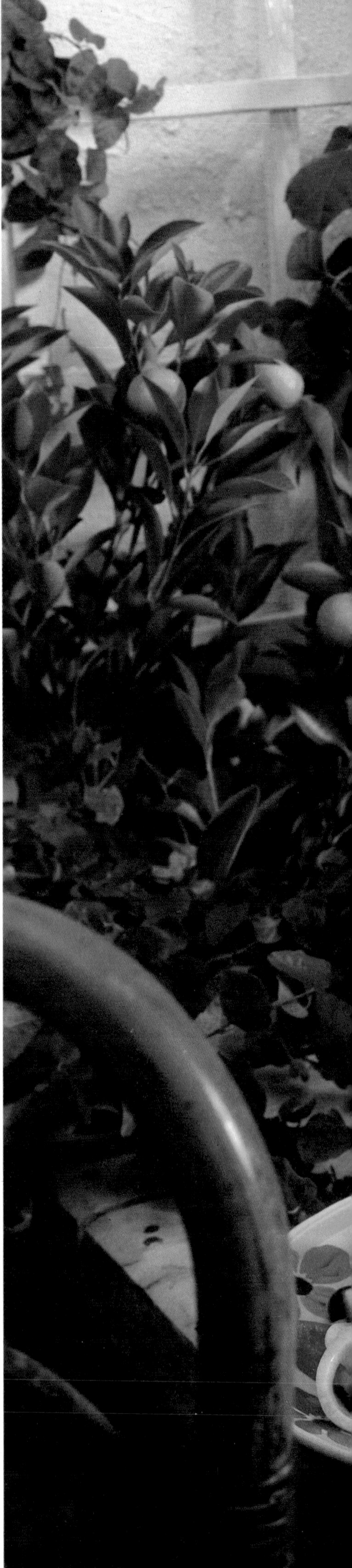

Left to right: Greek salad; Leaf salad; Courgette salad with mint and lemon

Πίνεται Παγωμένο
CLAUSS
ESTICA

Chinese Salad

Serves 4 – 6
Preparation time: 5 minutes

4 tablespoons French Dressing (page 152)
2 teaspoons soy sauce
50 g/2 oz button mushrooms, sliced
50 g/2 oz bean sprouts
4 spring onions, trimmed and chopped
225 g/8 oz Chinese cabbage, shredded

1. Mix the French dressing with the soy sauce in a salad bowl. Add the mushrooms and bean sprouts and toss to coat well. Leave to marinate for at least 10 minutes.
2. Just before serving, add the spring onions and Chinese cabbage and toss well.

Left: Hot potato sa
Right: Chinese sa

Hot Potato Salad

Preparation time: 5 minutes
Cooking time: 20 minutes

750 g/1½ lb new potatoes, scrubbed
large sprig mint
Dressing:
3 tablespoons oil
75 g/3 oz streaky bacon, rinded and chopped
1 bunch spring onions, trimmed and chopped
1 tablespoon wine vinegar
salt
freshly ground black pepper

1. Place the potatoes and mint in a saucepan and pour in just enough salted water to cover them. Cover the pan, bring to the boil and simmer for about 15 – 20 minutes until tender.
2. Meanwhile make the dressing. Heat the oil in a saucepan and fry the bacon for about 5 minutes until crisp. Remove the saucepan from the heat and stir in the spring onions, vinegar, salt and pepper.
3. Drain the potatoes and place them in a serving dish. Pour over the hot dressing.
4. Serve hot or cold.

Potato and Leek Layer

rves 4 – 6
eparation time: 10 minutes
oking time: 1½ hours

0 g/1 lb potatoes, peeled and thinly sliced
5 g/8 oz leeks, thinly sliced
teaspoon grated nutmeg
t
shly ground black pepper
0 ml/½ pint milk

1. Arrange the potatoes and leeks in layers in a 1.2 litre/2 pint casserole dish.
2. Sprinkle the layers with nutmeg, salt and pepper and finish with a layer of potatoes with a few leeks in the centre. Pour over the milk and cover.
3. Bake in a preheated oven at 190°C, 375°F, Gas Mark 5 for 1 hour.
4. Uncover and cook for a further 30 minutes until the potatoes are browned and tender, and most of the milk has been absorbed. Serve hot.

Celeriac Duchesse

eparation time: 15 minutes
oking time: 45 minutes

0 g/1 lb potatoes, peeled and diced
5 g/8 oz celeriac, peeled and diced
gg, beaten
t
shly ground black pepper
nched almonds

The vegetable purée may be prepared in advance, piped, covered and stored until required.

1. Place the diced potato and celeriac in a saucepan. Pour over just enough salted water to cover. Cover the pan, bring to the boil and simmer for 20 – 30 minutes until the vegetables are soft.
2. Drain the vegetables, then mash to a smooth purée. Beat in the egg, salt and pepper.
3. Leave the purée to cool slightly, then spoon the purée into a large piping bag fitted with a large, star nozzle. Pipe whirls of purée on to a lightly greased baking sheet. Top each whirl with a blanched almond.
4. Bake in a preheated oven at 200°C, 400°F, Gas Mark 6 for 15 – 20 minutes until heated through and golden brown. Serve hot.

Rosti Potatoes

rves 4 – 6
eparation time: 10 minutes
oking time: 30 minutes

g/2 lb potatoes, peeled
t
arge onion, peeled and grated
gg, beaten
shly ground black pepper
g/2 oz butter

1. If the potatoes are large, cut them into halves or quarters and place them in a saucepan. Pour over enough water to cover and add salt. Cover, bring to the boil and simmer for 5 minutes. Drain and leave to cool.
2. Coarsely grate the potatoes into a mixing bowl and add the grated onion. Stir in the beaten egg with salt and pepper.
3. Heat the butter in a frying pan and add the potato mixture, spreading it over the pan. Cook over a moderate heat, turning with a spatula when the underside becomes lightly browned (there is no need to turn all the potato at once – just lift a section on the spatula at a time and turn it over).
4. Cook for about 15 minutes until lightly browned throughout and crisp. Use the spatula to press the potato together to form a large pancake, then cook for 2 – 3 minutes until the underside is browned and crisp.
5. Turn the pancake over and cook the other side. It is easier to turn over, if you invert the pancake on to a plate then slide the pancake back into the pan to cook the other side.
6. Serve at once, cut into wedges.

VARIATION:

This dish may be made in advance. Cook the potatoes, as above, in the pan for 15 minutes until lightly browned, but do not press into a pancake. Turn the mixture into a shallow ovenproof dish and leave until required. Bake in a preheated oven at 190°C, 375°F, Gas Mark 5 for 30 minutes until heated through, crisp and browned.

From the top: Potato and leek layer; Celeriac duchesse; Rosti potatoes

Jerusalem Artichokes with Lemon and Herbs

Preparation time: 10 minutes
Cooking time: 15 minutes

750 g/1½ lb Jerusalem artichokes
grated rind and juice of 1 lemon
150 ml/¼ pint water
1 tablespoon fresh thyme leaves, stalks removed, or 1 teaspoon dried thyme
salt
freshly ground black pepper
1 tablespoon chopped fresh parsley, to garnish

1. Peel and thickly slice the artichokes. Place them immediately in a saucepan with the lemon rind, juice and water to prevent them from turning brown. Add the thyme, salt and pepper.
2. Cover the pan, bring to the boil and simmer for about 10 minutes until the artichokes are tender and nearly all the water has evaporated.
3. Sprinkle with parsley, add a little butter, if liked, and serve hot with veal, fish or poultry.

Beetroot in Orange Sauce

Preparation time: 10 minutes
Cooking time: 10 minutes

450 g/1 lb beetroot, cooked, peeled and diced
Sauce:
25 g/1 oz butter
1 small onion, peeled and finely chopped
1 tablespoon plain flour
150 ml/¼ pint milk
grated rind and juice of 1 orange
salt
freshly ground black pepper

1. Either gently fry the cooked beetroot in a little butter in a saucepan, turning it occasionally, or place it in an ovenproof dish, cover and heat in a moderate oven at 180°C, 350°F, Gas Mark 4 for 20 minutes.
2. Meanwhile make the sauce. Melt the butter in a saucepan and fry the onion gently for 5 minutes. Stir in the flour and then the milk. Bring to the boil, stirring until thickened and smooth. Add the orange rind and juice and return to the boil, stirring. Simmer for 2 minutes. Add salt and pepper to taste.
3. Pour the sauce over the hot beetroot in a serving dish.

Root Vegetable Casserole

Preparation time: 5 minutes
Cooking time: 1½ hours

750 g/1½ lb mixed root vegetables (carrots, parsnips, swedes, turnips), peeled and cut into 5 mm/¼ inch slices
1 tablespoon chopped fresh sage or 1 teaspoon dried sage
salt
freshly ground black pepper
150 ml/¼ pint chicken or vegetable stock
4 rashers bacon

1. Arrange the vegetables in layers in a 1.2 litre/2 pint casserole dish, sprinkling with the sage, salt and pepper. Pour over the stock and lay the bacon rashers across the top. Cover and bake in a preheated oven at 190°C, 375°F, Gas Mark 5 for 1 hour.
2. Uncover and cook for a further 30 minutes until the bacon is crisp and browned and the vegetables are just tender.

Carrots with Yogurt Parsley Sauce

Preparation time: 5 minutes
Cooking time: 20 minutes

450 g/1 lb carrots, topped, tailed, scrubbed or peeled
300 ml/½ pint chicken stock or water
150 ml/¼ pint plain, unsweetened yogurt
2 tablespoons chopped fresh parsley
salt
freshly ground black pepper

1. If the carrots are large, cut them into halves or quarters lengthways, otherwise leave them whole.
2. Place the carrots in a saucepan and pour over the stock or water. Bring to the boil and simmer for 15 minutes until the carrots are just tender.
3. If there is any liquid left, boil rapidly to reduce to about 2 tablespoons.
4. Remove the saucepan from the heat and immediately stir in the yogurt, chopped parsley, and salt and pepper. The heat from the carrots should be sufficient to heat the yogurt, but if necessary return the saucepan the flame and heat very gently. Do not allow the yogurt to boil or else it may curdle.
5. Transfer to a hot serving dish and serve at once with poultry or fish.

Back: Carrots with yogurt parsley sauce; Beetroot in orange sauce
Front: Root vegetable casserole; Jerusalem artichokes with lemon and herbs

Turnip and Watercress Purée

:paration time: 10 minutes
oking time: 30 minutes

) g/1 lb turnips, peeled and
liced
5 g/8 oz potato, peeled and
liced
) ml/1 pint water
t
shly ground black pepper
unch watercress

1. Place the diced turnips and potatoes in a saucepan with the water and salt. Cover and bring to the boil. Simmer for 20 – 30 minutes until the vegetables are very tender.
2. Remove the coarse stalks from the watercress and reserve a sprig for garnish. Add the watercress to the turnips, bring back to the boil and simmer for 1 minute. Drain and reserve the water.
3. Liquidize or sieve the vegetables to a purée, adding a little of the cooking water if necessary. Adjust the seasoning and reheat if necessary.
4. Turn into a warm serving dish and garnish with watercress. Serve as an accompaniment to roast meat.

Celery in Stilton Sauce

Preparation time: 5 minutes
Cooking time: 15 minutes

- 1 head of celery (about 450 g/ 1 lb)
- salt
- 25 g/1 oz butter
- 25 g/1 oz plain flour
- 300 ml/½ pint milk
- 100 g/4 oz Stilton cheese, grated or crumbled

This dish goes particularly well with roast pork but may be served with any roast meat.

1. Reserve the celery leaves for garnish, and cut the rest into sticks about 7.5 × 2.5 cm/3 × 1 inches.
2. Place the celery sticks in a saucepan and just cover with salted water. Bring to the boil and simmer for about 10 minutes until the celery is just tender.
3. To make the Stilton sauce, melt the butter in a saucepan and stir in the flour. Over a low heat pour in the milk, then bring to the boil, stirring constantly until the sauce thickens. Simmer for 2 minutes.
4. Reserve 25 g/1 oz of the Stilton for the top, remove the pan from the heat and stir in the remaining Stilton until melted.
5. Drain the celery and place in a hot serving dish. Pour over the Stilton sauce and sprinkle with the reserved Stilton.
6. Serve immediately, or lightly brown the cheese under the grill. Garnish with the reserved celery leaves.

Herb Baked Tomatoes

Preparation time: 10 minutes
Cooking time: 30 minutes

- 4 medium Mediterranean-type tomatoes or 4 large tomatoes
- 50 g/2 oz butter, softened
- 2 tablespoons chopped, fresh mixed herbs (thyme, marjoram, oregano, basil, chives) or 1 tablespoon dried mixed herbs
- 1 tablespoon chopped fresh parsley
- salt
- freshly ground black pepper

1. Cut the tomatoes in half and place them cut side up in an ovenproof dish.
2. Mix the butter with the herbs, salt and pepper and spread the mixture on top of the tomatoes.
3. Bake the tomatoes in a preheated oven at 190°C, 375°F, Gas Mark 5 for 30 minutes. Serve hot or cold with fish, steak or roast meats.

VARIATION:

A crushed garlic clove, or 1 tablespoon of finely chopped or grated onion, may be mixed with the butter and herbs before spreading on top of the tomatoes. This is a particularly good variation if using dried herbs.

Fennel in Cider Sauce

Preparation time: 3 minutes
Cooking time: 15 – 20 minutes

- 2 heads of fennel (about 450 g/ 1 lb)
- 300 ml/½ pint dry cider
- salt
- freshly ground black pepper
- 25 g/1 oz butter
- 25 g/1 oz plain flour

1. Wash and trim the fennel and reserve the feathery leaves for garnish.
2. Cut the heads into quarters lengthways and place them in a saucepan. Pour over the cider and add salt and pepper. Cover and simmer for 10–15 minutes until the fennel is just tender.
3. Drain, reserving the cooking cider, transfer the fennel to a warm serving dish and keep warm. Make the cider up to 300 ml/½ pint again with water.
4. Melt the butter in a small saucepan, stir in the flour. Over a low heat add the cider and water, then bring to the boil, stirring until thickened. Simmer for 2 minutes and taste and adjust the seasoning.
5. Pour the cider sauce over the fennel and garnish with the fennel leaves. Serve at once with roast meat or poultry.

Mixed Vegetable Fritters

reparation time: 15 minutes
'ooking time: 10 – 20 minutes

)0 g/4 oz plain flour
nch of salt
egg, separated
tablespoon oil
50 ml/¼ pint water
egetables:
large courgette, sliced
medium aubergine, roughly chopped
green pepper, cored, seeded and cut into 8
onion, peeled and cut into rings
) g/2 oz button mushrooms, or flat mushrooms, coarsely sliced
)0 g/4 oz Mozzarella cheese, sliced (optional)
l for deep-frying

Serve these vegetable fritters either as a first course or as a vegetable accompaniment to beef or grilled meat.

1. To make the batter, mix the flour and salt in a bowl, make a well in the centre and add the egg yolk. Add the oil and water and beat to a smooth batter.
2. Just before frying, whisk the egg white until stiff and fold it into the batter, using a large metal spoon.
3. Dip the prepared vegetables and the Mozzarella slices in the batter and fry in deep, hot fat at 180°C, 350°F for about 8 minutes until golden brown and crisp, turning frequently. Drain well on absorbent paper and serve immediately.
4. It may be necessary to cook the vegetable fritters in 2 or 3 batches, depending on the size of the pan. Drain the first batches well, place on a hot dish uncovered, and keep warm in the oven until all the fritters are cooked.

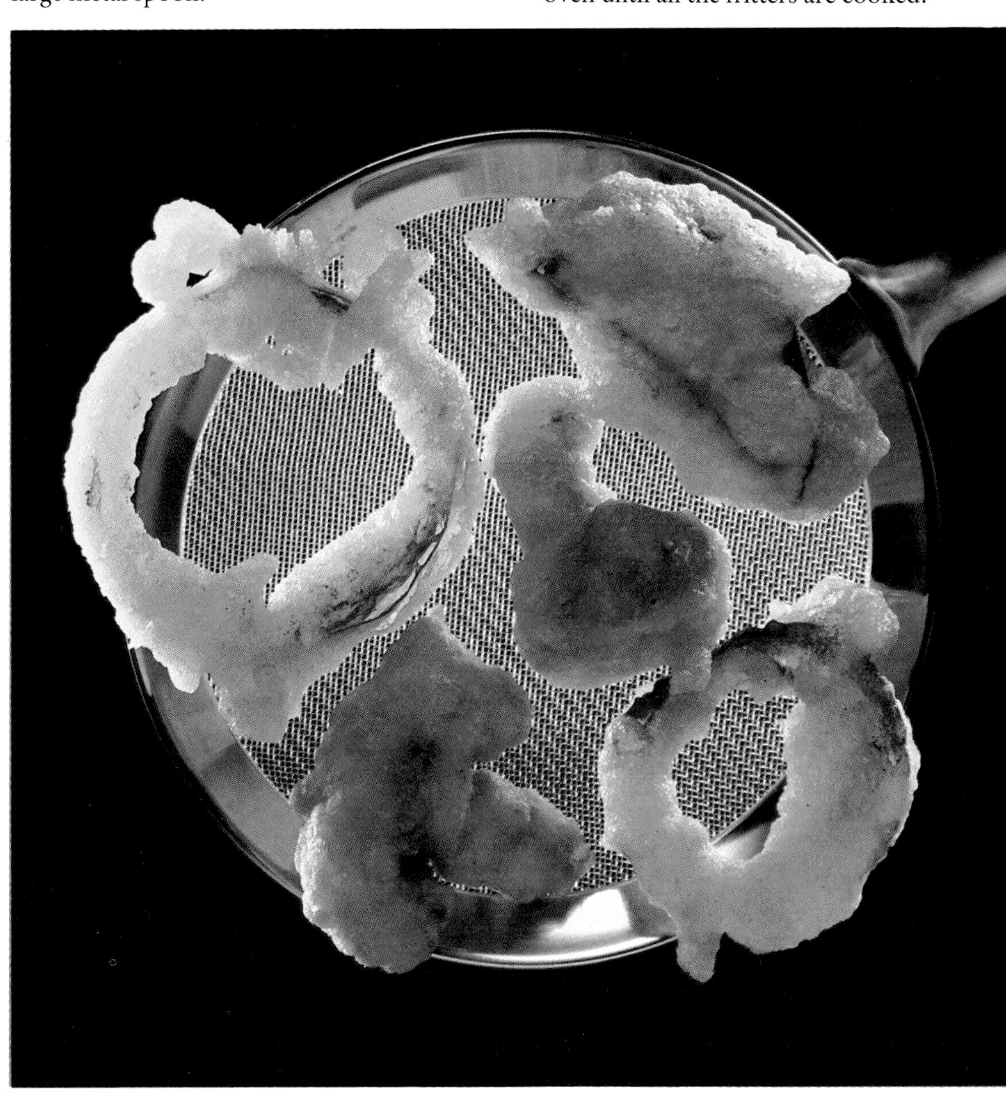

Braised Red Cabbage

eparation time: 10 minutes
oking time: 40 minutes

) g/1 lb red cabbage, shredded
arge onion, peeled and thinly sliced
arge cooking apple, peeled, cored and sliced
g/2 oz sultanas
) ml/¼ pint water, stock, or red or white wine
ablespoons wine vinegar
t
shly ground black pepper
ablespoon sugar

1. Place the cabbage, onion, apples and sultanas in a saucepan. Pour over the water and vinegar and sprinkle with the salt, pepper and sugar.
2. Cover and bring to the boil. Simmer for about 30 – 40 minutes until the cabbage is tender, stirring occasionally. If there is still some liquid left in the base, remove the lid and boil, stirring until the liquid evaporates.
3. This dish may also be cooked in the oven. Place all the ingredients in an ovenproof casserole, cover and bake in a preheated oven at 180°C, 350°F, Gas Mark 4 for about 1 hour, until tender.
4. Serve hot or cold with cold, roast or grilled meats, or fish.

Cauliflower Polonaise

Serves 4 – 6
Preparation time: 10 minutes
Cooking time: 20 minutes

1 medium cauliflower
600 ml/1 pint water
salt
freshly ground black pepper
50 g/2 oz butter
50 g/2 oz fresh breadcrumbs
2 hard-boiled eggs, finely chopped
grated rind and juice of ½ lemon
2 tablespoons chopped fresh parsley

1. Trim the coarse stalk from the base of the cauliflower but leave some of the smaller leaves attached.
2. Bring the water to the boil in a saucepan large enough to hold the cauliflower whole and add salt. Sit the base of the cauliflower in the boiling water, cover and simmer for about 15 minutes until just tender but not soft. (The cauliflower florets will cook in the steam and the stalk, which takes longer to cook, in the boiling water.)
3. Meanwhile make the sauce. Heat the butter in a saucepan and fry the breadcrumbs, stirring until lightly browned, about 5 minutes. Add the chopped hard-boiled egg, lemon rind and juice, parsley, salt and pepper and heat gently.
4. Drain the cauliflower and place in a warm, shallow serving dish. Spoon the topping on to the centre of the cauliflower and around the base of the dish. Serve at once with roast meat or poultry.

French Beans with Almonds and Lemon

Serves 4 – 6
Preparation time: 5 minutes
Cooking time: 10 minutes

450 g/1 lb French beans, topped and tailed
salt
50 g/2 oz butter
1 garlic glove, crushed
50 g/2 oz split almonds
1 tablespoon lemon juice
freshly ground black pepper

1. Place the beans in a saucepan of boiling salted water and simmer for about 5 minutes, until the beans are just tender.
2. Meanwhile, heat the butter in a saucepan and fry the garlic and almonds until lightly browned. Stir in the lemon juice and ground pepper.
3. Drain the cooked beans and add them to the pan. Cook, tossing gently until the beans are heated through. Serve at once.

French Braised Peas

Preparation time: 10 minutes
Cooking time: 15 minutes

1 kg/2 lb fresh peas, shelled, or 450 g/1 lb frozen peas
75 ml/3 fl oz water or chicken stock
4 sprigs fresh mint (optional)
8 spring onions, trimmed and chopped
1 teaspoon sugar
salt
freshly ground black pepper
1 small lettuce, trimmed and quartered
small sprigs of mint, to garnish

1. Place the peas in a saucepan and pour over the liquid. Add the mint, spring onions, sugar, salt and pepper. Place the lettuce wedges on top and cover the pan.
2. Bring to the boil and simmer for about 15 minutes until the peas are tender (frozen peas take less time to cook).
3. Pour into a serving dish with the liquid and garnish with sprigs of mint.
4. Serve hot with lamb, fish or poultry.

Left to right: French braised peas; Cauliflower polonaise; French beans with almonds and lemon

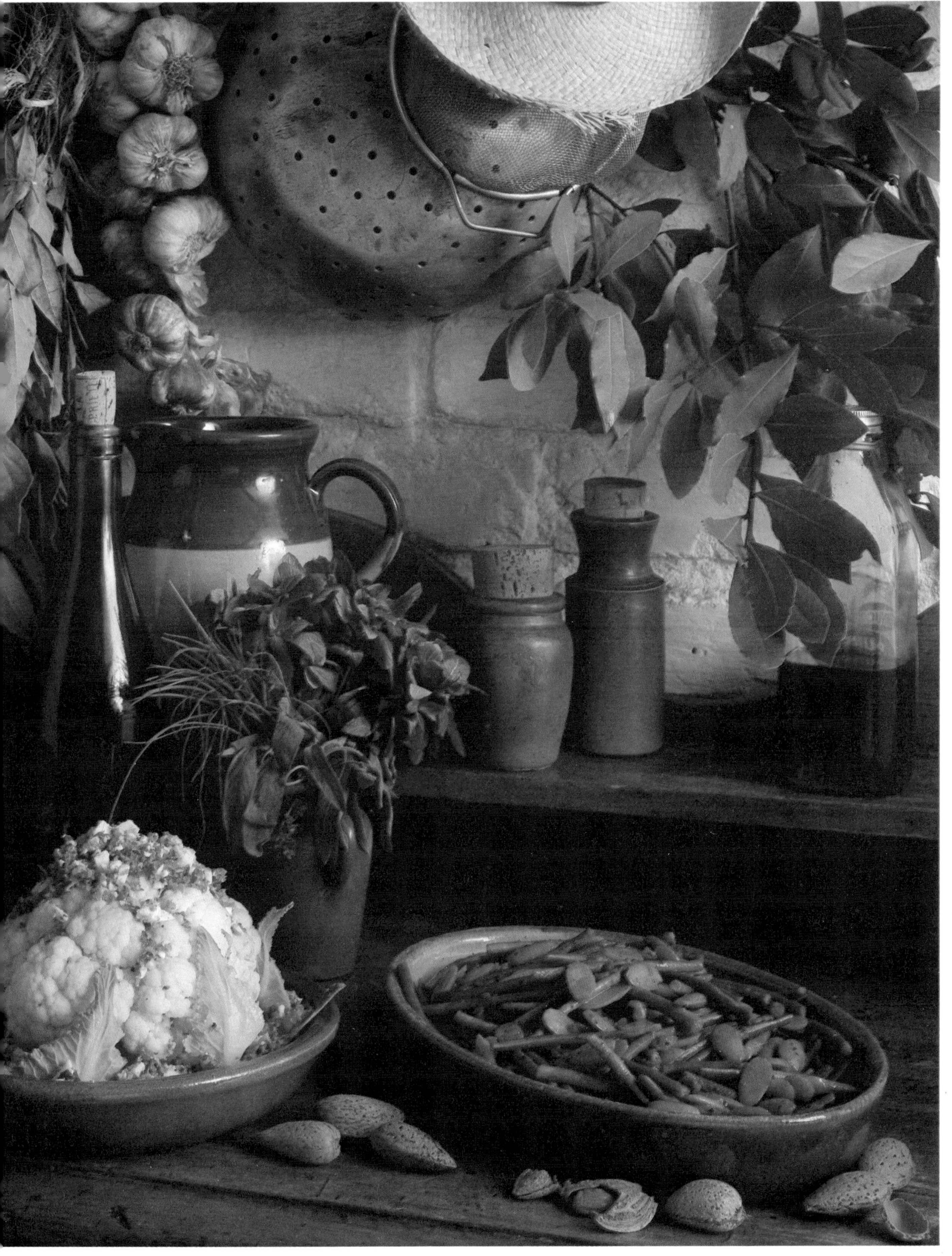

Leeks with Orange and Thyme

Preparation time: 5 minutes
Cooking time: 15 – 20 minutes

1 tablespoon oil
2 rashers streaky bacon, chopped
500 g/1¼ lb leeks, trimmed and sliced
grated rind and juice of 1 orange
1 tablespoon fresh thyme leaves or 1 teaspoon dried thyme
salt
freshly ground black pepper

1. Heat the oil in a saucepan and fry the bacon for 3 minutes. Add the leeks and fry for 2 minutes, stirring.
2. Make up the orange rind and juice to 150 ml/¼ pint with water, and add to the pan with the thyme, and salt and pepper.
3. Bring to the boil and simmer for 10 – 15 minutes, stirring occasionally until the leeks are just tender and most of the juice has evaporated.
4. Serve hot or cold.

Courgettes Niçoise

Preparation time: 5 minutes
Cooking time: 15 minutes

2 tablespoons oil
1 onion, peeled and chopped
1 garlic clove, crushed (optional)
450 g/1 lb courgettes, sliced
225 g/8 oz tomatoes, peeled and sliced
salt
freshly ground black pepper
1 tablespoon chopped fresh parsley, to garnish

1. Heat the oil in a pan and fry the onion, garlic and courgettes for 5 minutes or until lightly browned, turning occasionally. Stir in the tomatoes, with salt and pepper.
2. Cover the pan and cook gently for 5 – 10 minutes, stirring occasionally until the tomatoes are reduced to a pulp and the courgettes are just tender.
3. Turn into a serving dish and sprinkle with parsley.

Spring Greens with Bacon and Onion

Preparation time: 5 minutes
Cooking time: 10 minutes

2 tablespoons oil
2 rashers streaky bacon, rinded and chopped
1 large onion, peeled and sliced
1 garlic clove, crushed (optional)
450 g/1 lb spring greens or cabbage, shredded
150 ml/¼ pint chicken stock
salt
freshly ground black pepper

1. Heat the oil in a large saucepan and fry the bacon, onion and garlic for 5 minutes until lightly browned. Add the shredded spring greens and stock and bring to the boil. Simmer for 5 minutes, stirring occasionally until the greens are just tender. Remove greens to a serving dish and keep warm.
2. Boil rapidly to reduce the stock to about 4 tablespoons. Add salt and pepper to taste and pour over greens. Serve at once with poultry or roasts and casseroles.

Spinach Timbale

erves 4 as a main course or 6 – 8
s a vegetable accompaniment
reparation time: 5 minutes
ooking time: 1 hour

eggs
00 ml/½ pint milk
25 g/8 oz frozen, chopped
spinach, thawed
0 g/2 oz fresh breadcrumbs
0 g/2 oz Cheddar cheese, grated
4 teaspoon grated nutmeg
lt
eshly ground black pepper

1. Beat the eggs and the milk together in a bowl. Stir in the spinach, breadcrumbs, cheese, nutmeg, salt and pepper. Pour into a greased 1.5 litre/2½ pint ovenproof dish or a ring mould.
2. Bake in a preheated oven at 180°C, 350°F, Gas Mark 4 for about 1 hour (exact time depends on the depth of the dish) until the custard is set and slightly risen. Test with a skewer, which should come out clean.
3. Serve straight from the dish or leave for a few minutes before turning out. (If serving the timbale cold, leave it in the dish until cold before turning out.)
4. Serve hot with a Tomato Sauce (page 151) for a light main course.
5. Alternatively, serve the timbale by itself, hot or cold as a vegetable accompaniment to meat.

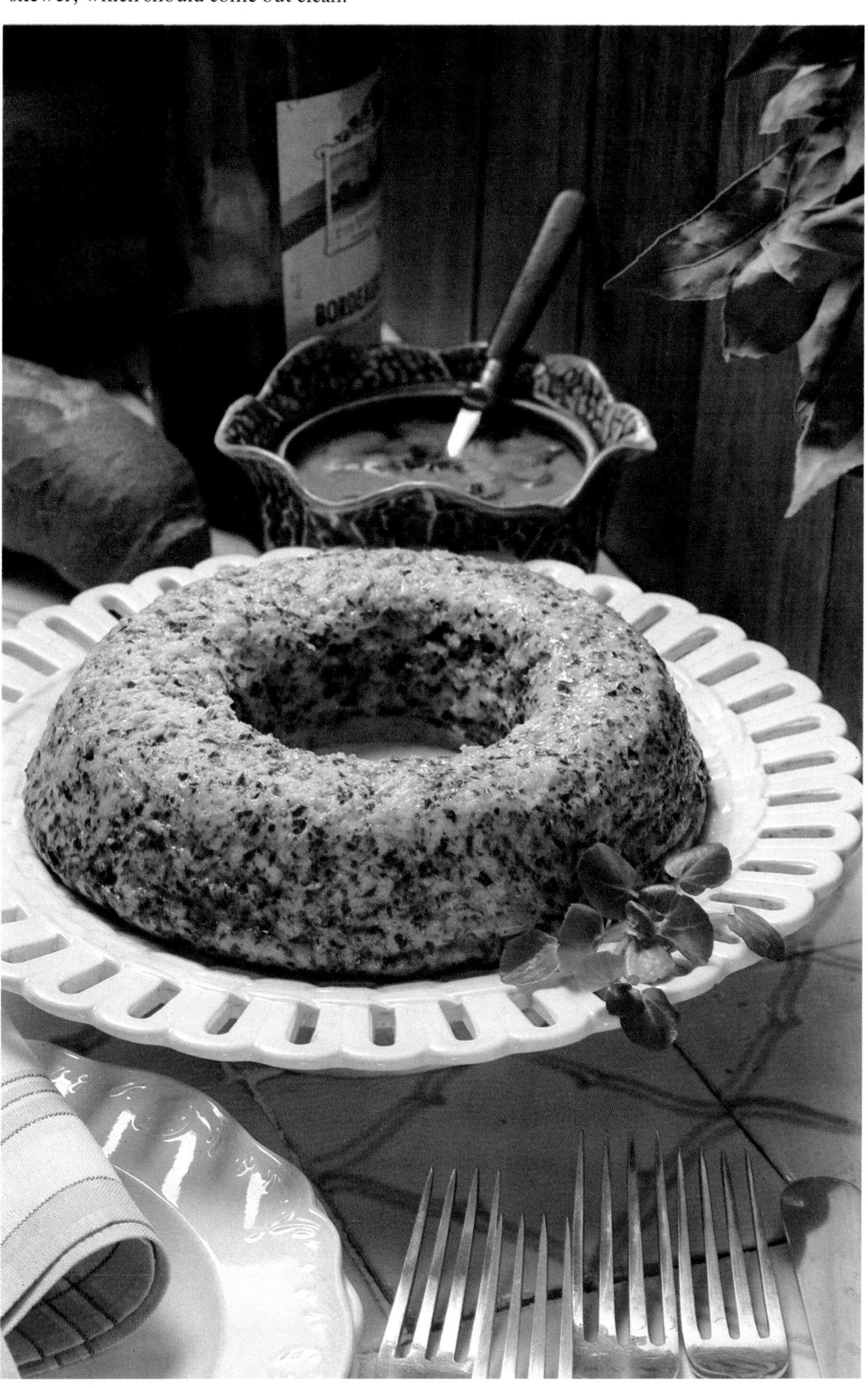

Rice, Pasta and Pulses

RICE

Almond and Herb Rice Ring

Serves 4 – 6 as a vegetable accompaniment
Preparation time: 20 minutes
Cooking time: 20 minutes

225 g/8 oz long-grain or medium-grain rice
salt
600 ml/1 pint water
4 tablespoons chopped fresh mixed herbs (chives, oregano, thyme, basil and parsley) or 2 tablespoons dried mixed herbs
1 oz butter
2 oz split almonds

This dish is ideal for a dinner party as it can be made in advance, chilled if kept overnight, and reheated still in the mould in a moderate oven for about 20 minutes when required.

1. Cook the rice in boiling salted water for 10 minutes. Add the chopped herbs and cook for a further 5 minutes until the rice is just tender. Drain thoroughly.
2. Melt the butter in a small pan and fry the almonds gently until golden brown, then remove the pan from the heat.
3. Lightly grease a 900 ml/18 cm 1½ pint/7 inch ring mould. Place the almonds in the base of the ring.
4. Spoon the rice into the mould, pressing it down firmly with the back of the spoon. Cover and bake in a preheated moderate oven or 180°C, 350°F, Gas Mark 4 for 20 minutes until heated through.
5. Cover the mould with a serving plate, invert and remove the mould. Serve at once.

Vegetable Pilaff

Serves 4 as a main course or 6 as a vegetable accompaniment
Preparation time: 10 minutes
Cooking time: about 30 minutes

1 tablespoon oil
1 onion, peeled and chopped
225 g/8 oz long-grain rice
600 ml/1 pint vegetable or brown stock
1 cinnamon stick or pinch of ground cinnamon
1 bay leaf
salt
freshly ground black pepper
Vegetables:
2 tablespoons oil
1 onion, peeled and sliced
1 garlic clove, crushed (optional)
450 g/1 lb courgettes, sliced
1 green pepper, cored, seeded and diced
100 g/4 oz button mushrooms
450 g/1 lb tomatoes, peeled and roughly chopped
1 tablespoon chopped fresh herbs (oregano, marjoram, basil and parsley) or 1 teaspoon dried mixed herbs
salt
freshly ground black pepper

1. To make the pilaff, heat the oil in a saucepan and fry the onion for 5 minutes. Add the rice and cook, stirring, for 1 minute. Pour in the stock and add the remaining ingredients.
2. Bring to the boil, stirring occasionally. Cover the pan and simmer gently for 15 – 20 minutes until the rice is cooked and all the stock has been absorbed.
3. Meanwhile, prepare the vegetables. Heat the oil in a saucepan and fry the onion, garlic and courgettes for about 5 minutes, stirring occasionally until the vegetables are lightly browned. Add the pepper and mushrooms and fry for 2 minutes. Add the tomatoes with the herbs, salt and pepper.
4. Cook for 10 – 15 minutes, stirring occasionally until the tomatoes are reduced to a pulp and the courgettes are just tender.
5. Transfer the pilaff to a warm serving dish and pour over the vegetables. Serve hot.

Left: Almond and herb rice ring
Right: Vegetable pilaff

Mushroom and Ham Risotto

Preparation time: 5 minutes
Cooking time: 30 minutes

25 g/1 oz butter
1 tablespoon oil
1 onion, peeled and chopped
100 g/4 oz mushrooms, sliced
100 g/4 oz cooked ham, diced
225 g/8 oz short-grain rice
600 ml/1 pint chicken stock
salt
freshly ground black pepper
25 g/1 oz grated Parmesan cheese

1. Heat the butter and oil in a large saucepan and fry the onion for 3 minutes. Add the mushrooms and ham and fry for 2 minutes, stirring constantly.
2. Add the rice and cook for a further minute, stirring. Pour over the stock, add salt and pepper and bring to the boil, stirring.
3. Cover the pan and simmer gently for 15–20 minutes until the rice is cooked, adding more stock if necessary, and the stock has been absorbed. Stir in the grated cheese and season to taste. Serve at once.

Savoury Rice Casserole

Serves 4 as a vegetable accompaniment
Preparation time: 10 minutes
Cooking time: 25–45 minutes

1 tablespoon oil
50 g/2 oz streaky bacon, rinded and chopped
1 onion, peeled and chopped
1 green pepper, cored, seeded and diced
225 g/8 oz long-grain rice
450 ml/¾ pint chicken or vegetable stock
4 medium tomatoes, peeled and chopped
¼ teaspoon mixed dried herbs
salt
freshly ground black pepper

1. Heat the oil in a large saucepan and fry the bacon and onion for 5 minutes. Add the green pepper with the rice and fry for 1 minute, stirring constantly.
2. Add the stock, tomatoes, herbs, and salt and pepper and bring to the boil.
3. Transfer the mixture to a casserole dish, cover and bake in a preheated moderate oven at 180°C, 350°F, Gas Mark 4 for 30–40 minutes until the rice is tender and all the liquid has been absorbed.
4. (Alternatively, cook in the saucepan for 15 minutes, covered.)

Left to right: Mushroom and ham risotto; Savoury rice casserole

Fried Rice

Serves 4–6
Preparation time: 10 minutes
Cooking time: 10 minutes

2 tablespoons oil
1 onion, peeled and chopped
50 g/2 oz streaky bacon, rinded and chopped
225 g/8 oz long-grain rice
100 g/4 oz cooked cold meat (or chicken, or prawns) shredded
50 g/2 oz cooked peas
2 eggs, beaten
1 tablespoon soy sauce
salt
freshly ground black pepper

1. Cook the rice in boiling salted water for about 15 minutes, until tender, drain and set aside to cool.
2. Heat the oil in a wok or large, heavy fryin pan, and fry the onion and bacon for 5 minute
3. Add the rice, meat and peas and fry over moderate heat for 3 minutes, stirring constantly, until the rice is lightly browned and heated through.
4. Make a hollow in the centre of the mixtur and pour in the eggs. Stir the eggs until they begin to set, then stir the egg into the surrounding rice mixture. Stir in the soy sauc and adjust the seasoning. Serve at once.

Rice Salad

rves 4–6
eparation time: 5 minutes
oking time: 20 minutes

5 g/8 oz long-grain rice
t
0 ml/1 pint water
0 ml/¼ pint French dressing
0 g/7 oz can sweetcorn, drained
pring onions, trimmed and chopped
small red pepper, cored, seeded and diced
g/2 oz walnuts, roughly chopped

1. Cook the rice in boiling salted water for about 15 minutes until tender (or 30–40 minutes if using brown rice). Drain the rice and place it in a bowl.
2. While the rice is still warm, pour over half of the dressing and toss.
3. Add the remaining ingredients and mix together. Allow to cool completely. Before serving, pour over the remaining dressing and toss again.

Spaghetti Carbonara

Preparation time: 5 minutes
Cooking time: 20 minutes

225 g/8 oz spaghetti
salt
25 g/2 oz butter
1 tablespoon olive oil
100 g/4 oz bacon or cooked ham, chopped
4 eggs
freshly ground black pepper
50 g/2 oz Parmesan cheese, grated
4 tablespoons cream (optional)

1. Cook the spaghetti in a large pan of boiling, salted water for 10–15 minutes until just tender. Drain.
2. Meanwhile, heat the butter and oil in a large pan and fry the bacon for 3 minutes. Add the drained spaghetti and toss lightly to mix.
3. Beat the eggs with salt and pepper and pour them over the spaghetti. Stir gently over a low heat until the eggs begin to thicken.
4. Stir in the Parmesan cheese, and cream if using, and serve at once.

Noodles with Spinach and Yogurt

Serves 4–6 as a starter or vegetable accompaniment
Preparation time: 5 minutes
Cooking time: 10–20 minutes

225 g/8 oz noodles
salt
50 g/2 oz butter
1 onion, peeled and chopped
225 g/8 oz packet frozen spinach, thawed
150 ml/¼ pint plain, unsweetened yogurt
¼ teaspoon ground nutmeg
freshly ground black pepper

1. Cook the noodles in a large pan of boiling salted water for 5–15 minutes (depending on whether the pasta is fresh or dried) until they are just tender.
2. Meanwhile make the sauce. Heat the butter in a large saucepan and fry the onion for 5 minutes. Add the spinach, yogurt, nutmeg, and salt and pepper and bring to the boil.
3. Drain the noodles and add them to the spinach mixture. Cook gently, stirring occasionally, until the noodles are heated through. Serve at once.

Tagliatelle with Fresh Tomato Sauce

Serves 6 as a starter or 4 as a light main course
Preparation time: 5 minutes
Cooking time: 5–15 minutes

225 g/8 oz tagliatelle
salt
2 tablespoons olive oil
1 onion, peeled and thinly sliced
1 garlic clove, crushed
450–750 g/1–1½ lb tomatoes, peeled and cut into wedges
1 tablespoon chopped fresh basil
freshly ground black pepper

1. Cook the tagliatelle in a large pan of boiling salted water for 5–15 minutes (depending on whether the pasta is fresh or dried) until it is just tender.
2. Meanwhile, make the sauce. Heat the oil in a saucepan and fry the onion and garlic for 5 minutes until lightly browned.
3. Add the tomatoes, basil and pepper and cook, stirring occasionally, for 5 minutes, until there is a thick sauce with whole pieces of tomato in it.
4. Drain the pasta and place it in a serving dish. Pour over the tomato sauce and serve.

Top left: Spaghetti carbonara
Bottom left: Noodles with spinach and yogurt
Right: Tagliatelle with fresh tomato sauce

Pasta Shell Salad

Serves 4 as a main course or 6 as a starter
Preparation time: 15 minutes
Cooking time: 10–15 minutes

225 g/ 8 oz pasta shells
salt
150 ml/¼ pint French Dressing (page 152)
1 tablespoon anchovy essence
1 teaspoon tomato purée
225 g/8 oz white fish, cooked and flaked (cod, haddock, coley or whiting)
200 g/7 oz can tuna fish, flaked
100 g/4 oz peeled prawns
freshly ground black pepper
1 lettuce, washed and drained
To garnish:
unpeeled prawns
slices of lemon
1 tablespoon chopped fresh parsley

1. Cook the pasta in a large pan of boiling salted water for 10–15 minutes until just tender.
2. Place the drained pasta in a bowl. Mix the French dressing with the anchovy essence and tomato purée and pour half of this over the pasta. Toss well and leave until cold.
3. Add the white fish, tuna fish and prawns to the pasta. Pour over the remaining dressing and toss lightly. Season to taste with pepper. Leave to marinate for at least 30 minutes in a cold place.
4. Line a serving dish, or individual dishes, with lettuce leaves and pile the pasta and fish salad in the centre. Garnish with unpeeled prawns, lemon slices and parsley.

Lasagne Verde

Preparation time: 45 minutes
Cooking time: 30 minutes

225 g/8 oz lasagne, green or white
Meat sauce:
1 tablespoon oil
1 onion, peeled and chopped
1 garlic clove, crushed
1 celery stick, chopped
50 g/2 oz streaky bacon, rinded and chopped
350 g/12 oz minced beef
25 g/1 oz plain flour
300 ml/½ pint beef stock
2 tablespoons tomato purée
2 teaspoons fresh oregano chopped or 1 teaspoon dried oregano
salt
freshly ground black pepper
Béchamel sauce:
450 ml/¾ pint milk
1 onion, peeled and quartered
2 sprigs parsley
1 bay leaf
25 g/1 oz butter
25 g/1 oz plain flour
¼ teaspoon ground nutmeg
salt
freshly ground black pepper
25g/1 oz grated Parmesan cheese

1. To make the meat sauce, heat the oil in a large saucepan and fry the onion, garlic, celery and bacon for 5 minutes. Add the minced beef and continue frying for 5 minutes, stirring until the meat is browned.
2. Stir in the flour, then add the stock, tomato purée, herbs, and salt and pepper. Bring to the boil, stirring, then cover and simmer gently for 30 minutes, stirring occasionally.
3. Meanwhile, make the béchamel sauce. Pour the milk into a saucepan and add the onion, parsley and bay leaf. Bring the milk to the boil, remove the saucepan from the heat and leave to infuse for at least 10 minutes.
4. Melt the butter in a saucepan and stir in the flour. Strain the flavoured milk through a sieve into the saucepan. Bring to the boil, stirring until the sauce is smooth and thick. Simmer for 2 minutes, then add the nutmeg and salt and pepper to taste.
5. Lower the sheets of pasta one at a time into a large pan of boiling salted water for 5–15 minutes (depending on whether the pasta is fresh or dried) until just tender. Adding a little oil to the pan helps to prevent the lasagne from sticking together.
6. Cook the lasagne in batches if necessary. Drain the lasagne and spread the pieces to dry on a clean tea towel.
7. Arrange layers of meat, pasta and Béchamel sauce in an ovenproof dish, finishing with a layer of Béchamel sauce. Sprinkle the top with Parmesan cheese. (The lasagne may be prepared in advance, chilled and baked when required.)
8. Bake in a preheated oven at 190°C, 375°F, Gas Mark 5 for 30 minutes until bubbling and golden brown on top. Serve at once.

Lentils with Tomatoes

Preparation time: 5 minutes
Cooking time: 1¼ hours

225 g/8 oz brown or green lentils
425 g/15 oz can tomatoes
600 ml/1 pint water
1 onion, peeled and chopped
1 tablespoon chopped fresh oregano, marjoram or basil, or 1 teaspoon dried herbs
salt
freshly ground black pepper
1 tablespoon chopped fresh marjoram or parsley, to garnish

Serve with grilled meats or chicken.

1. Place the lentils in a saucepan. Pour in the tomatoes with the juice from the can and roughly cut up the tomatoes.
2. Pour over the water and add the onion, herbs, and salt and pepper. Cover the pan and bring to the boil.
3. Simmer gently for 1–1¼ hours until the lentils are tender and most of the liquid has evaporated, but the mixture is still moist. Stir occasionally towards the end of the cooking time to prevent the lentils sticking.
4. Serve hot, sprinkled with chopped marjoram or parsley as a vegetable accompaniment. May also be served cold.

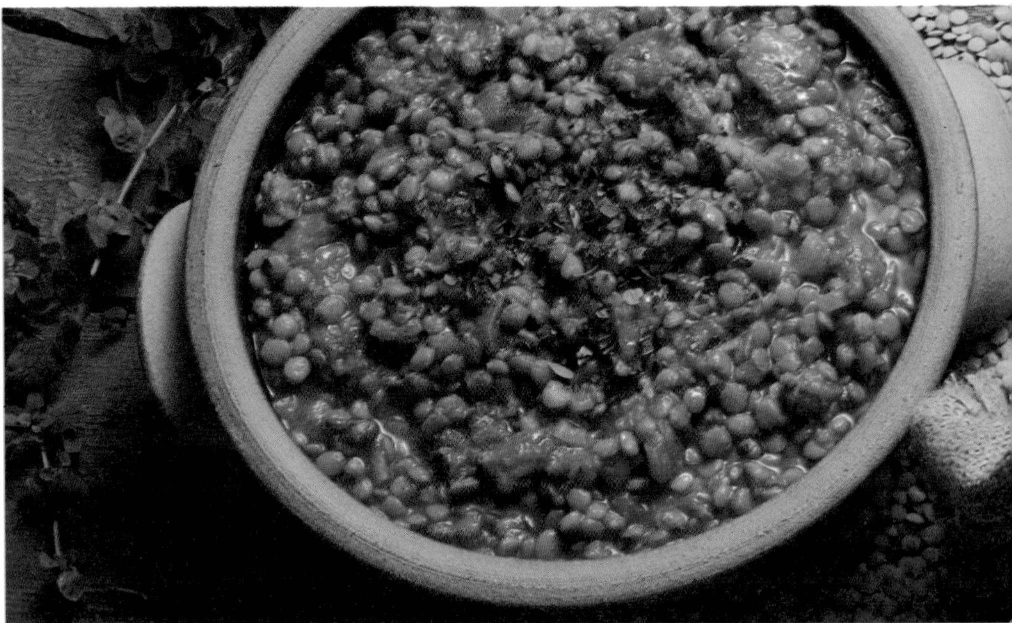

Left: Lentils with tomatoes
Right: Dhal

Whitebean Salad

Serves 4 as a salad or 6 as an hors d'oeuvre
Preparation time: overnight soaking or 2–3 hours
Cooking time: 1 hour

225 g/8 oz dried white beans (mixture of haricot, butter and black-eye peas)
600 ml/1 pint water
1 onion, peeled and chopped
1 bay leaf
salt
freshly ground black pepper
3 tablespoons olive oil
grated rind and juice of 1 small lemon
1 tablespoon capers
2 gherkins, sliced
2 tablespoons chopped fresh parsley
2 hard-boiled eggs, cut into wedges
8 black olives

1. Soak the beans in the water overnight, or cover with 600 ml/1 pint boiling water and leave to soak for at least 2 hours.
2. Drain the beans, reserve the liquid and make up to 600 ml/1 pint with water. Place the beans and the water in a saucepan and add the onion and bay leaf with salt and pepper.
3. Cover the pan and bring the water to the boil. Simmer for 45 minutes – 1 hour until the beans are tender. Drain the beans and leave to cool thoroughly.
4. To make the dressing, mix together the oil, lemon juice and rind, capers, gherkins, parsley, and salt and pepper. Pour half the dressing over the beans and leave to marinate for at least 30 minutes.
5. Turn the beans into a serving dish and arrange the hard-boiled eggs and olives on the top. Add the remaining dressing and serve.

Dhal

reparation time: 5 minutes
ooking time: 45 minutes

25 g/8 oz red lentils
00 ml/1 pint water
bay leaf
lt
eshly ground black pepper
g/1 oz butter or margarine
tablespoon oil
onion, peeled and finely chopped
garlic clove, crushed
teaspoon ground ginger or 1 teaspoon grated root ginger
teaspoon ground coriander
teaspoon ground cumin

1. Place the lentils in a saucepan and add the water, bay leaf, salt and pepper. Cover the pan and bring to the boil.
2. Simmer for 15–30 minutes until the lentils are swollen and the water has been absorbed to give a thickish purée.
3. Heat the butter and oil in a clean pan and fry the onion, garlic and root ginger, if using, for 5 minutes until lightly browned. Add the spices and cook for 1 minute. Add the cooked lentil purée and cook gently for 5 minutes.
4. Serve hot with rice or as an accompaniment to curry, or cold with a salad.

Flageolets with Rosemary

Serves 4–6
Preparation time: overnight soaking or 2–3 hours
Cooking time: 1 hour

225 g/8 oz dried green flageolet beans
600 ml/1 pint water
1 onion, peeled and chopped
1 garlic clove, crushed
1 tablespoon fresh rosemary leaves or 1½ teaspoons dried rosemary
1 bay leaf
salt
freshly ground black pepper
Sauce:
25 g/1 oz butter
25 g/1 oz plain flour
150 ml/¼ pint milk
salt
freshly ground black pepper
sprig of rosemary, to garnish

This is delicious served with roast lamb.

1. Soak the beans in the water overnight, or cover with 600 ml/1 pint boiling water and leave to soak for at least 2 hours.
2. Drain the beans, reserving the liquid and make up to 600 ml/1 pint with water. Place the beans and the liquid in a saucepan.
3. Add the onion, garlic, rosemary, bay leaf, and salt and pepper. Cover the pan and bring to the boil. Simmer for 45 minutes – 1 hour until the beans are tender. Drain the beans and reserve the cooking liquid.
4. To make the sauce, melt the butter in a saucepan and stir in the flour. Gradually stir the milk over a low heat with 150 ml/¼ pint of the cooking liquid.
5. Bring to the boil, stirring, until the sauce thickens. Simmer for 2 minutes and add salt and pepper to taste.
6. Fold the drained beans into the sauce and reheat. Serve hot, garnished with a sprig of rosemary.

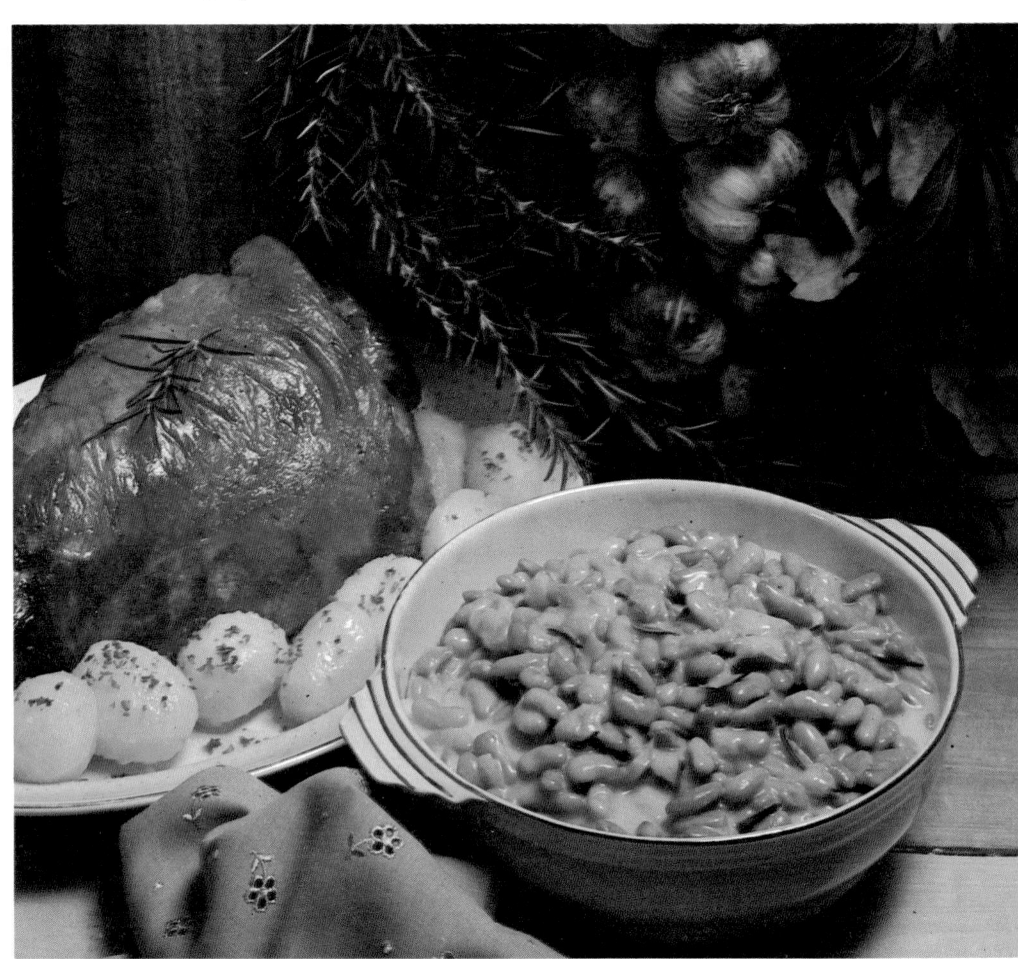

Kidney Bean Vegetable Casserole

Serves 4–6
Preparation time: overnight soaking or 2–3 hours
Cooking time: 2 hours

225 g/8 oz dried red kidney beans
600 ml/1 pint water
1 onion, peeled and chopped
2 celery sticks, sliced
1 green pepper, cored seeded and diced
1 bay leaf
salt
freshly ground black pepper

1. Soak the beans in the water overnight, or cover with 600 ml/1 pint boiling water and leave to soak for at least 2 hours.
2. Place the beans and their liquid in a casserole dish. Add the remaining ingredients and cover.
3. Bake in a preheated oven at 180°C, 350°F, Gas Mark 4 for 2 hours until the beans are tender and most of the liquid has been absorbed.
4. Serve hot as a vegetable accompaniment to hot or cold roast meat. This dish also tastes good served cold as a salad.

Italian Beans in the Oven

erves 4–6
reparation time: overnight
oaking or 2–3 hours
ooking time: 2–3 hours

25 g/8 oz dried haricot beans
00 ml/1 pint water
tablespoons olive oil
5 g/2 oz streaky bacon, rinded and chopped
onion, peeled and chopped
garlic clove, crushed
tablespoon chopped fresh sage or 1½ teaspoons dried sage
tablespoons chopped fresh parsley
rated rind and juice of ½ lemon
bay leaf
lt
eshly ground black pepper
tablespoon tomato purée or 2 tomatoes, skinned and roughly chopped
esh sage or sprig of parsley, to garnish

1. Soak the beans in the water overnight, or cover with 600 ml/1 pint of boiling water and leave to soak for at least 2 hours.
2. Heat the oil in a saucepan and fry the bacon, onion and garlic for 5 minutes until lightly browned. Add the beans with their liquid and all the remaining ingredients. Bring to the boil.
3. Transfer the mixture to a casserole dish, cover and bake in a preheated moderate oven at 180°C, 350°F, Gas Mark 4 for 2–3 hours until the beans are tender and most of the liquid has been absorbed.
4. Alternatively, cook on top of the cooker, in a covered saucepan until the beans are tender, adding a little more water if necessary.
5. Serve hot, garnished with fresh sage or a sprig of parsley.

Fish

Mackerel with Caper Dressing

Preparation time: 15 minutes
Cooking time: about 12 minutes

6 tablespoons oil
1 large garlic clove, crushed
juice of 1 large lemon
75 g/3 oz capers, rinsed and lightly crushed
salt
freshly ground black pepper
4 fresh mackerel, gutted and heads removed
2 tablespoons chopped fresh parsley or chives

1. Mix together the oil, garlic, lemon juice, capers, salt and pepper in a bowl, cover and leave to allow the flavours to blend.
2. Before cooking, slash the fish 3 times diagonally on each side, sprinkle with a little salt and pepper and arrange side by side on the grill rack.
3. Spoon the dressing over the fish. Cook under a pre-heated, moderately hot grill for about 5 minutes each side, turning once and basting with the dressing from time to time. If necessary, increase the heat towards the end to brown and crisp the skin.
4. Serve the fish with the pan juices, to which the parsley or chives have been added, spooned over.

VARIATION:

Instead of the caper dressing serve plain grilled fish with a tart fruit sauce–gooseberry is the traditional one, but rhubarb, damson or apple are equally good.

Trout with Hazelnuts

Preparation time: 10 minutes
Cooking time: 12–15 minutes

4 × 175 g/6 oz trout, cleaned, heads and tails left on, fins removed
salt
freshly ground black pepper
flour for coating
1 tablespoon oil
50 g/2 oz unsalted butter
75 g/3 oz hazelnuts
25 g/1 oz salted butter
4 tablespoons dry white breadcrumbs
2 tablespoons snipped chives or chopped fresh parsley
1 lemon, quartered, to garnish

1. Wash the trout, pat them dry with kitchen paper and season them inside and out with salt and pepper. (If using frozen trout, allow them time to thaw.) Just before cooking, roll the trout in flour, coating them evenly.
2. Heat the oil and unsalted butter in a large, heavy frying pan and, when the butter ceases to foam, put in the trout and cook gently for 12–15 minutes, turning carefully halfway through cooking.
3. Meanwhile, spread the hazelnuts in the grill pan and toast them gently for a few minutes until the skins burst, then rub them in a rough cloth to remove the skins. Chop the nuts coarsely.
4. When the fish are cooked through and golden, lift them out carefully, arrange side by side on a hot serving dish and keep hot.
5. Add the salted butter to the fat remaining in the frying pan (if it has over-browned wipe out the pan and start again, using 50 g/2 oz salted butter).
6. When the butter is hot, add the nuts and enough breadcrumbs to absorb all the fat. Fry fairly briskly, stirring, until golden brown and crisp. Stir in the chives or parsley with a little salt and pepper, and scatter immediately over the trout.
7. Garnish with lemon wedges and serve at once with boiled potatoes tossed in butter.

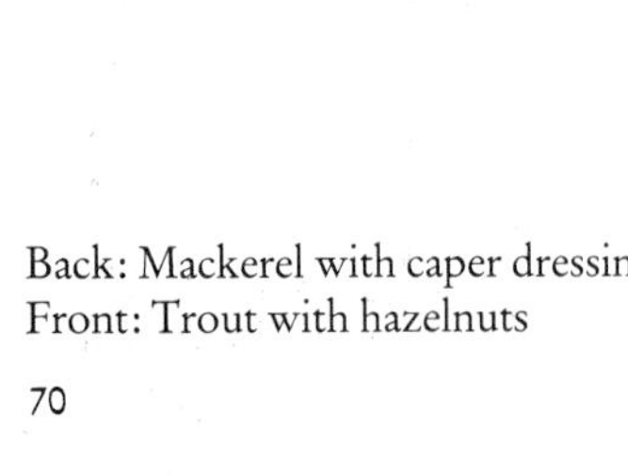

Back: Mackerel with caper dressing
Front: Trout with hazelnuts

Fish Pie

Preparation time: 20 minutes
Cooking time: 20–25 minutes

450 g/1 lb potatoes, peeled, boiled and drained, then mashed with 25 g/1 oz butter, salt and pepper and enough milk to make a creamy spreading consistency
Filling:
500 g/1¼ lb thick white fish fillets
300 ml/½ pint milk
1 thick slice onion
1 small bay leaf
4 peppercorns
salt
40 g/1½ oz butter
25 g/1 oz plain flour
50 g/2 oz grated cheese
225 g/8 oz tomatoes, skinned and chopped, or 50 g/2 oz peeled prawns
2 hard-boiled eggs, sliced
2 tablespoons chopped fresh parsley (optional)

A tasty, colourful fish pie makes a favourite family meal, and this one can be made without heating the oven. Use whatever kind of thick white fish fillets are available, for instance, whiting, cod, coley or haddock.

1. Rinse the fish under cold water, cut each fillet into 2 or 3 pieces and put into a saucepan.
2. Add the milk, onion, bay leaf, peppercorns and a little salt. Bring slowly to simmering point, then cover and cook very gently for 12–15 minutes.
3. Strain off the liquid and reserve for the cheese sauce.
4. Melt 25 g/1 oz butter in a clean saucepan, stir in the flour and cook gently for 1–2 minutes. Gradually stir in the reserved cooking liquid. When smoothly blended stir until boiling, then simmer gently for several minutes.
5 Meanwhile, remove any skin or bones from the pieces of fish and flake the flesh roughly. Discard the onion, bay leaf and peppercorns.
6. Stir into the sauce half the cheese, all the tomatoes or prawns, hard-boiled eggs, parsley if used, flaked fish and salt and pepper to taste. Mix gently over a low heat until thoroughly heated through.
7. Pour the mixture into a flameproof pie dish, spread the prepared potato topping over the top to cover it completely, and mark the surface with a fork.
8. Sprinkle with the remaining cheese, dot with flakes of the remaining butter and grill gently for a few minutes until the surface is golden and crisp.

VARIATION:

Aberdeen Fish Pie
Use smoked cod or haddock fillet instead of the white fish; omit the prawns and cheese.

Grilled Fish au Fromage

Preparation time: 10 minutes
Cooking time: 10–12 minutes

4 × 150–175 g/5–6 oz steaks or portions of white fish, skinned if necessary
salt
freshly ground black pepper
25 g/1 oz butter
100 g/4 oz finely grated Cheddar cheese, or a mixture of Gruyère and Parmesan
1 scant tablespoon French mustard
2–3 tablespoons single cream
2 firm tomatoes, sliced
watercress sprigs, to garnish

1. Wipe the fish with damp kitchen paper and season generously with salt and pepper.
2. Preheat the grill and melt the butter in a shallow flameproof dish large enough to hold the fish in a single layer.
3. Turn the fish in the melted butter, then grill under a moderate heat for about 4–5 minutes (under a low heat for 7–8 minutes if the fish is still frozen).
4. Meanwhile, put the cheese and mustard into a basin and beat in enough cream to make a soft mixture.
5. Turn the fish carefully, spread them evenly with the cheese mixture and continue grilling, very gently, for 5–6 minutes. When the surface is golden, but not overbrowned, arrange 2 slices of tomato on each portion and grill for a further minute.
6. Serve from the dish, garnished at the last moment with sprigs of watercress.

Above: Fritto misto di pesce
Right: Fish pie; Grilled fish au fromage

Fritto Misto di Pesce

reparation time: 30 minutes
:ooking time: 12–15 minutes

50 ml/¾ pint Fritter Batter (page 53)
25 g/8 oz thick fillet of haddock or hake
25 g/8 oz thin fillets of dab, plaice or sole
4 large, cooked prawns, shelled
small whole sardines or sprats, cleaned and beheaded
tablespoons plain flour
o garnish:
mon wedges
›rigs of parsley

1. Prepare the batter up to adding the egg whites, and leave it to rest in the refrigerator for about 30 minutes.
2. Cut the thick fish fillet into 2.5 cm/1 inch chunks and the thin fillets into 1 cm/½ inch wide diagonal strips.
3. Toss each variety of fish separately in the flour, including the prawns and sardines, and shake off any surplus flour. Arrange them in separate piles on a tray ready for coating.
4. Half fill a deep frying pan with oil and heat slowly until the thermometer registers 190°C/375°F.
5. Meanwhile, stiffly whisk the egg whites for the batter and fold them gently but thoroughly into the chilled batter.
6. When the fat is ready, fry each batch of fish separately. Dip each piece of fish in turn, in and out of the batter, using skewers.
7. Lower the fish into the hot fat and fry until crisp and cooked, about 1½–2 minutes for the small pieces, 3 minutes for the larger pieces.
8. Drain on crumpled kitchen paper and keep hot in a preheated oven at 150°C, 300°F, Gas Mark 2 until all the fish has been fried.
9. To serve, arrange the fish in groups on a hot dish, lined with absorbent paper. Garnish with lemon wedges and parsley and serve immediately accompanied by a tossed green salad and French bread.

Fillets of Sole au Vermouth

Preparation time: 15 minutes
Cooking time: 15 minutes

8 × 50–75 g/2–3 oz sole fillets, dark skin removed
salt
freshly ground black pepper
5 tablespoons water
5 tablespoons dry white Vermouth
1 shallot or very small onion, peeled and sliced
25 g/1 oz butter
175 g/6 oz button mushrooms, trimmed
2–3 teaspoons lemon juice
2 egg yolks
3 tablespoons double cream
paprika, to garnish (optional)

1. Season the fillets with salt and pepper and fold each in half with the skin-side inside.
2. Put the water, Vermouth and onion into a wide shallow pan and bring to simmering point. Add the fish, cover the pan and poach very gently for 8–10 minutes.
3. Meanwhile, melt the butter in a saucepan, add the mushrooms, 2 teaspoons of the lemon juice and a sprinkling of salt, cover and cook over a low heat for 2 minutes, shaking the pan frequently.
4. Lift the cooked fillets out with a perforated spoon and arrange them on a hot serving dish. Similarly lift out the mushrooms, and keep them warm.
5. Strain the fish poaching liquid into the pan in which the mushrooms were cooked and bring the combined liquids to the boil, stirring occasionally.
6. Blend the egg yolks and cream together and stir in several spoonfuls of the hot liquid, then pour back into the pan and heat gently, stirring continuously, until the sauce thickens enough to coat the back of the spoon. Do not allow the sauce to boil.
7. Add salt, pepper and lemon juice to taste and spoon the sauce over the fish. Scatter the mushrooms over and, if liked, garnish with paprika pepper.
8. Serve with small potatoes boiled and tossed in Maître d'hotel Butter (page 153).

Fillets of Whiting Gratinée

Preparation time: 15 minutes
Cooking time: 20 minutes

500–750 g/1¼–1½ lb whiting fillet
salt
freshly ground black pepper
50 g/2 oz butter
1 large onion, peeled and finely chopped
225 g/8 oz firm mushrooms, coarsely chopped (including stalks)
juice of ½ lemon
4 tablespoons dry white breadcrumbs
2 tablespoons finely grated strong cheese
chopped fresh parsley, to garnish

1. Wipe the fish with damp kitchen paper. Arrange the fillets flat, side by side, in a well buttered, shallow, ovenproof dish. Sprinkle the fish with salt and pepper.
2. Heat half of the butter in a saucepan and fry the onion very gently for 5 minutes, until beginning to soften. Add the mushrooms, stir and fry for another minute then add the lemon juice, salt and pepper.
3. Spoon the mixture evenly over the fish. Sprinkle the breadcrumbs mixed with the cheese over the surface and dot the rest of the butter over in small flakes.
4. Bake, uncovered, in the hottest part of a preheated oven at 200°C, 400°F, Gas Mark 6 for about 20 minutes (30 minutes if the fillets are frozen), until the fish is just cooked through and the surface golden. Sprinkle with parsley and serve from the dish.

Fish Fillets Provençale

Preparation time: 20–30 minutes
Cooking time: about 15 minutes

750 g/1½ lb white fish fillets, e.g. haddock, whiting, cod or coley, skinned
2 tablespoons seasoned flour
5 tablespoons olive oil
1 large onion, peeled, halved and thinly sliced
1–2 garlic cloves, crushed
450 g/1 lb tomatoes, peeled, seeded and chopped or 425 g/15 oz canned tomatoes, drained and chopped
2 tablespoons black or green olives (optional)
1 teaspoon caster sugar
salt
freshly ground black pepper
1 tablespoon chopped fresh herbs e.g. chives, chervil or parsley

1. Cut the fish into roughly 2.5 cm/1 inch cubes. Coat the fish in the seasoned flour, shaking off any surplus flour.
2. Heat 2 tablespoons of the oil in a frying pan and fry the onion very gently for 6–8 minutes, until soft and golden.
3. Add the garlic and fry for another minute, then add the tomatoes, olives, if using, sugar, and salt and pepper to taste. Stir for several minutes until the tomato begins to soften (if using fresh), then cover the pan and remove from the heat.
4. Meanwhile, heat the remaining oil in a large frying pan and, when sizzling hot, put in the pieces of fish and fry them over a moderate heat for about 10 minutes, turning frequently, until cooked through and lightly browned.
5. Using a perforated spoon, transfer the fish to a hot, shallow serving dish. Spoon the vegetables over the fish and sprinkle them with the herbs.

Back: Fish fillets provença
Front left: Fillets of sole au Vermou
Front right: Fillets of whiting gratin

Bretonne Style Dabs

eparation time: 15 minutes
oking time: about 20 minutes

x 350 g/12 oz whole dabs, cleaned, trimmed and beheaded
t
shly ground black pepper
ur for coating
g/2 oz unsalted butter
ablespoon oil
g/1½ oz salted butter
2 tablespoons finely chopped shallots or spring onions
g/2 oz shelled shrimps or small prawns
ablespoon capers
ce of 1 lemon
ablespoon chopped fresh herbs, i.e. parsley, chives and/or chervil, as available

This method of shallow frying can be used for any small, whole flat fish such as plaice or lemon sole, or for portion size fillets.

1. Wipe the fish with damp kitchen paper and season it generously with salt and pepper. Immediately before frying, coat both sides of the fish in the flour shaking off any surplus.
2. Heat 40 g/1½ oz of the unsalted butter and the oil in a large frying pan and, when hot, fry the fish in two batches, cooking them for 4–6 minutes each side, until golden and cooked through.
3. Arrange the fish on a hot serving dish and keep hot.
4. Meanwhile, heat the salted butter in a small saucepan and fry the shallot gently for a few minutes until soft, then add the shrimps, capers, lemon juice and herbs. Heat through.
5. Spoon the sauce over the fish and serve immediately with creamed potatoes.

Salmon Trout en Bellevue

Serves 6
Preparation time: 40 minutes
Cooking time: 45 minutes

1 × 1½ kg/3 lb salmon trout
salt
freshly ground black pepper
oil
600 ml/1 pint aspic jelly
To garnish:
spray of fresh tarragon, fennel or dill
3 medium tomatoes, halved, scooped out and filled with cooked peas (optional)
3 hard-boiled eggs, halved, yolks sieved and creamed with mayonnaise then piled into whites
½ cucumber, thinly sliced
Mayonnaise Chantilly (page 149), to serve

This is a cool, decorative dish for a summer party. Salmon trout average 1–1½ kg/2–3½ lb in weight and serve from 4–8 people. To preserve its delicate flavour, plan to cook and cool the fish on the day of the party rather than beforehand. If you haven't a large flat serving dish use a piece of board covered with foil. Powdered aspic jelly is available from most good delicatessens.

1. Wipe the fish with damp kitchen paper, scrape the body cavity clean and sprinkle it with salt and pepper.
2. Lay the fish on a large piece of well oiled foil and twist the foil edges together to form a loose but watertight parcel.
3. Place the parcel on a baking sheet and bake in the centre of a preheated oven at 180°C, 350°F, Gas Mark 4 for 45 minutes.
4. Meanwhile, make up the aspic jelly and leave to cool.
5. When the fish is cooked, remove the parcel from the oven and leave, unopened, to allow it to cool a little.
6. While the fish is still warm, open the parc and skin the fish. To do this, cut the skin around the head and across the tail and peel, away from the flesh. Roll the fish over and repeat on the other side.
7. Carefully transfer the fish to a flat serving dish. When the aspic is on the point of settin (if necessary, stir it over crushed ice until it coats the back of a metal spoon), spoon a thi film of jelly over the fish and leave to set.
8. Garnish the fish with a spray of herbs, co with a second layer of aspic and leave to set again. Chill the remaining aspic until stiff.
9. Chop the stiff aspic into small pieces and arrange the pieces along either side of the fish Set the filled tomatoes (if using) and eggs alternately in the aspic and border the dish with overlapping slices of cucumber.
10. Serve a Mayonnaise Chantilly separately in a sauce boat.

Smoked Haddock Kedgeree

rves 3–4
reparation time: 20 minutes
ooking time: 30 minutes

50 g/12 oz smoked haddock fillets
5 g/3 oz butter
medium onion, peeled and finely sliced
teaspoon curry powder
00 g/4 oz long-grain rice
5 g/1 oz currants (optional)
00 ml/½ pint water
eshly ground black pepper
-2 teaspoons lemon juice
lt, if necessary
tablespoon chopped fresh parsley
hard-boiled eggs, quartered lengthwise

1. Put the haddock fillets in a dish, cover them with boiling water and leave for 5 minutes. Drain, skin and divide the fillets into small pieces.
2. Heat 25 g/1 oz of the butter in a saucepan and fry the onion gently for 5 minutes, until soft but not browned. Stir in the curry powder and cook for a minute, then stir in the rice, currants, if using, and 300 ml/½ pint water.
3. Bring to the boil, reduce the heat, cover tightly and simmer very gently for 15 minutes.
4. Add the haddock and continue cooking gently, stirring frequently with a fork to prevent the mixture sticking to the pan, until all the liquid has been absorbed.
5. Stir in the remaining butter and season to taste with pepper, lemon juice and, if necessary, salt.
6. Pile the kedgeree into a hot serving dish, sprinkle with parsley and arrange the hard-boiled eggs around the edge.

Kippered Mackerel Salad

Preparation time: 15 minutes
Cooking time: 25 minutes plus cooling time

2 large kippered mackerel
½ cucumber
salt
4 firm tomatoes, peeled, seeded and diced
4–6 tablespoons bean-sprouts
Dressing:
3 tablespoons olive oil
1 tablespoon lemon juice
salt
freshly ground black pepper
1 tablespoon chopped fresh parsley, chervil or dill
1 tablespoon snipped chives

Kippered mackerel (which need a brief cook) and hot smoked mackerel (which are ready to eat) are usually interchangeable where recipes are concerned. Their rich flesh makes a substantial salad and is at its best when contrasted with crisp, refreshing fruit and vegetables.

1. Poach the kippered mackerel in their bags according to the label directions. Open the bags and set aside until cold.
2. Meanwhile, cut the cucumber into 5 mm/¼ inch dice, mix with 1 teaspoon salt and leave in a colander to drain for 30 minutes.
3. Rinse the bean-sprouts in cold water, drain thoroughly and chill in the refrigerator until ready to serve.
4. Shortly before serving mix all the dressing ingredients thoroughly in a bowl.
5. Rinse the cucumber under cold water and pat dry, then add to the dressing with the tomato and bean-sprouts; toss lightly together.
6. Cut each mackerel into 2 fillets, then cut each fillet lengthways into 2 pieces.
7. Arrange the pieces a little apart on individual serving dishes and spoon the salad down the centre. Alternatively, arrange in the same way on 1 large serving dish.

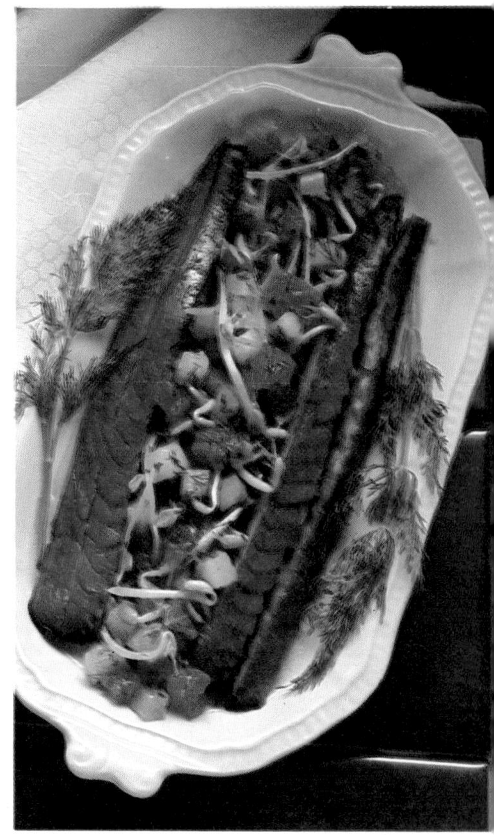

Fish Kebabs

Preparation time: 15 minutes, plus 3–4 hours marinating time
Cooking time: about 12 minutes

1 large green pepper, seeded and cut into 2.5 cm/1 inch squares
500 g/1¼ lb thick fish fillets, e.g. rock salmon, monkfish, gurnard, haddock or cod, skinned and cut into 2.5 cm/1 inch cubes
175 g/6 oz small mushroom caps
Basic Marinade (page 162)
6 bay leaves plus 2 from the marinade
4 small, firm tomatoes
To serve:
350 g/12 oz cooked savoury rice, to which plenty of chopped fresh parsley and chives has been added
1 lemon, quartered

1. Cover the green pepper with cold water, bring slowly to the boil and drain.
2. Put the blanched pepper, fish cubes and mushrooms into a basin and add the marinade. Stir well to coat the ingredients then cover and refrigerate for 3–4 hours, stirring occasionally.
3. When ready to cook, drain off and reserve the marinade. Discard the peppercorns.
4. Divide the ingredients equally and impale them on flat-bladed kebab skewers, adding 2 bay leaves per skewer. Make sure that you push the pieces fairly closely together into the centre of each skewer.
5. Preheat the grill and cook the kebabs und a moderate heat for about 12 minutes, turnin and basting with marinade from time to time Put a tomato on the end of each skewer for t last 5–6 minutes of cooking time. Alternatively, halve and grill them separately
6. To serve, lay the kebabs on a bed of savoury rice in a flat serving dish. Pour any remaining marinade over the kebabs, togethe with juices from the grill pan. Garnish with the lemon wedges.

Golden Fish Goujons

erves 4 as a starter, or 3 as a
ıain course
reparation time: 30 minutes,
lus 1 hour cooling time
:ooking time: about 10 minutes

50 g/1 lb filleted fish e.g. sole, lemon sole, dab, plaice or John Dory, skinned
tablespoons seasoned flour
(size 6) eggs, beaten with 2 teaspoons cold water
00 g/4 oz dry white breadcrumbs
il for deep frying
'o garnish:
·edges of lemon
ırigs of fresh parsley

These crisply fried strips of fish make a very acceptable alternative to whitebait.

1. Lay the fillets flat and cut each diagonally into 1 cm/½ inch wide strips.
2. Coat the pieces of fish, a few at a time, in seasoned flour, then in beaten egg and finally in breadcrumbs.
3. Spread the fish on a tray, cover loosely with greaseproof paper and leave in a cool place for an hour to 'set' the coating.
4. When ready to fry, heat a deep pan of oil to 190°C/375°F. Heat the frying basket in the fat at the same time.
5. Place a quarter of the goujons in a frying basket, lower them into the fat and fry for 1½–2 minutes until golden and crisp. Immediately lift out, turn the fish on to a baking sheet lined with crumpled kitchen paper, and keep hot in a preheated oven at 180°C, 350°F, Gas Mark 4.
6. Fry the remaining goujons in batches, making sure the fat regains the frying temperature between each batch.
7. To serve, pile the goujons into a hot doilie lined dish, garnish with lemon and parsley and serve immediately with a tartare sauce or garlic mayonnaise.

Gefullte Fish

:rves 4–6
'reparation time: about 1 hour
:ooking time: 20–30 minutes

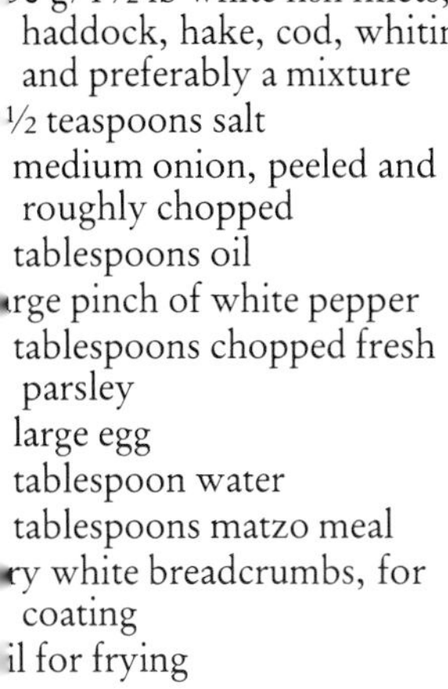

50 g/1½ lb white fish fillets, e.g. haddock, hake, cod, whiting, and preferably a mixture
½ teaspoons salt
medium onion, peeled and roughly chopped
tablespoons oil
ırge pinch of white pepper
tablespoons chopped fresh parsley
large egg
tablespoon water
tablespoons matzo meal
ry white breadcrumbs, for coating
il for frying

This is a traditional Jewish recipe for moist and tasty fish cakes that are equally good eaten hot or cold.

1. Wipe the fish with damp kitchen paper, sprinkle with the salt and leave in a cool place for half an hour. Skin the fish, cut it into pieces and mince the pieces coarsely with the chopped onion.
2. Mix together the oil, pepper, parsley, egg and water in a basin.
3. Add the minced fish and onion and the matzo meal and mix very thoroughly. The mixture should be stiff enough to hold its shape; if not, work in a little more water or matzo meal as necessary.
4. With wetted hands, form the mixture into balls, then flatten them into cakes. Coat the cakes in breadcrumbs and refrigerate until ready to fry.
5. Heat enough oil to cover the base of a large frying pan and, when sizzling hot, fry the cakes in batches, for 5–6 minutes each side, until golden and cooked through.
6. Serve hot with chips or creamed potatoes, or cold with a salad.

Scallops with Mushrooms and Parsley

Preparation time: 20 minutes
Cooking time: 10 minutes

10 large scallops
2 tablespoons oil
50 g/2 oz butter
2 shallots or 1 small onion, peeled and finely chopped
1 large garlic clove, crushed
salt
freshly ground black pepper
1 tablespoon plain flour
225 g/½ lb medium mushroom caps, quartered
juice of ½ large lemon
4–5 tablespoons dry white breadcrumbs
3 tablespoons chopped fresh parsley
1 lemon, quartered, to garnish

1. Wash the scallops, separate the roes and trim any hard white tissue from the sides of the cushions.
2. Heat half the oil and butter in a large frying pan and cook the onion very gently for 5 minutes, stirring from time to time. Stir in the garlic and cook for another minute.
3. Meanwhile pat the scallops dry with kitchen paper and cut the white cushions horizontally in halves. Season them with salt and pepper and then sprinkle lightly with the flour. Add them to the onion and garlic and cook gently for 5–6 minutes, stirring frequently.
4. Add the roes, mushrooms and lemon juice and cook gently, stirring, for another 3–4 minutes.
5. Meanwhile, heat the rest of the oil and butter in a small frying pan and fry the dried breadcrumbs, stirring frequently, until crisp and golden. Remove the pan from the heat and stir in the chopped parsley.
6. Taste and adjust the seasoning of the scallops, divide the mixture between 4 large, deep scallop shells or gratin dishes, sprinkle some crumbs and parsley over each and serve immediately, with wedges of lemon.

Left: Scallops with mushrooms and parsley
Right: Moules à la crème

Crab Mousse

eparation time: 20 minutes,
us at least 2 hours setting time

ant 300 ml/½ pint aspic jelly
5 g/8 oz crab meat, freed of all fragments of shell
tablespoons double cream
½ tablespoons finely grated Parmesan or hard, mature Cheddar cheese
teaspoon lemon juice
yenne pepper
t
eshly ground black pepper
large egg whites
garnish:
cucumber, sliced very thinly
hard-boiled eggs
tablespoon chopped fresh parsley

Crab is a rich fish and a relatively small amount of either fresh or frozen crab meat makes enough mousse for four. A fresh crab in its shell weighing about 750 g/1½ lb should yield about 225 g/8 oz crab meat. Use equal amounts of white and dark crab meat, and a small quantity of grated cheese to heighten the flavour. Powdered aspic jelly is available from most good delicatessens.

1. Dissolve the aspic jelly in 150 ml/¼ pint near boiling water. Stir in enough ice cubes to make the amount up to 250 ml/8 fl oz and to cool the jelly at the same time.
2. Put the crab meat into a bowl and beat it with an electric or rotary beater until reduced to a rough purée.
3. Beat in the cream, grated cheese, lemon juice, a little cayenne pepper, the liquid aspic jelly, and salt and pepper to taste. Set aside until cold and on the point of setting.
4. Whisk the egg whites until firm and fold them gently but evenly into the crab mixture. Turn the mixture into a serving bowl, cover and leave to set in the refrigerator for about 2 hours.
5. Just before serving, arrange the cucumber slices overlapping around the edge of the dish, the chopped egg whites in the centre, and scatter the sieved yolks and chopped parsley over the whites.

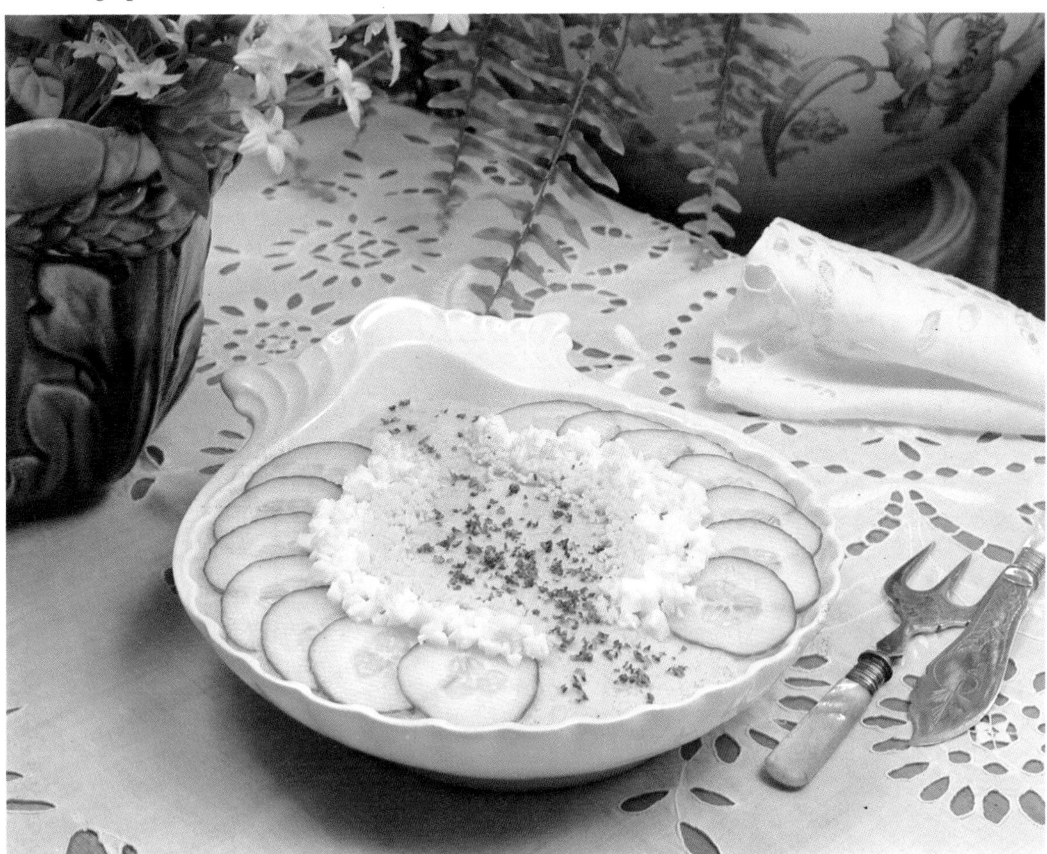

Moules à la Crème

eparation time: 30 minutes
oking time: 10–12 minutes

5 litres/4 pints fresh mussels
hallots or 1 medium onion, peeled and finely chopped
garlic clove, crushed
ew parsley stalks
ay leaf or small sprig thyme
0 ml/⅓ pint dry white wine or dry cider
shly ground black pepper
t, if necessary
0 ml/¼ pint double cream
opped fresh parsley, to garnish

This recipe requires fresh mussels in the shell. Look out for them during their season which lasts from late September until March, but buy only from reputable fishmongers who will not stock mussels unless they have been through an official cleansing process.

1. Scrub the mussels thoroughly, pull off the beards (the weed-like protrusions from between the shells) and discard. Wash the mussels in several changes of cold water. Discard any very heavy or broken mussels, or any that fail to shut when given a sharp tap.
2. Put the onion, garlic, herbs and wine or cider into a wide saucepan and bring to the boil.
3. Add the mussels to the pan, then cover and cook over high heat, shaking frequently, for about 5–6 minutes, until all the shells have opened. Discard any that do not open.
4. Transfer the mussels to a colander using a perforated spoon, discard the empty half of each shell and divide the mussels between 4 hot, shallow soup plates; keep warm.
5. To remove all traces of sand, immediately strain the cooking liquor through a muslin-lined strainer into a clean pan. Boil rapidly, uncovered, until reduced by half. Add the cream, boil rapidly until slightly thickened, taste and adjust the seasoning and pour the sauce over the mussels. Sprinkle with parsley and serve immediately.

Meat

BEEF

Steak, Kidney and Mushroom Pie

Serves 5–6
Preparation time: 25 minutes, using ready-made pastry
Cooking time: 3½–4 hours

225 g/8 oz ox kidney
750 g/1½ lb braising steak, cut into 5 × 2.5 cm/1 inch pieces
2 tablespoons plain flour
salt
freshly ground black pepper
300 ml/½ pint beef stock
100 g/4 oz small button mushrooms, trimmed
225 g/8 oz frozen puff pastry, thawed
a little beaten egg and milk, to glaze

The filling for this pie takes much longer to cook than the pastry and is therefore best made in advance, so that it has time to cook and cool completely before it is topped with pastry and baked.

1. Wash the kidney, remove any skin, core and cut it into small pieces.
2. Put the pieces into a large pudding basin and add the steak. Sprinkle the flour, seasoned generously with salt and pepper, over the meat and turn to coat the meat surfaces. Stir in the stock and cover the basin tightly with foil.
3. Stand the basin in a large saucepan filled with enough water to reach half way up the sides of the basin. Cover the pan tightly and simmer for 3–3½ hours, stirring once or twice, until the meat is just tender. Replenish the pan with hot water as necessary.
4. Remove from the heat and leave until completely cold.
5. Adjust the seasoning, add the mushrooms and turn into a 900 ml/1½ pint pie dish.
6. Roll out the pastry to make a cover for the pie, about 5 mm/¼ inch thick.
7. Cut strips from the pastry trimmings and use to cover the wetted rim of the dish. Damp the pastry rim and cover with the pastry top, pressing the edges together. Make a hole in the centre for the steam to escape. Decorate with thin pastry leaves and glaze the surface with egg and milk.
8. Bake above the centre of a preheated oven at 220°C, 425°F, Gas Mark 7 until the pastry is well risen and golden, about 25–30 minutes.

Flemish Beef in Beer

Serves 5–6
Preparation time: 20 minutes
Cooking time: 3 hours

1 kg/2 lb lean braising steak
40 g/1½ oz dripping or 3 tablespoons oil
450 g/1 lb medium onions, peeled and thinly sliced
3 garlic cloves, crushed
salt
freshly ground black pepper
150 ml/¼ pint well-flavoured beef stock
450 ml/¾ pint light ale
1 tablespoon brown sugar
sprig of parsley, thyme, small bay leaf and 3 × 5 cm/2 inch celery sticks, tied together
1 tablespoon cornflour
1½ tablespoons wine vinegar
To garnish:
1 tablespoon chopped fresh parsley or chives
slices of French bread, toasted and spread thickly with mustard butter (optional)

This delicious Flemish dish is very suitable for top of the stove cooking as thickening is added at the end.

1. Wipe the meat with damp kitchen paper, discard any excess fat and cut the meat into oblongs about 5 cm/2 inches long by 1 cm/½ inch thick.
2. Heat the dripping or oil in a large, flameproof casserole dish and fry the meat briskly, in two batches, for a few minutes until lightly browned on all sides. Using a perforated spoon, transfer the meat to a plate.
3. Lower the heat, add the onions and fry gently, stirring frequently, for 5–6 minutes. Stir in the garlic, and salt and pepper.
4. Add the stock and the beer and bring to th boil, stirring with a wooden spoon.
5. Return the meat to the casserole, add the sugar and bouquet of herbs. Cover tightly an simmer gently for 2½ hours, or until the mea is tender. Remove the bouquet of herbs.
6. Skim off any fat that has risen to the surfa of the casserole. Blend the cornflour with the vinegar, stir in a few spoonfuls of the hot liquid, then pour it into the casserole, stirring Simmer for a few minutes until thickened.
7. Sprinkle with parsley or chives and serve from the casserole, surrounded with the mustardy toasted bread slices.

Back: Flemish beef in beer
Front: Stifatho

Boeuf en Daube à la Provençale

rves 8
eparation time: 20 minutes
ooking time: about 4 hours

tablespoons olive oil
medium onions, peeled and sliced
× 175 g/6 oz piece unsmoked streaky bacon, cut into 1 cm/½ inch cubes
× 1½ kg/3 lb piece boneless braising beef: top rump, topside or de-fatted and rolled brisket
tablespoon plain flour
lt
eshly ground black pepper
large tomatoes, peeled and quartered
carrots, peeled and sliced
garlic cloves, crushed
thinly pared strips orange rind, 1 bay leaf, 1 sprig thyme, 2 parsley sprigs, tied together
i0 ml/¼ pint robust red wine
) g/2 oz small black olives, rinsed (optional)

The French custom of braising meat slowly with vegetables, herbs and wine is a very successful way of converting more muscular cuts of meat into tender, succulent dishes. The timing is not critical but cannot be hurried.

1. Heat the oil in a flameproof casserole which the meat fits into fairly closely. Add the onions and fry gently for 5 minutes, then add the cubed bacon and cook gently until the fat begins to run.
2. Meanwhile, wipe the meat with damp kitchen paper and dust lightly with flour, well seasoned with salt and pepper.
3. Increase the heat a little, put the meat into the pan and cook until lightly browned on each side.
4. Add the tomatoes, carrot, garlic, bouquet of herbs, a little salt and several grinds of pepper. Pour in the wine.
5. Bring to the boil, allow to simmer for a few minutes, then cover the pan tightly and transfer to a preheated oven at 150°C, 300°F, Gas Mark 2, and cook for about 4 hours or until the meat is tender when pierced with a skewer.
6. Turn the meat half way through the cooking and add the olives, if used, 30 minutes before the end.
7. To serve, remove the trussing string and arrange the meat on a hot serving dish and either leave whole or slice as much as required.
8. Skim off any fat from the gravy, remove the solid ingredients with a perforated spoon and arrange them around the meat. Remove and discard the bouquet of herbs.
9. Concentrate the rest of the gravy by boiling briskly for a few minutes, then taste and adjust the seasoning and pour it over the meat.
10. Serve with creamed potatoes and a green vegetable or follow with a green salad.

Stifatho

rves 6
eparation time: 30 minutes
ooking time: 2½ hours

tablespoons oil
kg/2 lb lean braising beef, cut into 2.5 cm/1 inch cubes
large onion, peeled and chopped
bay leaves
garlic clove, crushed
lt
eshly ground black pepper
tablespoons tomato purée
i0 ml/¾ pint water
kg/2 lb potatoes
iopped fresh parsley, to garnish

Choose good potatoes which keep their shape when cooked, otherwise the look of the dish will be spoiled.

1. Heat the oil in a heavy, flameproof casserole and fry the cubed meat fairly briskly, in two batches, turning until lightly browned on all sides. Transfer the meat to a plate, using a perforated spoon.
2. Lower the heat, add the onion to the pan and fry for 5 minutes, stirring occasionally.
3. Return the meat to the pan and add the bay leaves, garlic, and salt and pepper. Blend the tomato purée with the water, add to the casserole and bring to the boil, stirring. Cover the casserole tightly and simmer for 1½–2 hours, until the meat is almost tender.
4. Peel the potatoes and cut them into quarters if small, or into thick wedges if large. Stir the potatoes gently into the casserole, mixing them with the meat and gravy.
5. Cover and simmer for 15–20 minutes until the potatoes are tender and only a small amount of thick sauce remains.
6. Sprinkle with parsley and serve from the casserole.

Boeuf en daube à la provençale

Roast Beef, Yorkshire Pudding and Roast Potatoes

Serves 6–8
Preparation time: 30 minutes
Cooking time: 1¾ hours

1¼–1½ kg/2½–3 lb boned and rolled sirloin
40 g/1½ oz dripping or lard
750 g/1½ lb potatoes, peeled and cut into pieces roughly the size of a small egg
salt
1 tablespoon plain flour
freshly ground black pepper
300 ml/½ pint beef stock
Horseradish Sauce (page 152)
Yorkshire pudding:
100 g/4 oz plain flour
½ teaspoon salt
2 (size 5 or 6) eggs
300 ml/½ pint milk and water mixed

1. Weigh the joint and calculate the cooking time.
2. Select a roasting tin large enough to hold the meat and potatoes. Preheat the oven to 180°C, 350°F, Gas Mark 4 and put the roasting tin containing the fat in the oven to heat at the same time.
3. Meanwhile, cover the potatoes with cold, salted water, bring to the boil and simmer for 5 minutes, then drain thoroughly.
4. Wipe the meat with damp kitchen paper and rub the cut surfaces with the flour, well seasoned with salt and pepper. Insert a meat thermometer in the centre of the joint and place the meat, fat side uppermost, on a trivet.
5. Turn the potatoes in the hot fat to coat them, then stand the trivet and meat over the potatoes. Transfer to the centre of the oven and cook for 20 minutes per 450 g/1 lb plus 20 minutes, or until the thermometer registers 71°C/160°F for medium cooked meat (see times on page 165 for underdone or well done).
6. Meanwhile, make the Yorkshire pudding batter. Sift the flour and salt into a deep basin and make a well in the centre. Drop in the eggs, add half of the milk and water, and with a small wire whisk gradually draw the flour into the liquid and beat until smooth. Beat in the rest of the milk and water and refrigerate until needed.
7. When the meat is cooked, lift it out of the roasting tin and increase the oven heat to 220°C, 425°F, Gas Mark 7. Transfer the joint to a hot carving dish and leave in a warm place to rest for 15 minutes.
8. Using a perforated spoon, transfer the potatoes to a shallow ovenproof dish and return them to the oven to brown.
9. Pour a little of the hot fat from the roasting tin into each of 8 large bun tins and divide the batter between them. Cook in the hottest part of the oven for 15–20 minutes until well risen, crisp and golden.
10. Meanwhile, drain off any surplus fat from the roasting tin, add the stock, stir to dislodge the coagulated juices from the base of the tin and simmer gently.
11. Arrange the puddings around the joint and serve the potatoes, gravy and horseradish sauce separately.

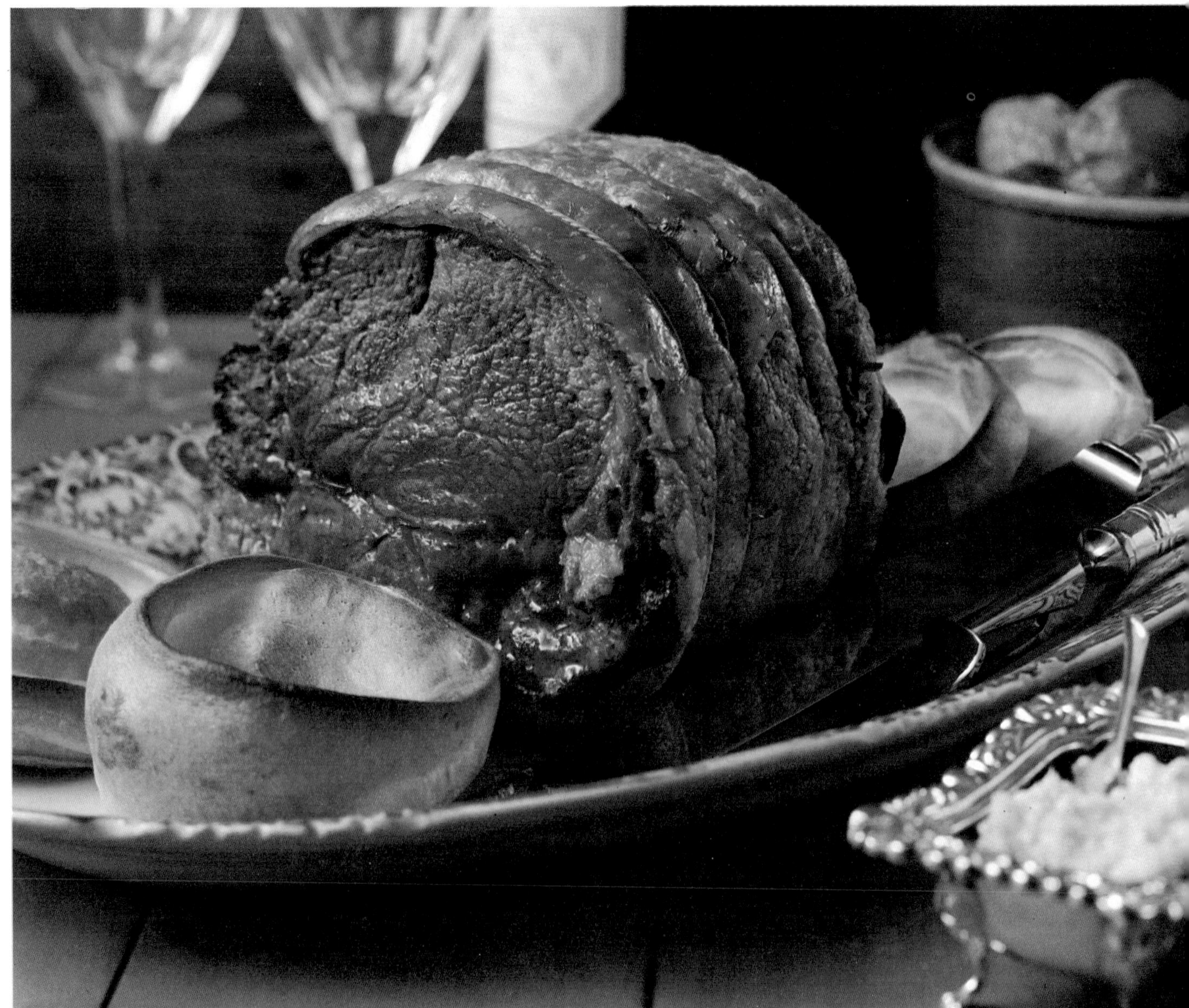

Minute Steaks with Mushrooms

reparation time: 15 minutes
Cooking time: 6–8 minutes

× 100–175 g/4 × 4–6 oz sirloin steaks, cut thinly
large garlic clove, peeled and halved (optional)
·eshly ground black pepper
tablespoon oil
5 g/3 oz butter
alt
50 g/12 oz button mushrooms, thinly sliced
uice of ½ lemon
tablespoon chopped chives or green of spring onion
tablespoon chopped fresh parsley
prigs of watercress, to garnish

1. Trim the steaks if necessary and wipe them with damp kitchen paper. Rub each side of the steak liberally with the cut garlic, if using, and season with pepper.
2. Heat the oil and half of the butter in a large, heavy based frying pan.
3. When the butter ceases to foam, put in the steaks and cook over a fairly brisk heat for 2 minutes each side, or a little longer if preferred. Season with salt, lift the steaks out of the pan, arrange them on a hot serving dish and keep hot.
4. Heat the remaining butter in the pan and add the mushrooms. Lower the heat and cook, stirring, for a few minutes until the mushrooms begin to soften.
5. Stir in the lemon juice and salt, and spoon the mushrooms and their juices over the steaks. Sprinkle with the herbs and serve garnished with watercress.

VARIATION:

Steak Diane
Pound 4 × 100 g/4 oz thin sirloin steaks with a wooden rolling pin until very thin. Fry steaks quickly for 1 minute each side in 25 g/1 oz butter and 1 tablespoon oil. Remove the frying pan from the heat, add 4 tablespoons medium dry sherry and 2 tablespoons brandy. Stand well back and set the alcohol alight with a match. When the flames die down, lift the steaks from the pan, season with salt and pepper and keep hot. Boil the pan juices and, after 1–2 minutes, when slightly reduced, stir in 25 g/1 oz butter in small pieces and 1 tablespoon chopped fresh chives and parsley. Pour the sauce over the steaks and serve at once.

Left: Minute steaks with mushrooms
Right: Steak Diane

Stuffed Fillet of Pork en Croûte

Serves 6–8
Preparation time: 30 minutes
Cooking time: 1¼ hours

25 g/1 oz butter
1 tablespoon oil
1 large onion, peeled and very finely chopped
225 g/8 oz firm mushrooms, chopped
finely grated rind and juice of ½ lemon
2 tablespoons chopped fresh parsley
2 tablespoons fine white breadcrumbs
salt
freshly ground black pepper
750 g/1¾ lb pork fillet in 2 pieces of similar length
1 × 375 g/13 oz packet frozen puff pastry, just thawed
beaten egg, to glaze

Lean, tender and boneless fillet of pork is an ideal meat for encasing in crisp pastry. As the meat is bland in flavour and inclined to be dry the stuffing needs to be moist and well flavoured.

1. Heat the butter and oil in a large frying pan and fry the onion gently for 5 minutes, until it begins to soften.
2. Add the mushrooms, stir, and cook for 1–2 minutes, then add the lemon rind, 1 tablespoon of the lemon juice, parsley, breadcrumbs, and plenty of salt and pepper. Leave to cool.
3. Trim any sinew or excess fat from the pork fillet. Lay the meat flat and cut each piece horizontally through the centre until almost, but not quite, in half, then open out and flatten the meat with a heavy rolling pin or large knife.
4. Sprinkle the fillets with salt and pepper and the remaining lemon juice. Sandwich the mushroom mixture between the two fillets, tuck in the ends and press into a neat oblong shape.
5. Roll out the pastry to a large oblong, 5 cm/2 inches longer and three times as wide as the meat. Trim the edges.
6. Transfer the meat to the centre of the pastry and damp the edges with cold water. Fold the sides over the centre and the ends inwards, pressing and sealing the edges.
7. Carefully invert the parcel on to a baking sheet so that the join is underneath. Decorate with pastry leaves and glaze the surface with beaten egg. Chill until ready to cook.
8. Bake for 30 minutes in the hottest part of a preheated oven at 200°C, 400°F, Gas Mark 6.
9. Reduce the heat to 180°C, 350°F, Gas Mar 4, and continue cooking for a further 45 minutes until the meat is thoroughly cooked. If necessary, cover the pastry with greaseproc paper to prevent over-browning.
10. To serve, transfer the roll carefully to a hot serving platter. Cut in thick slices and serve with braised celery, chicory or ovenbaked courgettes, and green beans.

Fruit Stuffed Belly of Pork

Serves 5–6
Preparation time: 15 minutes, plus overnight soaking
Cooking time: 1¾ hours

1–1¼ kg/2–2½ lb belly of pork, in one piece
about 1 tablespoon oil
salt
freshly ground black pepper
Stuffing:
8 large prunes, soaked overnight in water
1 large cooking apple, peeled, cored and chopped
50 g/2 oz fresh white breadcrumbs
finely grated rind and juice of ¼ lemon
1 egg, beaten
salt
freshly ground black pepper

Belly of pork is an economical cut that lends itself to splitting and filling with a fruity stuffing. Have the rind deeply and finely scored to encourage the crackling to crisp.

1. Wipe the meat with damp kitchen paper. With a sharp knife, cut horizontally through the centre of the joint, forming a wide pocket for the stuffing.
2. To make the stuffing, drain, stone and chop the prunes and mix thoroughly with all the other ingredients in a mixing bowl. Spread the stuffing evenly in the pocket made in the meat.
3. Stand the joint on a rack in a roasting tin, rub the skin with oil and sprinkle generously with salt and pepper. Cook in a preheated oven at 180°C, 350°F, Gas Mark 4 for 1¾ hours, or until the juices run colourless when the meat is pierced with a skewer.
4. Transfer the meat to a hot serving dish. Drain off any excess fat from the roasting tin and make a gravy from the juices in the usual way. Carve the meat downwards in fairly thick slices.

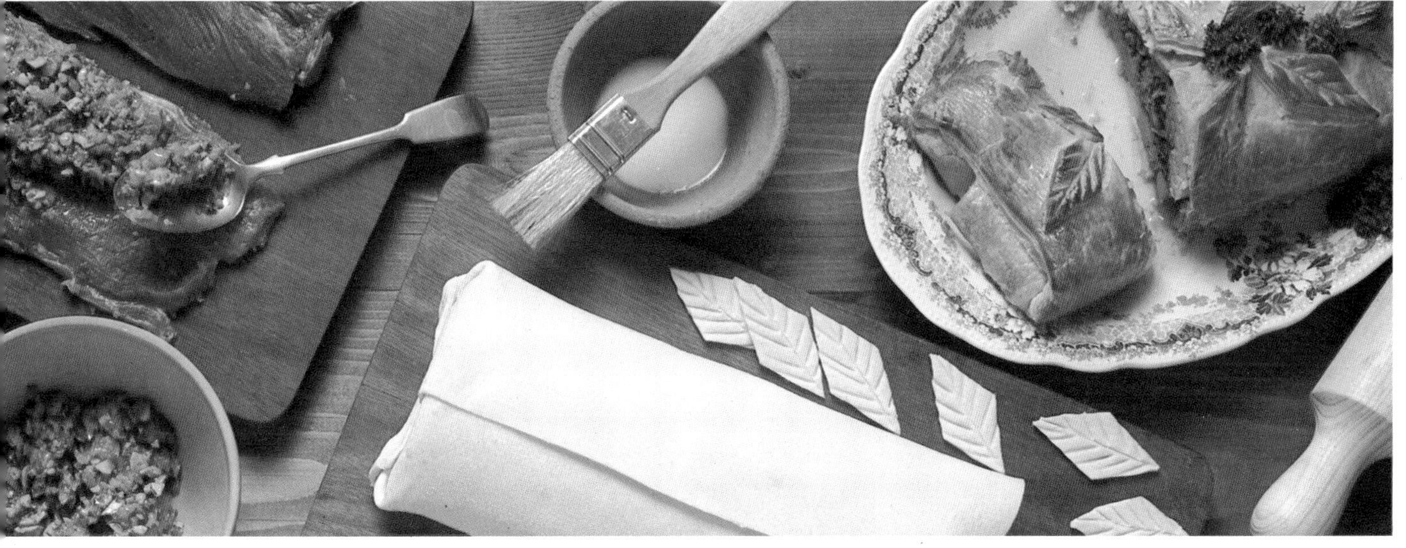

Spare Rib Chops Mandalay

·eparation time: 15 minutes
ooking time: about 30 minutes

spare rib chops
ittle oil
lt
eshly ground black pepper
uce:
tablespoons oil
small onion, peeled and finely chopped
× 225 g/8 oz can peeled tomatoes
tablespoons soft brown sugar
tablespoons wine vinegar
tablespoons tomato ketchup
teaspoons soy sauce

Spare rib chops are meaty shoulder cuts and not to be confused with the bony barbecued rib variety. The flavour is good if the chops are grilled slowly and basted frequently.

1. Wipe the meat with damp kitchen paper, rub both sides with a little oil, sprinkle with salt and pepper and arrange the chops side by side in a flameproof gratin dish.
2. To make the sauce, heat the oil in a small saucepan and fry the onion very gently for 5 minutes, stirring occasionally.
3. Add the tomatoes and their juice, the sugar, vinegar, tomato ketchup and soy sauce, and mash with a potato masher to break up the large pieces of tomato.
4. Bring to the boil and simmer, uncovered, for about 10 minutes, stirring occasionally, until fairly thick.
5. Seal the chops by cooking for 1 minute on each side under a preheated hot grill.
6. Pour the sauce over the chops, lower the heat and continue grilling, very gently, with the dish on the lowest position, for about 8–10 minutes each side, basting with sauce several times.
7. Serve hot with plain boiled rice and a crisply cooked green vegetable or salad.

Danish Spiced Frikadeller

Preparation time: 20 minutes, plus 1 hour cooling time
Cooking time: 15 minutes per batch

450 g/1 lb shoulder pork, finely minced
2 tablespoons plain flour
1 small onion, peeled and finely grated
½ teaspoon ground nutmeg or allspice
salt
freshly ground black pepper
150 ml/¼ pint milk
25 g/1 oz butter
4 tablespoons oil

Frikadeller are as popular in Denmark as hamburgers in America. Shoulder pork is a good cut to use, and they can be made entirely from minced pork or from a mixture of pork and veal.

1. Put the minced meat into a basin, stir in the flour, onion, nutmeg or allspice, and salt and pepper to taste.
2. Add the milk gradually, stirring vigorously until it is absorbed and the mixture is fairly soft. Cover and leave in a cool place for at least 1 hour.
3. Heat the butter and oil in a large, heavy based frying pan. Shape the meat mixture into ovals between 2 tablespoons and slide them into the hot fat.
4. Fry the meat shapes over a low heat until golden, then turn and fry the other side until cooked right through, about 15 minutes. The fricadeller should be golden and crisp outside but remain succulent in the centre.
5. Lift them out with a perforated spoon and keep hot until all the meat is cooked.
6. Serve as a main course with creamed spinach and boiled, or sauté, potatoes. Cold frikadeller are good sliced and used for open sandwiches.

Pork Spiedo

Preparation time: 15 minutes
Cooking time: 30 –40 minutes

2–3 slices firm white bread, cut 1 cm/½ inch thick
100 g/4 oz thinly sliced lean raw gammon
500 g/1¼ lb pork tenderloin, cut into 16 pieces
12 small bay leaves
olive oil
salt
freshly ground black pepper

This Italian kebab recipe is unusual in that it is cooked in the oven.

1. Remove the crusts and cut the bread into 16 cubes roughly the same size as the meat.
2. Remove any rind from the gammon and cut the meat into 16 pieces.
3. Divide the bread, gammon, pork and bay leaves equally between 4 kebab skewers, impaling them alternately.
4. Lay the filled skewers flat and side by side on a generously oiled baking sheet. Sprinkle them lightly with salt, generously with pepper, and then pour a little oil over each, turning to ensure that each bread cube is moistened with oil.
5. Bake in the centre of a preheated oven at 190°C, 375°F, Gas Mark 5 for 30–40 minute until the meat is cooked through and the bre crisp. Turn the skewers after 20 minutes.

Lamb Brodettato

eparation time: 20 minutes
ɔoking time: about 1 hour

g/1 oz butter
g/2 oz sliced pickled belly pork, rinded and cut in 5 mm/¼ inch dice
small onion, peeled and chopped
0 g/1½ lb boneless lean lamb cut in 2.5 cm/1 inch cubes
ablespoons plain flour
t
shly ground black pepper
ablespoons dry white vermouth
0 ml/½ pint light stock or water
small bay leaf
gg yolks
ce of ½ lemon
ablespoon chopped fresh parsley
easpoon chopped fresh marjoram or ½ teaspoon dried marjoram

Use lean shoulder or leg meat for this refreshing Italian version of a traditional Middle Eastern dish.

1. Melt the butter in a flameproof casserole dish and fry the pork and onion over a medium heat for 2 minutes.
2. Add the cubed lamb and cook, stirring frequently, for 6–8 minutes until the meat surfaces are seared and the onion turns golden.
3. Add the flour, and salt and pepper and cook, stirring, for 1–2 minutes.
4. Add the vermouth and simmer for several minutes, then stir in the stock.
5. Add the bay leaf, bring to the boil, then reduce the heat to very low, cover and leave to simmer gently for 45 minutes, or until the meat is tender when pierced with a fork.
6. Before serving, beat the egg yolks, lemon juice, parsley and marjoram together in a basin and stir in about 4 tablespoons of the hot liquid from the pan.
7. Return this mixture to the casserole, stirring continuously, and cook over very low heat until the sauce thickens slightly. Do not allow the sauce to boil. Taste and adjust the seasoning, discard the bay leaf and serve immediately.

Greek Lamb Kebabs

eparation time: 20 minutes,
ıs 4 hours to marinate
ɔoking time: 8–12 minutes

0 g/1½ lb boneless leg fillet of lamb
t
shly ground black pepper
easpoon dried marjoram
small onions, peeled
ablespoons olive oil
ablespoon lemon juice
8 bay leaves
garnish:
non wedges
rigs of parsley

1. Trim any excess fat from the lamb and cut the meat into 2 cm/¾ inch cubes. Put the meat in a bowl, season with salt and pepper and sprinkle with the marjoram.
2. Cut the onions into quarters, add the thick outer layers to the meat and reserve the inner cores for a tomato salad to serve with the kebabs.
3. Add the oil and lemon juice to the meat and onion, stir gently, cover and leave in a cool place to marinate for at least 4 hours.
4. To cook, divide the ingredients between 4 flat kebab skewers and impale a piece of onion and half a bay leaf between every 2 pieces of cubed meat.
5. Cook under a preheated hot grill for 8–12 minutes, until the meat is well browned outside but still juicy within.
6. Turn the skewers once and keep the kebabs well basted with the marinade throughout the cooking.
7. Arrange the skewers on a bed of parsley sprigs, garnish with lemon wedges and serve with crusty bread and a tomato salad.

VARIATION:

For a snack meal, serve the kebabs in warm pitta bread.

Guard of Honour with Apricot Rice

Serves 5–6
Preparation time: 30 minutes, plus 2 hours soaking time
Cooking time: 1½ hours

2 best ends of neck of lamb, chined
salt
freshly ground black pepper
Apricot rice stuffing:
50 g/2 oz butter
1 medium onion, peeled and chopped
225 g/8 oz long-grain rice, cooked and drained
100 g/4 oz dried apricots, soaked 2 hours in boiling water, drained and chopped
3 tablespoons seedless raisins, soaked 2 hours in warm water, then drained
2 tablespoons flaked almonds
½ teaspoon ground ginger
½ teaspoon ground cinnamon
½ teaspoon ground coriander
salt
freshly ground black pepper
To garnish:
cutlet frills
sprigs of watercress

For a special meal two best ends of neck of lamb can be transformed into this important looking and easily carved roast. Ask the butcher for a whole best end from one carcass, divided in half, skinned and then chined, leaving the long rib bones intact. You now have two identical joints of 5 or 6 cutlets each, depending on the size of the lamb. Allow two cutlets per person.

1. To make the stuffing, melt the butter in a saucepan and fry the onion very gently for 10 minutes, stirring frequently. Add the remaining ingredients and mix thoroughly.
2. Wipe the meat with damp kitchen paper. With a sharp knife remove the chine bones and cut away any surplus fat or cartilage. Cut 4 cm/1½ inches of meat from the thin ends of the joint, then scrape the exposed bones as cleanly as possible. Season the joints with salt and pepper.
3. Stand the joints on their thick ends, skin-sides facing outwards, and push them together so that the exposed bones cross each other alternately.
4. Skewer the joints firmly together at the base and push some of the stuffing into the central cavity.
5. Stand the joint upright in a roasting tin and cover the exposed bones with foil to prevent them burning. Cook in the centre of a preheated oven at 180°C, 350°F, Gas Mark 4 for 1¼–1½ hours, depending on preferences of taste.
6. Cook the remaining stuffing in a covered casserole during the last 30 minutes of cooking time.
7. When cooked, transfer the joint to a large serving dish, remove the foil and skewers and slip cutlet frills over the exposed bones.
8. Pile the extra stuffing at either end and garnish the sides with watercress. Serve with gravy (made from the de-fatted pan juices in the usual way) and a green vegetable.

Roast Loin of Lamb Persille

Serves 6–8
Preparation time: 20 minutes
Cooking time: 2 hours

1½–1¾ kg/3½–4 lb loin of lamb
1 large garlic clove, peeled and halved
salt
freshly ground black pepper
65 g/2½ oz butter
75 g/3 oz fine dry white breadcrumbs
3 tablespoons chopped fresh parsley
1 teaspoon finely chopped lemon thyme or ½ teaspoon dried thyme
finely grated rind and juice of ½ lemon

1. Wipe the meat with damp kitchen paper. Peel off the thin, papery skin covering the back fat and with a sharp knife score the fat into a diamond pattern.
2. Rub the cut halves of garlic all over the cut meat surfaces, the underside of the joint and the fat, then sprinkle generously with salt and pepper.
3. Stand the joint, fat-side uppermost, on a rack in a roasting tin. Spread a little of the butter over the fat, place in the centre of a preheated oven at 180°C, 350°F, Gas Mark 4 and cook for 1½ hours.
4. Meanwhile, melt the rest of the butter in a small saucepan, add the breadcrumbs, parsley, thyme and lemon rind and mix well.
5. Take the roasting tin from the oven and increase the oven heat to 200°C, 400°F, Gas Mark 6. Squeeze the lemon juice over the joint, press the crumb mixture evenly all over the fat side of the meat.
6. Return the joint to the oven and continue cooking for 20–30 minutes, until the crumbs are golden and crisp.
7. Serve the joint with gravy made from the skimmed pan drippings.

Left: Guard of honour with apricot rice
Right: Roast loin of lamb persille

Noisettes of Lamb Jardinière

rves 6
eparation time: about 30 inutes
ooking time: 15–20 minutes

arge noisettes of lamb
t
eshly ground black pepper
g/2 oz butter
arge mushroom cups, stalks removed (optional)
easpoons lemon juice (optional)
garnish:
ablespoons freshly cooked peas, drained (optional)
ourgettes Niçoise (page 56)

Ask your butcher to cut the noisettes from a loin or best end of lamb. Those from the latter are smaller and less meaty than the former. Allow 1 loin or 2 neck noisettes per person.

1. Season the noisettes with salt and pepper. Heat 40 g/1½ oz of the butter in a large frying pan and, when it ceases to foam, put in the noisettes and fry gently for 4–6 minutes each side, depending on thickness.
2. Lift the cooked noisettes from the pan, cut and remove the surrounding string and arrange around the edge of a hot serving dish.
3. Add the remaining butter to the pan and fry the mushroom cups for 3–4 minutes, if using, basting them with the pan juices and sprinkling them with the lemon juice and a little salt.
4. Arrange a mushroom, cup side upwards, on each noisette and fill the cups with peas. Carefully pile the hot Courgettes Niçoise into the centre of the dish and serve.

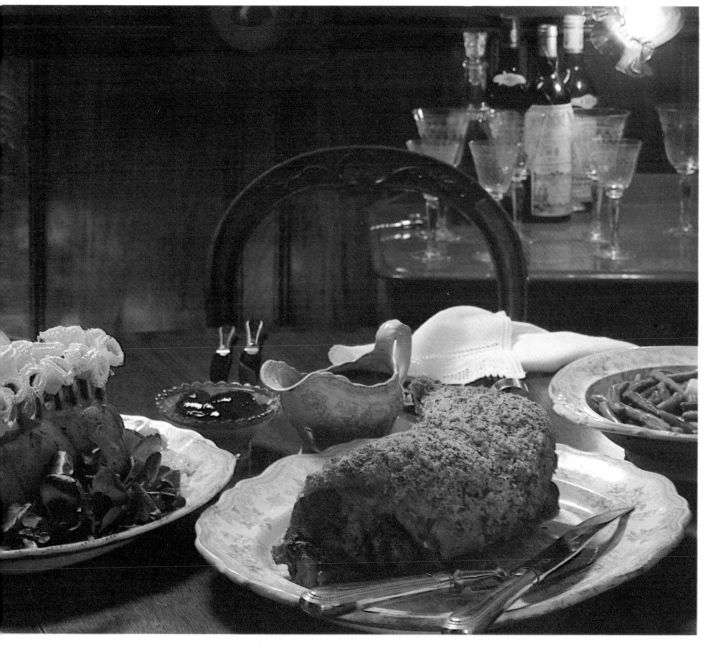

Creamy Lamb Korma

Preparation time: 20 minutes, plus 2 hours to marinate
Cooking time: 1½ hours

2 teaspoons cumin seeds
1 tablespoon coriander seed
300 ml/½ pint plain, unsweetened yogurt
1 teaspoon ground turmeric
½ teaspoon freshly ground black pepper
450 g/1 lb lean, boneless lamb, cut into 1 cm/½ inch cubes
40 g/1½ oz ghee or unsalted butter
1 medium onion, peeled and chopped
2 garlic cloves, crushed
1 × 2.5 cm/1 inch piece fresh root ginger, peeled and finely chopped, or ¼ teaspoon ground ginger
½ teaspoon ground cloves
1 teaspoon ground cardamom
3 tablespoons ground almonds
150 ml/¼ pint double cream
½ teaspoon salt
2–3 teaspoons lemon juice
To serve:
175–225 g/6–8 oz raw long-grain rice, cooked
To garnish:
1 tablespoon blanched and shredded almonds (optional)
1 lemon, quartered

Kormas are mild but rich creamy curries made from fresh meat and with a spicy rather than 'hot' flavouring.

1. Put the cumin and coriander seeds in a small dry pan and heat gently for a minute or so to release the aromatic oils, then transfer them to a mortar and pound until pulverised.
2. Put the yogurt into a deep basin and stir in the pounded cumin and coriander, the turmeric and the pepper. Add the meat, mix well, cover and refrigerate for 2 hours.
3. Melt the fat in a heavy based saucepan and fry the onions very gently, stirring occasionally, for 5 minutes. Add the garlic, ginger, cloves and cardamom and continue cooking gently for 3–4 minutes.
4. Add the meat and the marinade and the ground almonds and bring to the boil. Boil briskly for a few minutes, then cover tightly and simmer very gently for 1¼ hours, or unti the meat is tender. Stir occasionally and add a little water, if necessary.
5. Stir in the cream, add salt and lemon juice to taste and simmer for several minutes until well blended.
6. Pile the korma into a hot serving dish bordered with rice, scatter the almonds over the surface and arrange lemon wedges at eithe end of the dish.
7. Serve various sambals in small bowls, for instance, sliced bananas tossed in lemon juice, grated coconut, mango chutney and cucumbe raita (diced cucumber mixed with grated onio and plain, unsweetened yogurt).

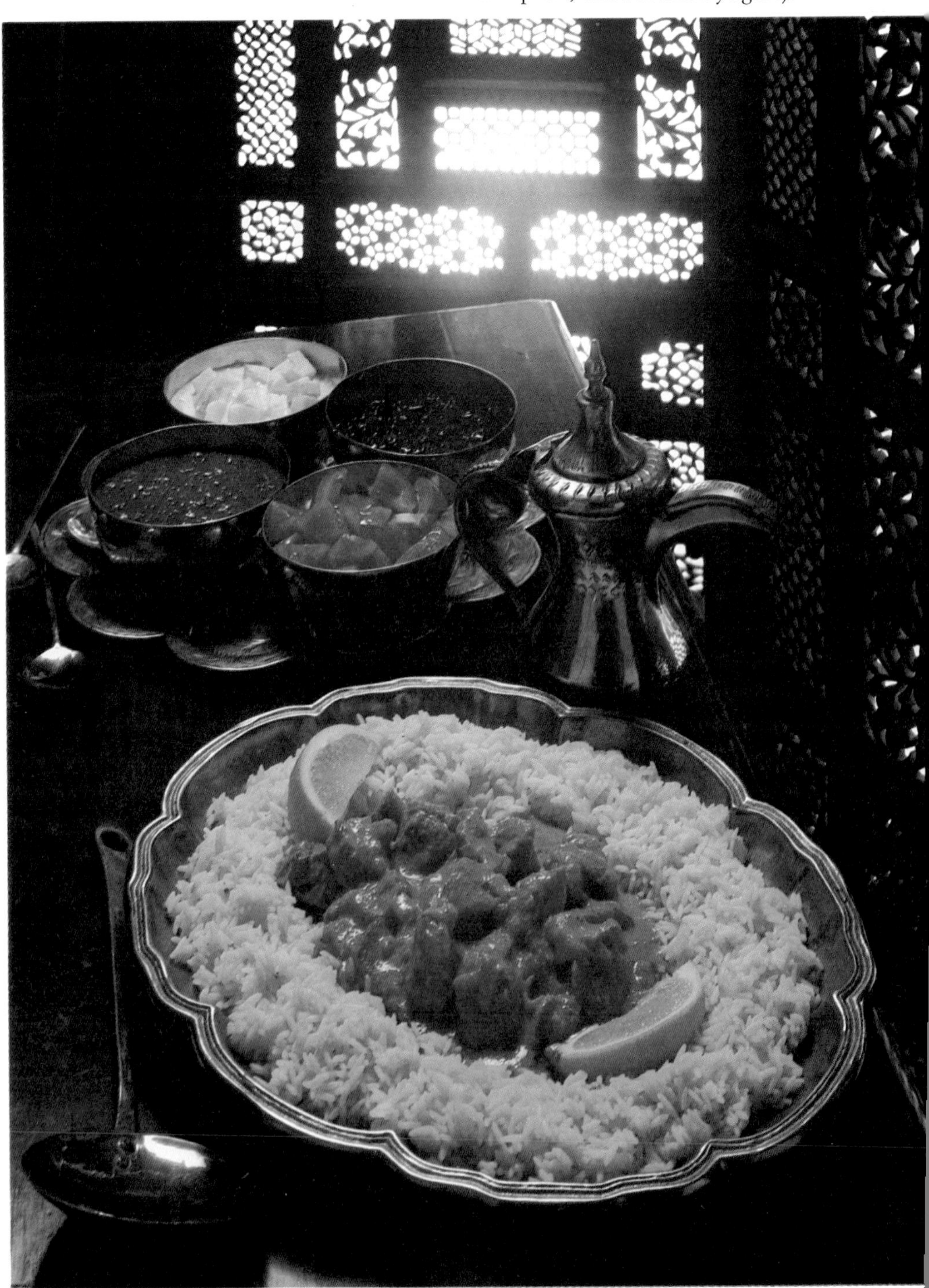

BLAND 7/10

Creamy Lamb Korma

eparation time: 20 minutes,
us 2 hours to marinate
ooking time: 1½ hours

teaspoons cumin seeds
tablespoon coriander seed
)0 ml/½ pint plain, unsweetened yogurt
teaspoon ground turmeric
2 teaspoon freshly ground black pepper
50 g/1 lb lean, boneless lamb, cut into 1 cm/½ inch cubes
0 g/1½ oz ghee or unsalted butter
medium onion, peeled and chopped
garlic cloves, crushed
× 2.5 cm/1 inch piece fresh root ginger, peeled and finely chopped, or ¼ teaspoon ground ginger
½ teaspoon ground cloves
1 teaspoon ground cardamom
3 tablespoons ground almonds
150 ml/¼ pint double cream
½ teaspoon salt
2–3 teaspoons lemon juice
To serve:
175–225 g/6–8 oz raw long-grain rice, cooked
To garnish:
1 tablespoon blanched and shredded almonds (optional)
1 lemon, quartered

Kormas are mild but rich creamy curries made from fresh meat and with a spicy rather than 'hot' flavouring.

1. Put the cumin and coriander seeds in a small dry pan and heat gently for a minute or so to release the aromatic oils, then transfer them to a mortar and pound until pulverised.
2. Put the yogurt into a deep basin and stir in the pounded cumin and coriander, the turmeric and the pepper. Add the meat, mix well, cover and refrigerate for 2 hours.
3. Melt the fat in a heavy based saucepan and fry the onions very gently, stirring occasionally, for 5 minutes. Add the garlic, ginger, cloves and cardamom and continue cooking gently for 3–4 minutes.
4. Add the meat and the marinade and the ground almonds and bring to the boil. Boil briskly for a few minutes, then cover tightly and simmer very gently for 1¼ hours, or until the meat is tender. Stir occasionally and add a little water, if necessary.
5. Stir in the cream, add salt and lemon juice to taste and simmer for several minutes until well blended.
6. Pile the korma into a hot serving dish bordered with rice, scatter the almonds over the surface and arrange lemon wedges at either end of the dish.
7. Serve various sambals in small bowls, for instance, sliced bananas tossed in lemon juice, grated coconut, mango chutney and cucumber raita (diced cucumber mixed with grated onion and plain, unsweetened yogurt).

FROM THE ENCYCLOPEDIA of CREATIVE COOKERY

Wiener Schnitzel

eparation time: 15 minutes
ooking time: 6–8 minutes

× 100 g/4 oz veal escalopes, beaten until thin
large lemon, cut in half
ablespoons plain flour
t
eshly ground black pepper
arge egg, beaten with 1 tablespoon cold water
g/3 oz dry white breadcrumbs
and butter for frying
garnish:
emons, quartered
all pickled gherkins, cut into fans (optional)

For good schnitzel you need thin unbroken slices of milk fed veal cut across the grain of the meat from the upper part of the leg.

1. Wipe the meat with damp kitchen paper. Rub the cut lemon over each side of the escalopes, squeezing the lemon a little to release the juice, cover and refrigerate until ready to cook.
2. Put the flour, well seasoned with salt and pepper, on one plate, the beaten egg on another and the breadcrumbs on a third.
3. Coat the escalopes one by one, first with flour, then with egg and finally with breadcrumbs, ensuring that they are evenly coated at each stage. Shake off surplus crumbs and chill the escalopes for 10 minutes.
4. Heat the oil and butter in a heavy based frying pan. When the butter ceases to foam, put in the escalopes and fry fairly briskly for about 3 minutes each side, until cooked through and golden. Avoid overcooking and drying the meat.
5. Drain the escalopes on kitchen paper, arrange them on a hot serving dish and garnish with lemon wedges and gherkins. Serve with sauté potatoes and a green salad.

VARIATIONS:

Veal Escalopes Parmigiana
Prepare and cook the escalopes as for Wiener Schnitzel, but mix 3 tablespoons grated Parmesan cheese with the breadcrumbs. Arrange the cooked escalopes flat in a flameproof dish and spread each with 1 tablespoon home made Tomato Sauce (see page 151) and cover with a thin slice of Bel Paese or Mozzarella cheese. Cook under a preheated moderate grill just until the cheese melts and bubbles.

Veal Escalopes Modena
Prepare and cook the escalopes as for Wiener Schnitzel, then arrange flat in a flameproof dish. Cover each escalope with a thin slice of Parma ham, and cover that with a thin slice of Fontina, Bel Paese or processed Gruyère cheese. Cook under a preheated hot grill just until the cheese melts.

Spinach Stuffed Braised Veal

Serves 6–8
Preparation time: 30 minutes
Cooking time: 2 hours

- 1–1½ kg/2–2½ lb boneless breast or shoulder of veal, suitable for stuffing
- salt
- freshly ground black pepper
- 2 teaspoons lemon juice
- a little seasoned flour
- 25 g/1 oz butter, softened
- 4 tablespoons dry white wine or dry white vermouth

Stuffing:

- 25 g/1 oz butter
- 1 small onion, peeled and finely chopped
- 225 g/8 oz fresh spinach leaves, washed, shaken dry and shredded
- 225 g/8 oz pork sausage meat
- 2 tablespoons grated Parmesan cheese
- 1 tablespoon chopped fresh parsley
- 1 egg, beaten

The stuffing keeps the veal beautifully moist while cooking and makes an interesting colour contrast when carved. Veal does not keep well, so plan to cook it within one day of buying.

1. To make the stuffing, melt the butter in a saucepan and fry the onion gently for 5 minutes, stirring occasionally.
2. Add the spinach and cook, stirring frequently, for 5–6 minutes until the leaves have wilted and their moisture has evaporated. Remove from the heat, mix in the sausage meat, Parmesan, parsley and egg.
3. Wipe the meat on both sides with damp kitchen paper. Lay the meat flat, boned-side uppermost, and sprinkle with salt, pepper and lemon juice. Fold the meat in half and, with needle and thread, sew up two sides to form a 'bag' for the stuffing.
4. Fill the bag loosely with stuffing and sew up the open end.
5. Coat the stuffed joint lightly with seasone flour and put in an ovenproof casserole dish. Spread the butter on top of the meat, cover tightly and cook in a preheated oven at 160°C 325°F, Gas Mark 3 for about 2 hours.
6. After 30 minutes cooking pour the wine o vermouth over the meat and continue cooking, basting with the pan juices from tim to time.
7. To serve, lift the meat into a hot dish, pull out the strings and carve in thick slices.
8. Skim the fat off the cooking juices, taste and adjust the seasoning and spoon the juices over the meat. Serve hot with young carrots, French beans and sauté potatoes. Any meat left over is good served cold with salad.

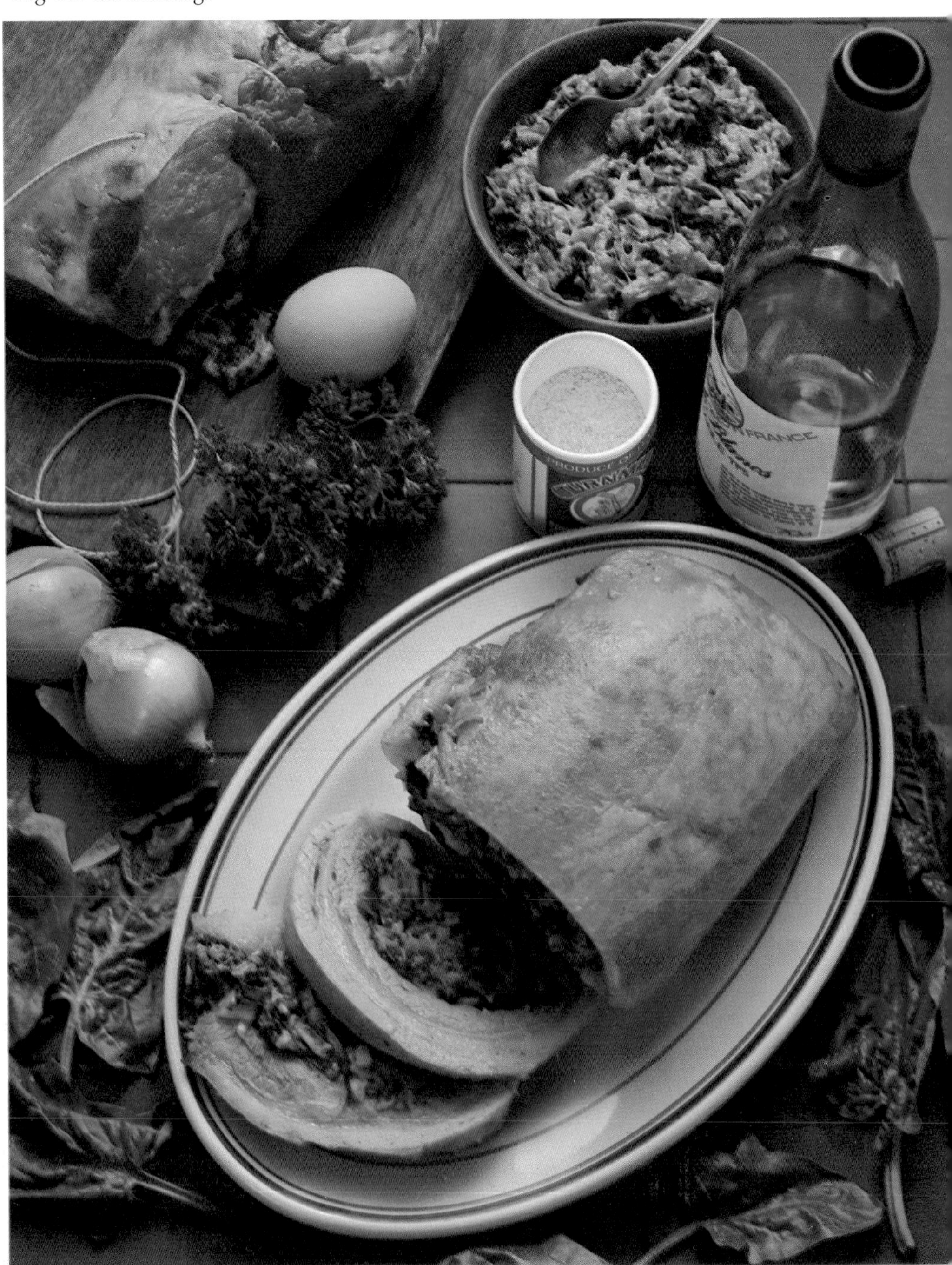

Neapolitan Veal Rolls

eparation time: 20 minutes
ooking time: 20–25 minutes

small escalopes of veal, weighing 40–50 g/1½–2 oz each
g/3 oz cooked ham, very thinly sliced
g/2 oz Bel Paese or Gruyère cheese
g/2 oz sultanas, washed
g/1 oz pine nuts, or blanched, slivered almonds
g/2 oz chopped fresh parsley
lt
eshly ground black pepper
tablespoon olive oil
g/1 oz butter
0 ml/¼ pint dry white wine or dry white vermouth and water mixed

1. Lay the pieces of veal between two sheets of cling film or damp greaseproof paper and beat them gently with a rolling pin until very thin. Remove the top layer of paper and lay a small slice of ham on each piece of veal.
2. Chop the cheese into very small dice and mix with the sultanas, nuts, parsley, and salt and pepper. Divide this stuffing between the pieces of meat, roll up each in turn and secure with white cotton.
3. Heat the oil and butter in a wide saucepan and fry the rolls fairly briskly, turning as necessary, until lightly browned all over. Pour in the wine, cover tightly and simmer very gently for 20–25 minutes until tender, turning once during cooking.
4. Lift out the rolls, remove the cotton and arrange on a hot serving dish.
5. Boil the pan juices rapidly, uncovered, until well reduced and slightly syrupy, then pour the juice over the rolls. Serve with broccoli spears or French beans, and creamed potatoes.

Blanquette de Veau

rves 4–6
eparation time: 30 minutes
ooking time: 1¼ hours

kg/2 lb boneless shoulder or breast of veal, cut into 4 cm/1½ inch cubes
lt
lemon
carrot, peeled and quartered
onion, peeled and quartered
ouquet garni
00 ml/1 pint chicken stock
g/1 oz butter
g/1 oz plain flour
5 g/8 oz firm button mushrooms
(size 2) egg yolks
0 ml/¼ pint single cream
eshly ground black pepper
garnish:
angles of fried bread
out 3 tablespoons cooked peas

1. Place the meat in a saucepan with 1 teaspoon salt, a slice of the lemon and cold water to cover. Bring slowly to the boil, then drain through a colander and rinse the meat under the cold tap.
2. Return the blanched meat to the rinsed pan with the carrot, onion, herbs and chicken stock. Bring to simmering point, cover tightly and simmer gently for 1 hour or until tender.
3. Strain off and reserve the liquid; discard the vegetables and herbs, leaving the meat in the pan.
4. Melt the butter in another saucepan, add the flour and cook, stirring, for 2 minutes. Add 450 ml/¾ pint of the strained cooking liquid all at once and whisk until boiling and thickened, then simmer for 5 minutes.
5. Add the mushrooms and 1 tablespoon lemon juice and simmer for another 5 minutes.
6. Blend together the egg yolks and cream in a bowl, stir in 2 tablespoons of the hot stock, then add all to the saucepan, stirring.
7. Heat very gently until lightly thickened, but do not allow to boil.
8. Add the meat and heat through gently without boiling. Season to taste with salt, pepper and lemon juice.
9. Transfer the mixture to a shallow gratin dish, surround with fried bread triangles and scatter the peas over the surface. Serve with French beans and boiled potatoes.

Kidney Strogonoff

Preparation time: 20 minutes, plus 30 minutes soaking time
Cooking time: about 20 minutes

- 1 tablespoon oil
- 50 g/2 oz butter
- 2 medium onions, peeled and thinly sliced
- 175 g/6 oz button mushrooms, thinly sliced
- 450 g/1 lb lamb's or veal kidneys, soaked in cold water for 30 minutes
- 2 tablespoons dry white vermouth
- salt
- freshly ground black pepper
- 150 ml/5 fl oz soured cream
- 1 tablespoon chopped fresh parsley, to garnish
- 225 g/8 oz raw long-grain rice, cooked, to serve

Increase the amount of cream if you like a richer sauce, and if no soured cream is available use double cream soured with 1 teaspoon lemon juice.

1. Melt the oil and 25 g/1 oz of the butter in a large frying pan and fry the onions gently for about 10 minutes until they begin to soften. Add the mushrooms and stir gently for another 2–3 minutes.
2. Meanwhile, drain the kidneys, peel off the skin, if any, and snip out the white central core with scissors; slice them as thinly as possible.
3. Increase the heat, add the remaining butter and, when melted, put in the sliced kidneys. Cook fairly quickly for about 5 minutes, turning the kidneys frequently until their reddish colour changes to brown.
4. Pour in the vermouth and boil for a minute or two.
5. Reduce the heat to very low and stir in the soured cream, and salt and pepper to taste. Simmer gently for 3–5 minutes until the sauce is creamy. Serve the kidneys on a bed of boiled rice and sprinkle with chopped parsley.

Liver and Onions

Preparation time: 15 minutes
Cooking time: 20 minutes

- 4 tablespoons olive oil
- 350 g/12 oz onions, peeled and thinly sliced
- ¼ teaspoon dried sage
- salt
- freshly ground black pepper
- 400–450 g/14 oz–1 lb calf's or lamb's liver, in one piece
- 1 tablespoon wine vinegar
- 1 tablespoon water
- 2 tablespoons chopped fresh parsley

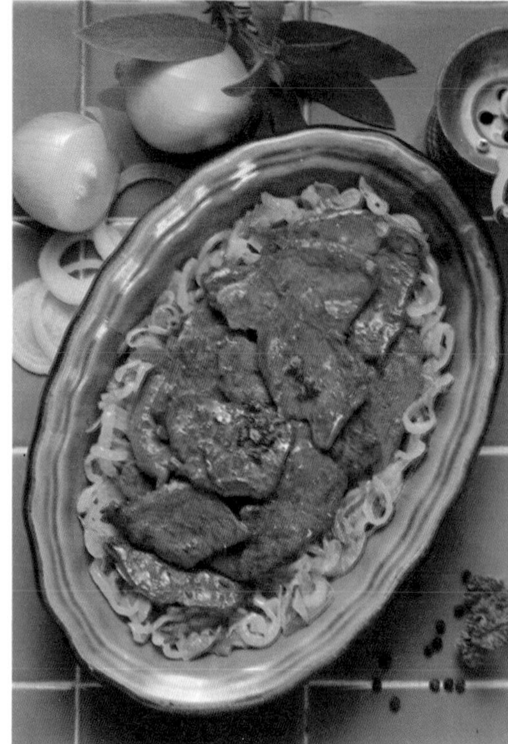

1. Heat 2 tablespoons of the oil in a large, heavy-based frying pan. When hot, put in the onions and cook over a low heat, stirring frequently, for 15–20 minutes, until the onions are soft and golden.
2. Stir in the sage and a little salt and pepper, then spread the mixture over the base of a hot serving dish Keep hot.
3. While the onions are cooking lay the liver on a chopping board, cut out any veins and slice it horizontally as thinly as possible, about 3 mm/⅛ inch thick. Pat each slice dry with kitchen paper and cut into pieces roughly 4 cm/1½ inches square.
4. Using kitchen paper, wipe clean the pan in which the onions cooked.
5. Pour the remaining oil into the pan and, when sizzling hot, put in the pieces of liver and fry briskly, turning frequently, for 2–3 minutes, until the liver changes colour on the outside but is still juicy inside. Add salt and pepper and pile the liver on top of the onions
6. Add the vinegar and water to the frying pan, boil for a few seconds, stirring and scraping up the juices from the base of the pan and pour over the liver. Sprinkle with parsley.

Skewered Sweetbreads in Bacon

eparation time: 2–3 hours
ooking time: 12 minutes

50 g/1 lb lamb's sweetbreads
lt
eshly ground black pepper
2 rashers thin cut smoked streaky bacon, rinded
0 g/1½ oz butter
0 g/2 oz dry white breadcrumbs
o serve:
00 ml/½ pint bread sauce
rigs of watercress

1. Cover the sweetbreads with lightly salted cold water and soak them for several hours, changing the water occasionally, until all traces of blood have disappeared and the breads, if frozen, have thawed.
2. Drain, cover the sweetbreads with fresh cold water, bring slowly to the boil and simmer for 2 minutes. Drain, cover with cold water and leave to cool.
3. With a sharp knife cut away any thick pieces of skin and membrane.
4. Divide the prepared sweetbreads into walnut-size pieces and season them lightly with pepper. Lay the bacon rashers flat on a board and stretch them with a heavy knife until very thin.
5. Cut the bacon into lengths, wrap each length around a piece of sweetbread and impale each roll on a skewer, dividing the rolls between 4 skewers.
6. Preheat a grill to medium and cook the sweetbread rolls for 10–12 minutes, turning several times, until the bacon is crisp.
7. Meanwhile, melt the butter in a frying pan and, when hot, fry the breadcrumbs for 5–6 minutes, stirring constantly, over a moderate heat until golden.
8. To serve, lay the skewers on a hot serving dish, scatter the fried breadcrumbs over them and garnish with watercress. Serve the hot bread sauce separately in a sauceboat.

Braised Oxtail

eparation time: 20 minutes
ooking time: about 4 hours

½ kg/2½ lb oxtail, cut in pieces
tablespoons oil
large onions, peeled and sliced
medium carrots, peeled and cut in chunks
celery sticks, cut into 4 cm/1½ inch lengths
tablespoons plain flour
50 ml/1¼ pints beef stock
tablespoons tomato purée
bay leaves
rig of thyme
lt
eshly ground black pepper
tablespoon chopped fresh parsley

This can be cooked in advance and when the casserole is cold, the solidified fat can be lifted off before reheating. Any excess sauce makes an excellent soup base.

1. Wipe the pieces of oxtail with a damp paper towel and trim away any excess fat. Heat the oil in a large flameproof casserole. When hot, fry the pieces of oxtail, in batches, removing them with a perforated spoon to a plate as soon as they are lightly browned on all sides.
2. Lower the heat a little, add the onions, carrots and celery and fry, stirring frequently, for 5 minutes.
3. Stir in the flour and cook for a minute, then stir in the stock and tomato purée. Bring to the boil, add the bay leaves, thyme, and salt and pepper.
4. Return the pieces of oxtail to the pan and mix them with the sauce. Cover the casserole and transfer to a preheated oven at 150°C, 300°F, Gas Mark 2 and cook for 3½–4 hours until the meat is very tender.
5. To serve immediately, skim off the surface fat, remove the bay leaves and thyme, adjust the seasoning and sprinkle with parsley.

Pressed Ox Tongue

Preparation time: 20 minutes, plus soaking time if necessary
Cooking time: 3½–4½ hours according to size (or 1¼–1½ hours in a pressure cooker)

- 1 pickled ox tongue, soaked in cold water, if necessary
- 1 small onion, peeled
- 1 large carrot, peeled and sliced
- 1 celery stick, sliced
- 12 black peppercorns, slightly crushed
- 2 bay leaves

An ox tongue usually weighs between 1¼ and 1¾ kg/2½ and 4 lb, and is excellent for a hot meal, followed by cold meat the next day. As cold tongue reheats in a sauce very successfully and carves more economically it is best to cook and shape the tongue in advance.

Pickled tongue sometimes needs 2–4 hours soaking in cold water before cooking, so follow the label directions or seek the butcher's advice.

1. Rinse the tongue in cold water and place it in a large pan, or pressure cooker, with cold water to cover. Bring slowly to the boil and skim. Add all the other ingredients and bring back to boiling point.
2. Cover the pan tightly and barely simmer for 3½–4½ hours, until the tongue is very soft when pierced in the thickest part with a skewer.
3. Alternatively, pressure cook at 15 lb pressure for 1¼–1½ hours.
4. When cooked, leave the tongue in the cooking water until cool enough to handle.
5. Lift out the tongue, peel off the thick skin and remove any small bones or gristle from the root end.
6. Curl the tongue around and fit it tightly into a small cake tin approximately 15 cm/6 inches wide and 7.5 cm/3 inches deep. Cover with a saucer which fits inside the tin and press with some heavy weights. Leave overnight in a cool place to set.
7. To unmould, dip the tin briefly in hot water and invert on to a plate. Serve cold with Cumberland Sauce (page 151) and a selection of salads.

To serve hot in Madeira Sauce:
For 4–6 portions make about 450 ml/¾ pint Madeira Sauce (page 147). Slice 350–450 g/12 oz–1 lb tongue and arrange overlapping slices in a shallow dish. Pour the sauce over, cover with foil, and reheat gently in a preheated oven at 150°C, 300°F, Gas Mark 2. Alternatively serve the whole hot tongue and hand the sauce separately. Serve with carrots, cauliflower and boiled potatoes.

Orange Glazed Corner of Gammon

erves 8
reparation time: 10 minutes, lus soaking time
ooking time: 1½ hours

½ kg/3 lb corner of gammon, soaked for 1–2 hours in cold water
bay leaves
ice of 1 orange
0 g/2 oz soft brown sugar
few cloves
seedless orange, peeled and thinly sliced, to garnish
auce:
ooking juices from the gammon, made up to 300 ml/½ pint with water
teaspoons cornflour
tablespoons bitter orange marmalade
5 g/½ oz butter
eshly ground black pepper

This small, boneless, triangular shaped joint is ideal for a small roast. For a larger joint up to 2¾ kg/6 lb, cook middle gammon in the same way, using twice the amount of glaze and cooking for 25 minutes per 500 g/1 lb.

1. Drain the gammon and wrap it loosely in a large piece of foil with the bay leaves beneath. Place the foil parcel on a rack in a roasting tin and cook in the centre of a preheated oven at 190°C, 375°F, Gas Mark 5, for 1 hour.
2. Remove the parcel from the oven, open the foil and strip off the rind. Score the fat surface in a large diamond pattern and spoon the orange juice over it. Press the brown sugar evenly over the fat and stud with cloves.
3. Leave the foil around the lower part of the joint to keep the meat moist, and return the joint to the oven for a further 30 minutes to complete the cooking and brown the glaze.
4. Lift the joint on to a hot serving dish and garnish with the orange slices.
5. Pour the liquid which has collected in the foil into a measuring jug and make up to 300 ml/½ pint with water.
6. To make the sauce, pour the liquid into a small saucepan, add the cornflour blended smoothly with 2 teaspoons cold water, and the marmalade. Stir until boiling, taste and adjust the seasoning and simmer for 2 minutes. Stir in the butter and serve with the gammon.

Devilled Pineapple Gammon Steaks

reparation time: 10 minutes
ooking time: 12 minutes

× 100–175 g/4–6 oz smoked gammon steaks
5 g/1 oz melted butter
tablespoon French or green pepper mustard
tablespoons demerara sugar
fresh pineapple rings, or canned, drained
o garnish:
ushrooms brushed with oil and grilled in the pan beneath the bacon
prigs of watercress

1. Cut off the rind and snip the fat at 1 cm/½ inch intervals around the gammon steaks to prevent them curling under the grill.
2. Brush one side with melted butter and cook under a preheated medium grill for 5 minutes.
3. Turn the steaks over, brush with butter, spread lightly with mustard and sprinkle with a little sugar. Grill for another 3 minutes.
4. Arrange a slice of pineapple on each steak, brush with the remaining butter and sprinkle with sugar. Grill for a further 2 minutes, if necessary increasing the heat to lightly glaze and brown the pineapple.
5. Garnish with the mushrooms and a sprig of watercress.

Poultry and Game

CHICKEN

Coq au Vin Rouge

Preparation time: 40 minutes
Cooking time: about 1 hour

1½ kg/3 lb roasting chicken, jointed (page 173)
1 medium onion, peeled and sliced
1 small carrot, peeled and sliced
150 ml/¼ pint water
450 ml/¾ pint red wine (robust Burgundy, Beaujolais or Macon)
salt
freshly ground black pepper
100 g/4 oz unsmoked streaky bacon, sliced 5 mm/¼ inch thick, rinded
1 tablespoon oil
25 g/1 oz butter
12 button onions, peeled
1–2 garlic cloves, crushed
1 bay leaf
sprig of thyme
2 tablespoons brandy
100 g/4 oz firm button mushrooms
Beurre manié:
25 g/1 oz butter creamed with 2 tablespoons plain flour
To garnish:
crescents of butter fried bread
1 tablespoon finely chopped fresh parsley

1. Place the giblets, back bone and trimmings from the jointed chicken into a saucepan.
2. Add the onion, carrot, water, wine and a little salt and pepper and simmer, uncovered, for 30 minutes, until well reduced.
3. Fry the bacon strips gently in a saucepan with the oil, butter and button onions, shaking the pan frequently, for several minutes.
4. Meanwhile wash the chicken portions and pat dry with paper towels. Season with salt and pepper, place skin side down in the pan with the bacon, onions, cloves, bay leaf and thyme, and fry until golden, about 10 minutes.
5. Pour the brandy into a heated ladle, ignite and pour flaming over the chicken, shaking the pan gently until the flames die.
6. Strain the reduced wine and stock into the pan and bring to the boil. Cover, and simmer very gently for 35 minutes, adding the mushrooms for the last 10 minutes of cooking.
7. Transfer the chicken, bacon, mushrooms and onions with a perforated spoon to a serving dish and keep warm. Discard the herbs.
8. Reduce the liquid to about 300 ml/½ pint by boiling rapidly uncovered, if necessary.
9. Add the beurre manié in small pieces to the liquid, stirring constantly, and simmer until the sauce thickens to a glossy coating consistency. Taste and adjust the seasoning and pour the sauce over the chicken.
10. Dip the croûtons in the parsley and arrange around the edge of the dish.

Chicken Breasts Italiana

Preparation time: 20 minutes
Cooking time: 15–20 minutes

4 chicken breasts
1 tablespoon plain flour
salt
freshly ground black pepper
1 tablespoon oil
50 g/2 oz butter
100 g/4 oz button mushrooms, finely sliced
2 tablespoons grated Parmesan or hard, mature Cheddar cheese
6 tablespoons Marsala
2 tablespoons chicken stock

1. Prepare the chicken breasts as escalopes (page 173) and keep refrigerated.
2. Coat the chicken with the flour seasoned with salt and pepper. Heat the oil and 25 g/1 oz of the butter in a large frying pan and, when hot, fry the chicken breasts gently for 6–7 minutes on each side, turning once, until golden.
3. Transfer the meat to a shallow, flameproof dish and keep warm.
4. Add the remaining butter to the pan and, when hot, fry the sliced mushrooms briskly for about 3 minutes, stirring frequently.
5. Remove from the pan with a perforated spoon and spread the mushrooms over the chicken breasts. Sprinkle on the cheese.
6. Pour the Marsala and the stock into the frying pan and boil rapidly until reduced to half the quantity. Spoon this liquid over the chicken, then place the dish under a preheated moderate grill for 3–4 minutes, just until the cheese melts.

Left: Chicken breasts Italiana
Right: Coq au vin rouge

LE FI
le débat

Tarragon Chicken en Cocotte

Serves 4–6
Preparation time: 20 minutes
Cooking time: 1½ hours

1 × 1½ kg/3 lb roasting chicken
salt
freshly ground black pepper
50 g/2 oz butter
8 sprigs fresh tarragon or 1 teaspoon dried tarragon
1 tablespoon oil
1 medium onion, peeled and sliced
1 medium carrot, peeled and sliced
1 celery stick, sliced
450 ml/¾ pint chicken stock
1 tablespoon cornflour
2 tablespoons medium sherry
2 tablespoons chopped fresh tarragon or parsley
a few whole tarragon leaves, to garnish

1. Rinse the chicken under running cold water, drain and pat dry with paper towels. Season the body cavity with salt and pepper and insert 15 g/½ oz of the butter and half of the sprigs or dried tarragon.
2. Truss the bird if necessary.
3. Heat the oil and remaining butter in a flameproof casserole. Place the chicken breast-down in the dish and adjust the heat so that the chicken browns in 3–5 minutes but the fat is not hot enough to discolour.
4. Turn the chicken at intervals to brown the sides and then the back; this gentle browning process takes a total of 10–15 minutes.
5. Lift out the chicken on to a plate.
6. Add the onion, carrot and celery to the pan and fry gently in the same fat for 5 minutes. Sprinkle with a little salt and pepper and add the rest of the sprigs or the dried tarragon.
7. Replace the bird on top of the vegetables and cover with kitchen foil and the lid. Transfer to a preheated oven at 180°C, 350°F, Gas Mark 4 and cook for 1 hour 20 minutes. Pierce the thickest part of the thigh with a metal skewer and if the juices run clear the bird is cooked.
8. Lift the chicken on to a hot serving dish, discard any trussing strings and keep hot.
9. Add the stock to the pan and boil for a few minutes, stirring to free any sediment from the base of the pan. Skim off any surface fat. Stir in the cornflour blended with the sherry and bring to the boil. Stir until the sauce thickens slightly.
10. Taste and adjust the seasoning, strain the sauce into a hot sauce boat and stir in the herbs.
11. Immediately before serving, garnish the breast of the bird with a few fresh tarragon leaves and spoon over a little of the sauce.

French Roast Chicken with Herb Baked Tomatoes

Serves 4–6
Preparation time: 20 minutes
Cooking time: 20 minutes per 450 g/1 lb, plus 20 minutes

1½–1¾ kg/3–4 lb roasting chicken
65 g/2½ oz butter, softened
2 tablespoons chopped fresh herbs; parsley, tarragon, chervil, as available
1 garlic clove, crushed (optional)
salt
freshly ground black pepper
squeeze of lemon juice
To garnish:
Herb Baked Tomatoes (page 52)
sprigs of fresh watercress

This simple French method of roasting chicken ensures a crisp golden skin and a juicy, succulent breast. The buttery cooking juices form a small amount of natural gravy, and instead of a stuffing the bird is served with herb and garlic flavoured tomatoes baked in the oven at the same time.

1. Note the weight of the bird and calculate the cooking time. Reserve the giblets for stock or soup and freeze if not required immediately.
2. Wash the chicken under running cold water, drain and carefully pat the outside dry with paper towels.
3. Cream half of the butter with the herbs, garlic, if used, and season well with salt and pepper. Insert the mixture into the body cavity. Tie the legs together.
4. Lay the bird on its side in a small roasting tin and spread half the remaining butter over the exposed surfaces. Transfer to a preheated oven at 190°C, 375°F, Gas Mark 5 and cook for one-third of the calculated time.
5. Turn the bird on to its other side, spread with the remaining butter and cook for a similar time.
6. Turn the bird breast-up, baste it with the juices which have collected in the pan and complete the cooking. Pierce the thickest part of the thigh with a metal skewer and if the juices run clear the bird is ready to serve.
7. Lift the bird from the roasting tin, tilting it so that the juices run back into the tin, and arrange on a hot dish.
8. Discard the trussing strings and garnish the bird with the tomatoes and sprigs of watercress.
9. Add a squeeze of lemon juice to the pan juices, taste and adjust the seasoning, reheat and serve in a hot sauce boat.

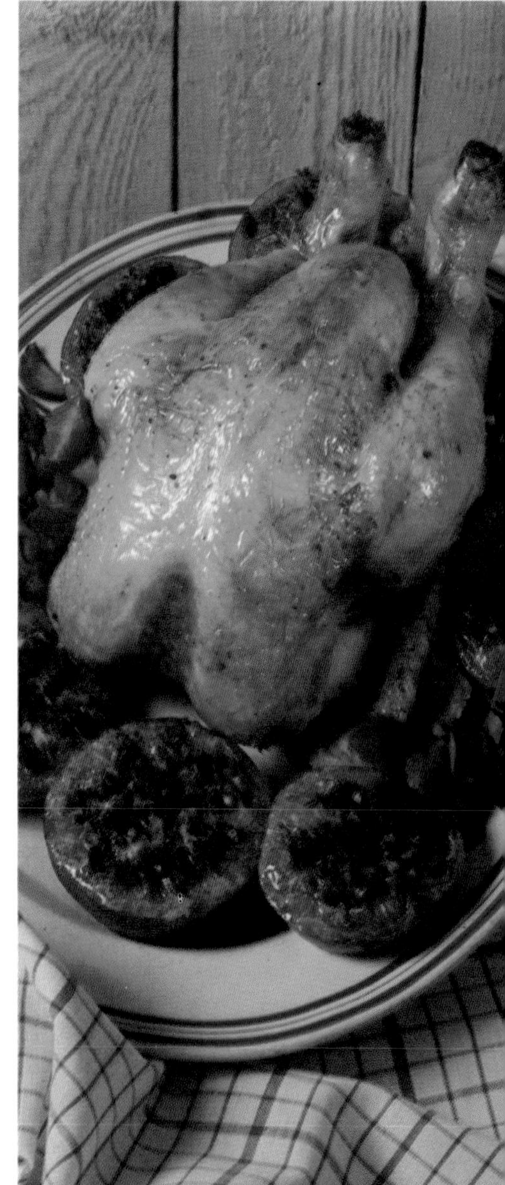

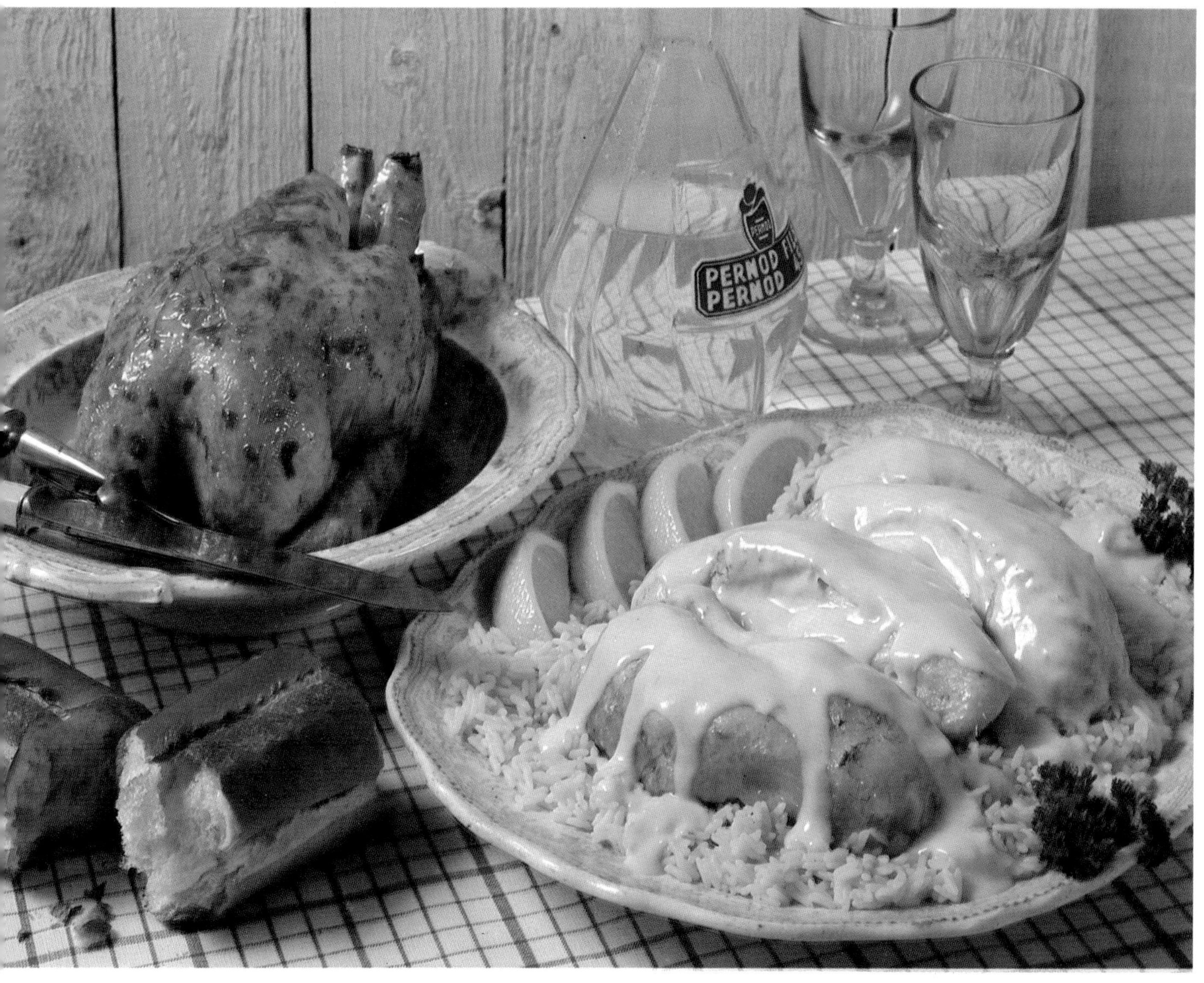

Lemon Chicken with Rice

eparation time: 15 minutes
ooking time: $1\frac{1}{4}$ hours

4–1½ kg/2½–3 lb roasting chicken
lt
medium onion, peeled
small bay leaf
emon
carrot, peeled and quartered
celery sticks, chopped
black peppercorns
0 ml/1 pint water
ice:
5 g/6 oz long-grain rice
0 ml/¾ pint water
teaspoon salt
chicken stock cube
uce:
0 ml/¾ pint hot stock strained from the chicken
g/1½ oz butter
g/1½ oz plain flour
egg yolk
tablespoons single cream
ice of ½ lemon
rigs of parsley, to garnish

This recipe uses a roasting chicken, but you can use a boiling fowl instead; in that case increase the liquid to cover the thighs of the bird and simmer for two hours or until tender.

1. Prepare the chicken for cooking. Sprinkle the body cavity with salt and insert the onion and the bay leaf. Cut the lemon in half, rub one cut surface over the chicken and reserve the other half for garnishing.
2. Place the bird in a deep pan with a tight fitting lid. The bird must fit fairly snugly.
3. Add the washed giblets, a thin strip of lemon rind, the carrot, celery, peppercorns, 1 teaspoon salt and the water.
4. Bring to simmering point, cover the pan tightly and simmer gently for about 1 hour, or until the chicken is tender and the juices run clear when the bird is pierced with a skewer.
5. Half an hour before the chicken is cooked put the rice, water, salt and stock cube into a saucepan. Bring to the boil, stir to dissolve the cube, cover tightly and cook over low heat until the rice is tender and all the liquid absorbed.
6. To make the sauce, strain 450 ml/¾ pint stock from the chicken, but leave the chicken in the pan to keep hot. Melt the butter in a small saucepan, stir in the flour and cook gently, stirring, for 2 minutes.
7. Gradually add the hot stock, stirring briskly until smoothly blended.
8. Return the pan to the heat and cook, stirring continuously, until the sauce boils and thickens, then simmer gently for 5–10 minutes.
9. Mix the egg yolk with the cream, stir in 2 tablespoons of the hot sauce, then pour into the sauce and stir over low heat for 1 minute, but do not allow to boil. Add lemon juice to taste and adjust the seasoning.
10. Mix 3–4 tablespoons of sauce into the rice and spoon on to a hot serving dish.
11. Carve the chicken into joints, arrange on the rice and coat the chicken with the remaining sauce. Garnish with the reserved lemon half, cut into wedges, and with sprigs of parsley.

Above left: Tarragon chicken en cocotte
Above right: Lemon chicken with rice

Greek Island Grilled Chicken

Preparation time: 30 minutes, plus at least 4 hours to marinate
Cooking time: 25–30 minutes

4 chicken quarters
Marinade:
4 tablespoons olive oil
4 tablespoons lemon juice
strip of thinly pared lemon rind
6 black peppercorns, slightly crushed
3 sprigs thyme
1 garlic clove, crushed
1 teaspoon salt

This is a very simple dish, but one that needs plenty of time for the chicken to absorb the flavours of the lemon and herb marinade. If circumstances do not permit grilling outdoors over charcoal in the Greek manner, the chicken still tastes delicious grilled in the conventional way. Serve with a crisp green salad and (optionally) a chilled Yogurt and Cucumber Dressing (page 152).

1. Wipe the chicken pieces with a damp kitchen paper towel.
2. Mix all the marinade ingredients together in a deep dish. Add the chicken pieces, turn them in the marinade, then cover and refrigerate for at least 4 hours, turning them once or twice.
3. Preheat the grill to medium.
4. Drain the chicken pieces, reserving the oil and lemon marinade.
5. Remove the grill rack and arrange the chicken, cut side uppermost, in a single layer in the grill pan. Position the pan 13–15 cm/ 5–6 inches below the source of heat and grill gently for 12–15 minutes.
6. Turn the chicken portions, brush with marinade and continue grilling gently for another 12–15 minutes, until the skin is golden and the juices run clear when the deepest part of the thigh is pierced with a fine skewer.
7. Baste the chicken portions with the marinade frequently throughout the cooking.

Casseroled Chicken in Quick Barbecue Sauce

Preparation time: 15 minutes
Cooking time: 1¼ hours

1 kg/2 lb chicken portions
1 tablespoon plain flour
salt
freshly ground black pepper
2 tablespoons oil
25 g/1 oz butter
Sauce:
1 small onion, peeled and finely chopped
275 g/10 oz can cream of tomato soup
2 tablespoons soft brown sugar
1 tablespoon Worcestershire sauce
1 tablespoon wine vinegar
2 teaspoons prepared mustard

Chicken thighs or drumsticks, or a quartered small chicken may be used for this recipe. Serve with buttered rice and a green vegetable.

1. Coat the chicken portions lightly with the flour seasoned with salt and pepper.
2. Heat the oil and butter in a large frying pan, and when hot fry the chicken portions fairly briskly, turning, until golden all over.
3. Lift out the pieces and transfer them to a casserole.
4. Fry the onion in the same fat for a minute, then add all the other ingredients and simmer together for 10 minutes. Pour this over the chicken and cover the dish.
5. Cook in a preheated oven at 180°C, 350°F, Gas Mark 4 for 1 hour.

Oven Fried Cheesy Chicken

*reparation time: 15 minutes
ing ready cut portions; 25
inutes if jointing a whole
icken*
ooking time: 35–40 minutes

× 1–1¼ kg/2–2½ lb chicken, cut into 4 quarters (page 173) or 4 × 225 g/8 oz chicken portions
lt
eshly ground black pepper
g/3 oz butter
small garlic clove, crushed
g/2 oz fresh white breadcrumbs
g/2 oz mature Cheddar cheese, finely grated
garnish:
lemon, quartered
rigs of watercress

Serve this easy to prepare dish with sauté potatoes and a green salad. When cold the chicken pieces are equally good for picnics or packed lunches.

1. Wipe the chicken pieces with a damp paper towel and sprinkle generously with salt and pepper.
2. Melt the butter slowly with the garlic in a saucepan.
3. Meanwhile, mix together the breadcrumbs, cheese and 1 teaspoon salt and spread in a shallow dish.
4. Brush the pieces of chicken all over with the melted butter, then press, one by one, into the breadcrumb mixture, turning to coat both sides. Press the crumbs in place using a palette knife.
5. Arrange the portions, skin side up and side by side, in a shallow baking tin. Scoop out the garlic with a perforated spoon and trickle the remaining butter evenly over the exposed chicken surfaces.
6. Bake, uncovered, in a preheated oven at 190°C, 375°F, Gas Mark 5 for 35–40 minutes, until the juices run clear when the chicken is pierced with a skewer and the coating is crusty and golden brown.
7. Arrange on a hot dish and garnish with lemon wedges and watercress, or serve cold.

Above left: Greek island grilled chicken
Above right: Oven fried cheesy chicken
Below: Casseroled chicken in quick barbecue sauce

Foil roast turkey

Preparation time: about 40 minutes
Cooking time: see chart on page 172

1 oven-ready turkey
salt
freshly ground black pepper
50 g/2 oz butter, softened
Stuffing (for recipes and quantities see page 175)

Accompaniments:
1 pork chipolata per person, grilled, baked or fried
liver and bacon rolls, 1 per person (page 172)
Bread or Cranberry Sauce (pages 150 and 151)

Once the bird goes into the oven this method of cooking turkey leaves you free until shortly before dishing up time. If cooking a frozen bird follow the label directions and the chart for thawing on page 172. Prepare the giblet stock, sauces and stuffings in advance and refrigerate them, but do not stuff the bird until shortly before cooking. To enable the heat to circulate freely through the carcass only the neck end is stuffed. Calculate the cooking time according to the weight of the bird plus the stuffing; see the chart on page 172.

1. Rinse the bird under running cold water, drain and pat the skin dry with paper towels.
2. Season the body cavity with salt and pepper and insert about 15 g/½ oz butter.
3. Stuff the neck end of the bird and hold in place by securing the flap of neck skin to the back of the bird with the wing tips or small skewer. Truss if necessary.
4. Place the bird breast-up on a rack. Stand the rack in a roasting tin and spread the remaining butter all over the turkey. Cover loosely with a large piece of oiled kitchen foil and twist it around the rim of the roasting tin.
5. Transfer to a preheated oven at 180°C, 350°F, Gas Mark 4 and cook until 30 minutes before the calculated time. Remove the foil, baste the bird with the juices from the pan and continue cooking, uncovered, for the remaining time.
6. Pierce the thickest part of the thigh with a metal skewer and if the juices run clear the bird is cooked. If they are slightly pink cook for 15 minutes then test again.
7. When cooked, lift the bird on to a hot serving dish, remove the trussing string and the skewers and leave the turkey to firm up for 15 minutes before carving.
8. Meanwhile, pour off the surface fat from the roasting tin, add 600 ml/1 pint Giblet Stock, stir well to release the sediment from the base of the tin, then allow to simmer gently to reduce and concentrate the flavour until ready to serve. Taste and adjust the seasoning and pour into a hot gravy boat.
9. Arrange the chipolatas, bacon rolls and extra stuffing balls around the bird before carving.

VARIATION:

For an alternative method of cooking small turkeys breast-down to begin with, follow the directions, oven temperature and timing for French Roast Chicken (page 104).

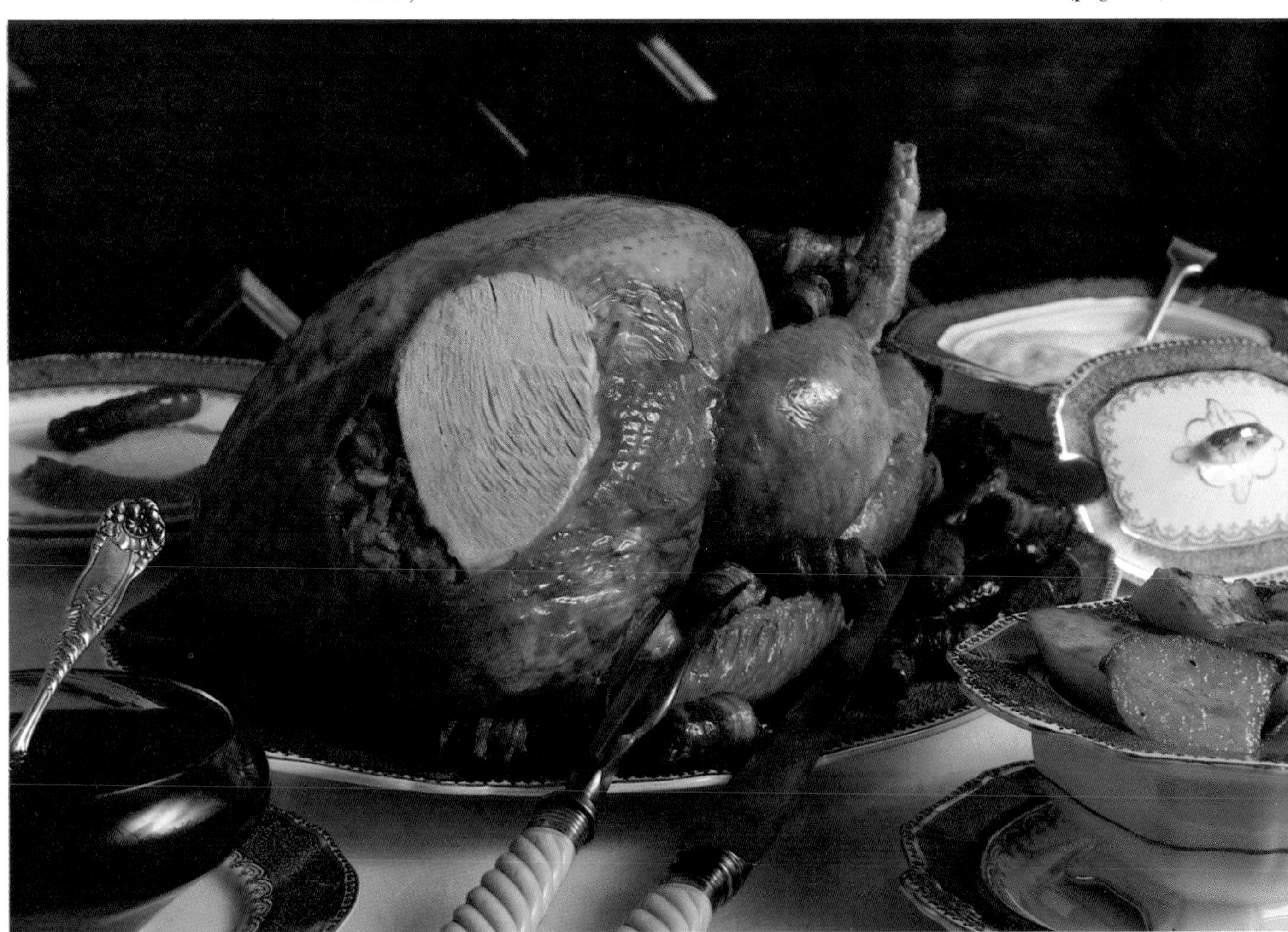

Turkey Escalopes in Cream Sauce

·eparation time: 10 minutes
ooking time: 15–20 minutes

)0–450 g/14–16 oz turkey breast
tablespoon oil
5 g/1 oz butter
2 lemon
lt
eshly ground black pepper
little plain flour
tablespoons dry white vermouth
tablespoons chicken stock
50 ml/¼ pint double cream
o garnish:
25 g/8 oz button mushrooms
ueeze of lemon juice
aprika pepper

1. Remove and discard any skin or membrane from the turkey meat.
2. Cut the meat into evenly thick slices and divide into portions, then lay the slices between pieces of cling film or damp greaseproof paper and beat carefully with a rolling pin until no more than 5 mm/¼ inch thick.
3. Heat the oil and butter in a large frying pan with a lid.
4. Meanwhile, rub the cut lemon over the turkey slices, then season them with salt and pepper and dust lightly with flour.
5. When the oil is hot add the turkey slices and fry fairly briskly until golden on both sides, about 5 minutes. Pour in the vermouth and the stock, let it bubble for a minute or two, then cover the pan and cook very gently for 10 minutes.
6. Meanwhile, simmer the button mushrooms in a little water with a squeeze of lemon juice and salt.
7. Check that the turkey is tender by piercing with a fork, and if so, lift on to a hot serving dish and keep warm.
7. Stir the cream into the pan juices and allow to boil gently until thickened to a coating consistency. Taste and adjust the seasoning, adding a few drops of lemon juice, if liked, and pour it over the turkey. Dust with a little paprika and arrange the drained mushrooms at either end of the dish.

VARIATION:

Turkey Escalopes Cordon Bleu
Prepare the escalopes and brown them in oil and butter as above. Cover them with slices of good quality lean ham cut to the size of the escalopes, and top the ham with a thin slice of a good 'melting' cheese such as Bel Paese or Gruyère.
Add 3 tablespoons chicken stock to the pan, cover tightly with the lid and cook gently for about 10 minutes, until the turkey is tender and the cheese melted. Serve with the pan juices spooned over.

ack: Turkey escalopes cordon bleu
ront: Turkey escalopes in ·eam sauce

Turkey Portions Creole

·eparation time: 20 minutes
ooking time: about 1½ hours

kg/2 lb turkey portions
tablespoons plain flour
lt
eshly ground black pepper
tablespoon oil
5 g/1 oz butter
medium onions, peeled and thinly sliced
large green pepper, cored, seeded and sliced
garlic clove, peeled and crushed
)0 g/14 oz can peeled tomatoes
bay leaf, sprig of thyme and parsley, tied together
50 ml/¼ pint chicken stock or water

This is a simple but colourful way of cooking turkey portions such as thighs, drumsticks or wings. Serve with boiled rice, allowing 40–50 g/1½–2 oz rice per portion. Turkey portions vary in size, so check the cooking time.

1. Coat the turkey portions in the flour, well-seasoned with salt and pepper.
2. Heat the oil and butter in a large frying pan with a lid and, when hot, fry the turkey portions fairly briskly until golden on all sides.
3. Lower the heat, add the onion and stir to coat with fat, then cook gently for 5 minutes. Sprinkle in the remaining flour, stir for a minute, then add the green pepper, garlic, tomatoes and juice, herbs and stock or water.
4. Bring to the boil, stirring, cover tightly and simmer very gently for 1¼ hours or until the turkey is tender.
5. When cooked, lift the turkey pieces on to a hot serving dish, carving into portions if necessary, and keep hot.
6. Discard the herbs from the sauce and boil it rapidly, uncovered, until reduced to a coating consistency. Taste and adjust the seasoning and pour the sauce over the joints.

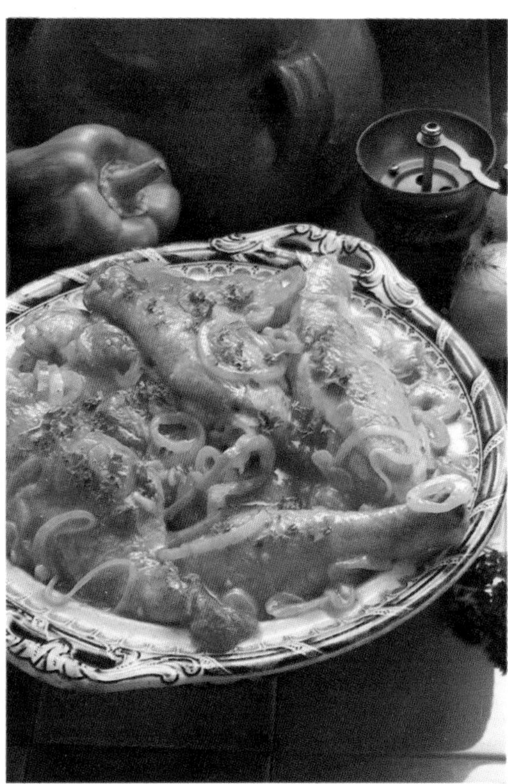

Roast Stuffed Turkey en Gelée

Serves 15–20
Preparation time: 2 hours, plus 3 hours on the day
Cooking time: 3–3½ hours

1 × 3½–4½ kg/8–10 lb turkey
salt
freshly ground black pepper
juice of ½ lemon
40 g/1½ oz butter, softened
Stuffing:
350 g/12 oz gammon rashers, cut 1 cm/½ inch thick
225 g/8 oz raw, lean veal
40 g/1½ oz butter
1 medium onion, peeled and finely chopped
450 g/1 lb pork sausage meat
50 g/2 oz fresh white breadcrumbs
finely grated rind and juice of 1 lemon
2 tablespoons chopped fresh parsley
2 small eggs, beaten
15 g/½ oz pistachio nuts, skinned (optional)
freshly ground black pepper
Garnish:
600 ml/1 pint aspic jelly
piece of cucumber
a few radishes
a few stuffed olives
sprigs of watercress

A boned and stuffed turkey served cold is a good choice for a buffet meal as all the cookin is done the day before. Commercially made aspic jelly is available at most delicatessens, and should be made up according to instructions on the packet.

1. Prepare the stuffing before boning the bird. Discard the rind from the gammon rasher, remove the fat and cut into 1 cm/½ inch dice. Coarsely mince the gammon meat with the veal.
2. Melt the butter in a saucepan and fry the onion gently for 5 minutes until soft but not coloured.
3. Remove the saucepan from the heat, add the minced meats, diced gammon fat, sausage meat, breadcrumbs, lemon rind and juice, parsley, beaten eggs, pistachio nuts, if used, and a few grinds of black pepper. Mix very thoroughly, cover and leave to cool.
4. Bone the turkey following the directions o page 174.
5. Spread the bird open, skin side down, tuck the leg and wing pieces inside and season all ov with salt, pepper and lemon juice. Arrange th stuffing down the centre.
6. Fold the neck and tail ends inwards and bring the two sides together. With a trussing needle threaded with a long length of fine string, sew the edges together leaving a loose end to pull the string out after cooking.
7. Turn the turkey over, press into a neat shape and place on a rack in a roasting tin.
8. Smear the softened butter all over the bird Cover loosely with a large, well-oiled piece o foil and twist around the edges of the roasting tin.
9. Cook in a preheated oven at 180°C, 350°F, Gas Mark 4 for 3–3½ hours or until the juice run clear when the turkey is pierced with a metal skewer. Remove the foil for the last 20 minutes to brown the skin.
10. When cooked, remove the bird from the roasting tin but leave it on the rack in a cool place until cold.
11. Pull out the trussing string and refrigerate the bird overnight.
12. Next day, prepare the aspic and leave unt on the point of setting.
13. Stand the bird on the rack over a tray and spoon about half of the jelly along the centre, encouraging it to run down and coat the sides.
14. Cut the radishes and olives into very thin circles. Pare strips of cucumber skin and cut into leaves and stalks. Arrange these in a flower pattern on top of the bird.
15. Coat with a second layer of barely liquid aspic jelly. Leave to set.
16. Carefully lift the bird on to a flat serving dish or board. Cut a few slices from one end and leave the remainder whole. Garnish with any leftover aspic jelly, chopped, and with sprigs of watercress.

Maharanee Turkey Mayonnaise

rves 8–10
eparation time: 30 minutes
ooking time: 10 minutes

kg/2 lb cold, boneless, cooked turkey meat
uce:
ablespoons oil
g/3 oz onion, peeled and finely chopped or grated
arge dessert apple, peeled, cored and chopped
ablespoons curry powder
ablespoon plain flour
0 ml/¼ pint chicken stock
ablespoons apricot jam
o 3 teaspoons lemon juice
0 ml/1 pint thick mayonnaise
t
shly ground black pepper
ablespoons whipping cream
garnish:
ard-boiled eggs, quartered
rigs of watercress
ablespoon flaked almonds, fried and lightly browned in oil
or 100 g/4 oz black grapes, halved and seeded

A mildly devilled but very creamy mayonnaise is the perfect foil for cold turkey, a meat which is naturally bland in flavour and inclined to be dry. If the turkey has to be cooked specially, a boneless roast is a good choice. Attractively garnished this dish makes a splendid centre-piece for a cold buffet, and a rice, herb and cucumber salad is a good partner.

1. Remove any skin or sinew from the turkey meat and cut into small, neat slices. Cover and refrigerate while preparing the sauce.
2. Heat the oil in a frying pan and gently fry the onion and the apple for about 10 minutes until soft but not coloured.
3. Add the curry powder and flour, stir and cook gently for another 1–2 minutes, stirring occasionally.
4. Stir in the chicken stock, and continue stirring. Cook for several minutes until the mixture becomes a thickish paste.
5. Stir in the jam and 1 teaspoon of the lemon juice. Cool a little, then press through a sieve into a bowl. Cover and leave to go cold.
6. Add the mayonnaise and mix thoroughly.
7. Taste and adjust the seasoning, adding salt, pepper and lemon juice to taste, and stir in enough cream to make a thick, creamy sauce.
8. Mix about two-thirds of the sauce with the turkey and arrange in a shallow serving dish. Stir the rest of the cream into the remaining sauce and pour over the turkey.
9. Surround the dish alternately with quartered eggs and sprigs of watercress and scatter the centre with the browned almonds or with the black grapes.

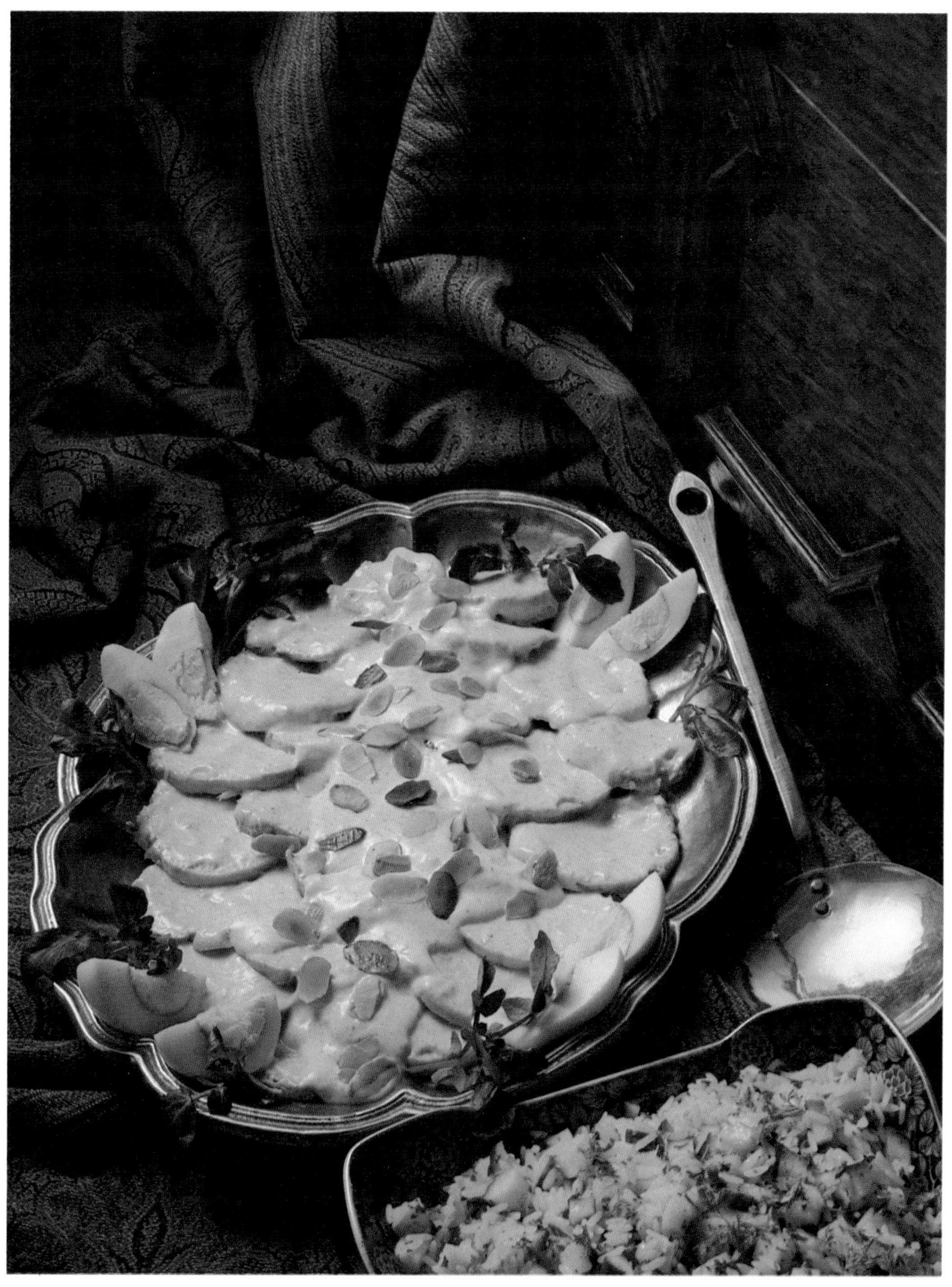

Honey Roast Duckling

Serves 3–4
Preparation time: 20–30 minutes
Cooking time: 2–2½ hours

1 × 2¼–2¾ kg/5–6 lb duckling
salt
freshly ground black pepper
1 small onion, peeled
2 tablespoons clear honey
1 tablespoon boiling water
4 crisp lettuce leaves
2 large seedless oranges, peeled and thinly sliced
1 small ripe pineapple, prepared and sliced or 1 × 225 g/8 oz can pineapple slices, drained
4 sprigs watercress
6 tablespoons French Dressing

1. Remove the giblets and reserve for making stock or freeze until needed.
2. Rinse the duckling under running cold water, drain and pat dry with paper towels. Prick the skin all over with a fork. Sprinkle the body cavity with salt and pepper and insert the onion.
3. Place the bird breast-up on a rack in a roasting tin and sprinkle with salt. Roast in the centre of a preheated oven at 180°C, 350°F, Gas Mark 4, allowing 30 minutes per 450 g/1 lb.
4. After 1 hour of cooking strain off the fat from the roasting tin. Blend the honey with the hot water and spoon this over the surface of the duck. Continue cooking for the estimated time, basting the duckling two or three times with the pan juices.
5. Check that the juices run clear when the thigh is pierced with a fine skewer, then remove the duck from the oven and leave to become cold.
6. Shortly before serving, prepare the salads on individual plates. Use a lettuce leaf for the base and arrange several overlapping orange slices topped with a slice of pineapple.
7. Fill the central pineapple hole with a sprig of watercress and sprinkle each salad with French dressing (page 152).

Duckling à l'Orange

rves 2
eparation time: 20 minutes
ɔoking time: 2–2¼ hours

× 1½–1¾ kg/3½–4 lb duckling
t
·shly ground black pepper
small onion, peeled
.arge seedless oranges, washed
:ablespoons granulated sugar
0 ml/¼ pint chicken stock
ice of ½ lemon
:ablespoons Grand Marnier or other orange liqueur
rigs of watercress, to garnish

1. Remove the giblets. Wash the duckling and giblets under running cold water, then drain and pat dry with paper towels.
2. Prick the duck's skin all over with a fork. Sprinkle the body cavity with salt and pepper and insert the onion, duck liver and 4 strips of finely pared orange rind.
3. Place the giblets in the bottom of a roasting tin and place the duck breast-up on a rack over them. Sprinkle the duck lightly with salt.
4. Roast in a preheated oven at 180°C, 350°F, Gas Mark 4 for 30 minutes per 450 g/ 1 lb.
5. Meanwhile, pare the rind thinly from one of the oranges with a potato peeler. Cut the rind into matchstick strips, and place in a saucepan covered with water. Simmer for 6–8 minutes and then drain.
6. Peel one orange to remove both the white pith and the skin, then divide the flesh into individual segments. Squeeze the juice from the other orange.
7. In a small, heavy saucepan, dissolve the sugar in 2 tablespoons water, then boil fast until caramelized. Immediately add the hot stock (take care, because the hot liquid may splutter) and heat until the caramel dissolves.
8. Pierce the thickest part of thigh with a metal skewer and if the juices run clear the duck is cooked.
9. Lift the duck on to a board, carve into 4 portions, arrange these in a serving dish and keep warm.
10. Pour off the fat from the roasting tin, add the stock and dissolved caramel, orange and lemon juices and the liqueur. Heat, stirring to release the sediment from the base of the tin and boil rapidly until well reduced and flavoured.
11. Taste and adjust the seasoning and strain the sauce over the duck . Scatter the rinds over the portions and garnish with the orange segments and sprigs of watercress.

Pheasant Braised with Cabbage

Serves 6–8
Preparation time: 20 minutes
Cooking time: 1¼–1¾ hours

50 g/2 oz bacon fat or butter
1 onion, peeled and chopped
2 celery sticks, thinly sliced
1¼ kg/2½ lb winter cabbage, coarsely shredded
6 tablespoons stock, water or dry white wine
8 juniper berries, crushed
salt
freshly ground black pepper
2 oven-ready pheasants
4 rashers bacon, rinded
25 g/1 oz butter
1 tablespoon oil

Braising is an excellent method of cooking either young pheasants, or older birds of indeterminate age. The juices permeate the vegetables with their rich flavour and the birds remain beautifully moist.

1. Melt the bacon fat or butter in a large, flameproof casserole and fry the onion and celery gently for a few minutes.
2. Add the cabbage, stir to mix thoroughly with the fat, and cook gently for 5 minutes, stirring often.
3. Add the stock, water or dry white wine, the juniper berries, if used, and salt and pepper to taste. Continue to cook gently while preparing the pheasants.
4. Wash the pheasants under running cold water, drain and pat dry with paper towels. Sprinkle inside and out with salt and pepper and tie the legs together.
5. Stretch the bacon rashers out thinly with the blade of a knife and tie them over the breasts of the pheasants with fine string.
6. Heat the oil and butter in a frying pan and when hot, brown the pheasants lightly on all sides.
7. Transfer the pheasants to the casserole, moving the cabbage aside so that it surrounds and covers them. Cover the casserole tightly.
8. Cook in a preheated oven at 160°C, 325°F, Gas Mark 3 for 1 hour if young birds, 1½ hours (or until tender) for older birds.
9. Lift out the pheasants and remove the trussing strings. Arrange a bed of braised cabbage on a hot serving dish and lay the whole, or carved, pheasants on top.

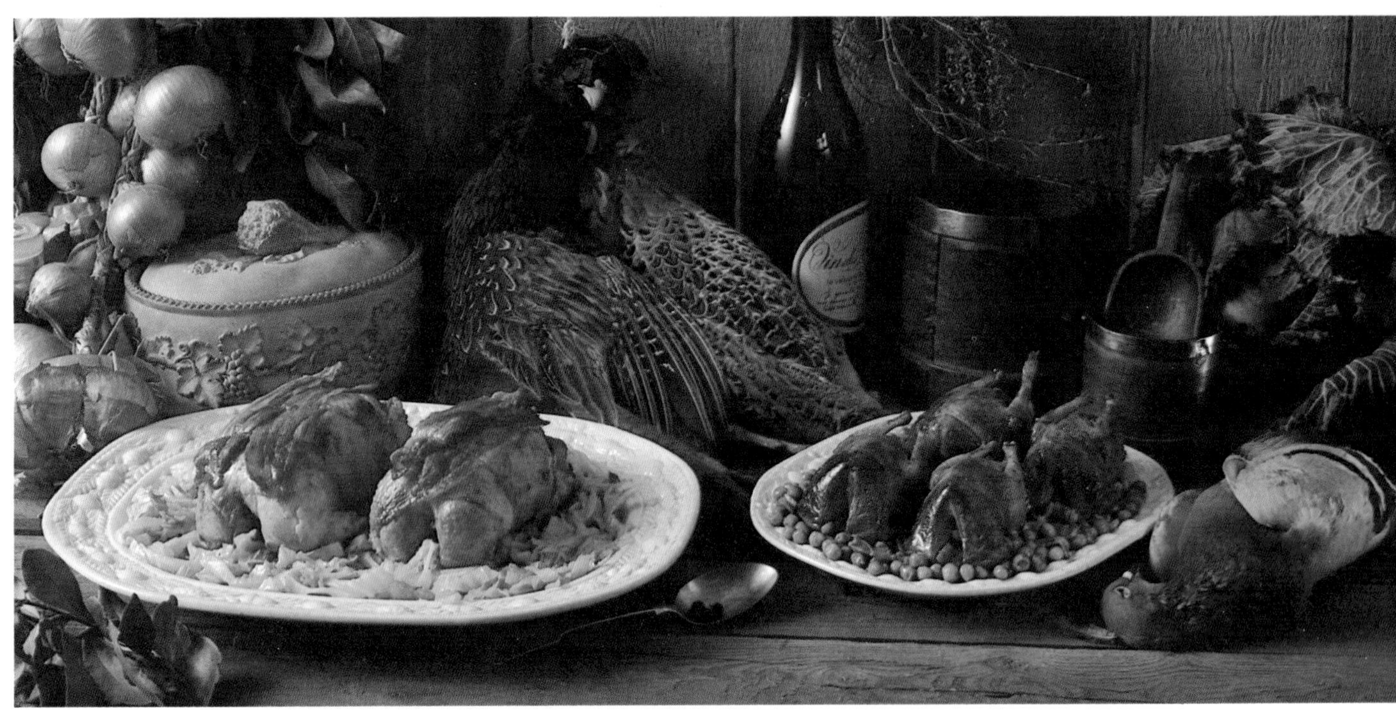

Pigeons Braised with Peas

Preparation time: 20 minutes
Cooking time: 2–2¼ hours

4 young, oven-ready pigeons
salt
freshly ground black pepper
2 tablespoons oil
25 g/1 oz butter
6 rashers streaky bacon, rinded and diced
1 large onion, peeled and chopped
4 tablespoons dry white vermouth or wine
300 ml/½ pint chicken stock
450 g/1 lb shelled peas
1 teaspoon sugar

Pigeons tend to be rather dry birds so braising is one of the best ways of cooking them. Choose young wood pigeons which should cook in about 1½ hours, but allow 2 hours in case they are older. This makes a good choice for special occasions.

1. Wash the pigeons under running cold water, drain and pat dry with paper towels. Season them inside and out with salt and pepper and tie their legs together.
2. Heat the oil and butter in a large, flameproof casserole and fry the bacon and onion together gently for 5 minutes.
3. Increase the heat, add the pigeons and cook, turning as necessary, until golden brown on all sides.
4. Add the vermouth or wine and the stock, bring to simmering point, cover the casserole tightly and simmer very gently for 1–1½ hours or until the pigeons are almost tender. Check the pan now and then to make sure there is enough liquid, adding more stock if necessary.
5. Add the peas and sugar, cover and continue simmering for 20–30 minutes until the peas and the pigeons are tender. Taste and adjust the seasoning and serve from the casserole.

Above left: Pheasant braised with cabbage
Above right: Pigeons braised with peas

Rabbit in Cider with Mushrooms

eparation time: 20 minutes,
us soaking time
ooking time: 1¼ hours

kg/2 lb rabbit joints
lt
ablespoon vinegar
ablespoon oil
g/1 oz butter
0 g/4 oz unsmoked streaky bacon in thick slices, rinded and diced
medium onions, peeled and sliced
ablespoons plain flour
0 ml/½ pint dry cider
0 ml/¼ pint stock or water
0 g/4 oz button mushrooms, wiped with a damp cloth
bay leaf, sprig of thyme, strip of lemon zest, tied together
eshly ground black pepper

Rabbit is an undervalued meat but it makes an excellent casserole and can nowadays be bought jointed and ready for the pot.

1. Soak the rabbit joints for several hours in cold, lightly salted water and the vinegar. Drain and pat dry with paper towels.
2. Heat the oil and butter in a flameproof casserole and fry the rabbit joints quickly, turning to brown all over. Lift out and reserve.
3. Add the bacon and onions to the pan and fry gently, stirring occasionally, for about 10 minutes.
4. Sprinkle in the flour, stir and cook for 1–2 minutes, then gradually stir in the cider and stock and bring to the boil.
5. Return the rabbit to the pan with the mushrooms, bay leaf, thyme and lemon zest and salt and pepper to taste.
6. Cover the casserole and simmer very gently for 1 hour or until the rabbit is tender when pierced with a skewer.
7. Remove the herbs, check the seasoning and serve from the casserole.

Partridges with Grapes

eparation time: 20 minutes
ooking time: 30–40 minutes

0 g/1 lb white grapes (Muscat, when available)
× 275 g/10 oz young, oven-ready partridges
lt
eshly ground black pepper
g/3 oz butter
tablespoon oil
ice of ½ lemon

Partridges are in season from 1st September to 1st February. The delicacy of young birds is shown at its best if they are cooked very simply with butter, allowing one bird per person. Older birds may be large enough to serve 2 portions each, and are best casseroled with a little liquid. This makes an impressive dish which is well worth the extra cost for a special occasion.

1. Skin, halve and seed half of the grapes and reserve the remainder.
2. Rinse the birds under running cold water, drain and pat dry with paper towels. Sprinkle them inside and out with salt and pepper. Insert a small piece of butter and 8 of the skinned, halved grapes into the body cavity of each bird.
3. Heat the oil and remaining butter in a wide flameproof casserole, and when hot, add the birds and fry, turning, until lightly browned.
4. Leave the birds breast-down in the casserole and cover with the lid. Transfer to a preheated oven at 200°C, 400°F, Gas Mark 6 and cook for 20–40 minutes, depending on the size of the birds. Pierce the thigh with a fine skewer to check if the birds are tender.
5. Meanwhile, roughly chop the reserved whole grapes (or purée them in an electric blender) then press through a sieve.
6. Lift the birds on to a hot serving dish and keep warm. Remove the trussing strings.
7. Add the grape and lemon juices to the buttery juices in the casserole and heat gently, stirring to release any coagulated residue from the base of the pan.
8. Add the remaining skinned and halved grapes, reheat gently and pour around the birds.

ack: Rabbit in cider with ushrooms
ont: Partridges with grapes

Puddings and Desserts

COLD PUDDINGS

Glazed Cherry Flan

Preparation time: 35 minutes
Cooking time: 20 minutes

175 g/6 oz Flan Pastry, made with 175 g/6 oz flour, pinch of salt, 100 g/4 oz butter, 1 teaspoon sugar and 1 egg + 1 teaspoon water (page 177)

Filling:

25 g/1 oz plain flour
25 g/1 oz caster sugar
1 egg, beaten
300 ml/½ pint milk
a few drops of almond essence
225 g/8 oz fresh cherries, trimmed and stoned or 1 × 425 g/15 oz can cherries, drained

Glaze:

2 teaspoons arrowroot
150 ml/¼ pint water
1 teaspoon sugar

This flan has a creamy almond flavoured filling topped with cherries.

1. Line a 21 cm/8½ inch fluted flan ring or flan dish with the pastry. Place the dish on a baking sheet. Chill for 10 minutes then bake blind in a preheated oven at 200°C, 400°F, Gas Mark 6 for 20 minutes. Allow to cool.
2. Meanwhile, make the confectioner's custard by blending the flour, sugar and egg well together in a basin.
3. Heat the milk, then pour it on to the mixture stirring well.
4. Return the mixture to the saucepan, reheat until boiling and simmer for 2 minutes, stirring all the time. Add the almond essence. Cover and allow to cool.
5. Spread the cooled custard over the base of the baked flan case. Arrange the cherries neatly over the custard.
6. To make the glaze, blend the arrowroot with a little water in a bowl. Add the sugar and the remaining water.
7. Pour the mixture into a saucepan and bring to the boil, stirring all the time until the glaze becomes transparent. Brush over the fruit.
8. Serve the flan chilled.

VARIATIONS:

Use strawberries, raspberries, apricots, peaches or grapes instead of the cherries.

French Apple Flan

Preparation time: 30 minutes
Cooking time: 25 minutes

150 g/6 oz Pâte Sucrée, made with 150 g/6 oz flour, pinch of salt, 75 g/3 oz butter, 75 g/ 3 oz caster sugar and 3 egg yolks (page 178)
300 ml/½ pint apple purée, made with 450 g/1 lb cooking apples, 50 g/2 oz sugar and 25 g/ 1oz butter
2 red dessert apples
25 g/1 oz melted butter
6 tablespoons apricot jam
3 tablespoons water

A classic French dish which has become a firm favourite in this country too.

1. Line a 20 cm/8 in flan ring with the pâte sucrée. Place the flan ring on a baking sheet.
2. Prick the pastry with a fork and bake blind in a moderately hot, preheated oven at 190°C, 375°F, Gas Mark 5 for 15 minutes.
3. Remove from the oven and allow to cool slightly before filling with the apple purée.
4. Quarter, core and slice the dessert apples and place them in overlapping circles on top of the purée. Brush with melted butter and return to oven at 200°C, 400°F, Gas Mark 6 for about 10 minutes, until the apples are tinged brown. Protect the pastry edges with foil if necessary.
5. To make the glaze, heat the apricot jam with the water in a saucepan and allow to boil for 3 minutes.
6. Cool the glaze, then sieve it and brush it over the apples.
7. Chill the flan, then serve with cream.

Gooseberry Soufflé

Preparation time: 40 minutes

225 g/8 oz fresh gooseberries, trimmed
100 g/4 oz caster sugar
3 eggs (size 1 or 2), separated
3 tablespoons water
2 teaspoons gelatine powder
2 tablespoons water
150 ml/¼ pint whipping cream, lightly whipped
2 drops green colouring (optional)
To decorate:
150 ml/¼ pint whipping cream, lightly whipped
25 g/1 oz chocolate, grated
25 g/1 oz chopped mixed nuts (optional)

This not only looks impressive but tastes delicious, so is worth making for a special occasion.

1. Cut a doubled strip of greaseproof paper, folded up 5 cm/2 inches at the bottom long enough to wrap around the outside of a 13 cm/5 inch soufflé dish and to overlap slightly. The paper must be deep enough to reach from the bottom of the dish to 5 cm/2 inches above the top. Secure the paper around the dish with string or paper clips.
2. Brush the inside of the greaseproof paper above the rim with melted butter.
3. Put the gooseberries in a pan with 25 g/1 oz of the sugar and 1 tablespoon water and cook for about 10 minutes. Rub the gooseberries through a sieve.
4. Put the egg yolks, remaining sugar and 3 tablespoons of water in a heatproof basin and whisk over a saucepan of hot water until thick and creamy.
5. Remove the saucepan from the heat and continue whisking until the mixture is cool.
6. Place a small basin containing 2 tablespoons of water over a pan of hot water, sprinkle the gelatine over and allow to dissolve. When cool, pour in a thin stream into the egg mixture and stir.
7. Place the bowl in the refrigerator until the mixture is just beginning to set.
8. Remove the bowl from the refrigerator and stir in the gooseberry purée, cream and green colouring, if used.
9. Whisk the egg whites and fold them into the gooseberry mixture using a large metal spoon. Pour into the soufflé dish and leave for 4 hours in the refrigerator to set.
10. To serve, carefully remove the greaseproof paper using a wet-bladed palette knife. Decorate the top with whirls of whipped cream and grated chocolate. Press chopped nuts around the sides, if desired.

VARIATIONS:

Lemon Soufflé
Use the grated rind and juice of 2 lemons. Decorate with lemon slices, nuts and cream.

Orange Soufflé
Use the grated rind and juice of 1½ medium oranges. Decorate with orange slices, nuts and cream.

Coffee Soufflé
Use 5 tablespoons strong black coffee. Decorate with caramelized coffee beans, nuts and cream.

Chocolate Soufflé
Stir 50 g/2 oz melted cooking chocolate into the egg mixture with the gelatine. Decorate with cream and nuts.

Raspberry, Strawberry or Apricot Soufflé
Use 150 ml/¼ pint fruit purée. Decorate with some retained fresh fruit, nuts and cream.

Fresh Raspberry Mousse

Serves 6
Preparation time: 30 minutes

750 g/1½ lb raspberries (fresh or frozen)
25 g/1 oz gelatine
4 tablespoons cold water
100 g/4 oz caster sugar
2 tablespoons lemon juice
3 egg whites
150 ml/¼ pint whipping cream, lightly whipped
To decorate:
25 g/1 oz flaked almonds, toasted
whole raspberries

1. Pass most of the raspberries through a sieve, but retain some for decoration.
2. Sprinkle the gelatine over the cold water in a saucepan and leave for a few minutes. Add the sugar and lemon juice and dissolve over a low heat. Remove from the heat and stir into the raspberry purée.
3. Transfer the mixture to a basin and place in the refrigerator until just beginning to set.
4. Whisk the egg whites until just holding their shape and fold the cream and egg whites into the setting purée, using a large metal spoon. Pour the mousse mixture into a serving bowl and chill until firm.
5. Decorate with toasted flaked almonds and raspberries.

Strawberry Crème Caramel

reparation time: 25 minutes
ooking time: 1 hour 15 minutes

)0 g/4 oz granulated sugar
50 ml/¼ pint water
)0 ml/1 pint milk
eggs, beaten
25 g/8 oz fresh strawberries, washed, hulled and halved
opping:
) g/2 oz demerara sugar

1. Put the sugar and the water in a heavy-based pan and heat gently until dissolved. Bring to the boil and boil rapidly until a golden caramel.
2. Warm the milk in a saucepan and pour in the caramel, using a wooden spoon to work the caramel over a low heat until it dissolves.
3. Mix the beaten eggs with the caramel milk and pour into a 1.2 litre/2 pint soufflé dish or shallow flan dish. Add the strawberries, cover the dish with foil and place it in a small roasting tin half filled with water.
4. Bake in a preheated oven at 160°C, 325°F, Gas Mark 3 for 1¼ hours until set. Allow to cool completely.
5. Sprinkle the surface with demerara sugar and place under a preheated hot grill until the sugar has caramelized. Serve immediately.

Fresh Fruit Salad

reparation time: 25 minutes

)0 ml/8 fl oz medium dry white wine
)0 ml/8 fl oz water
teaspoon rum flavouring (optional)
-2 tablespoons sugar
red eating apples, cored and sliced
peaches, sliced
oranges, peeled and sliced
pears, peeled and diced
)0 g/4 oz fresh red cherries, stalked and stoned, or black grapes
bananas, peeled and sliced
g/1 oz toasted flaked almonds, to decorate

1. Pour the wine into a saucepan and boil for 3 minutes to drive off the alcohol.
2. Add the water, rum flavouring (if using) and sugar, and stir to dissolve the sugar. Cool quickly then pour into a fruit bowl. Add the apples, peaches, oranges, pears, cherries and bananas.
3. Chill in the refrigerator for a few hours.
4. Just before serving, sprinkle the toasted flaked almonds over the top. Serve with pouring cream.

VARIATIONS:

Use any fruits in season.

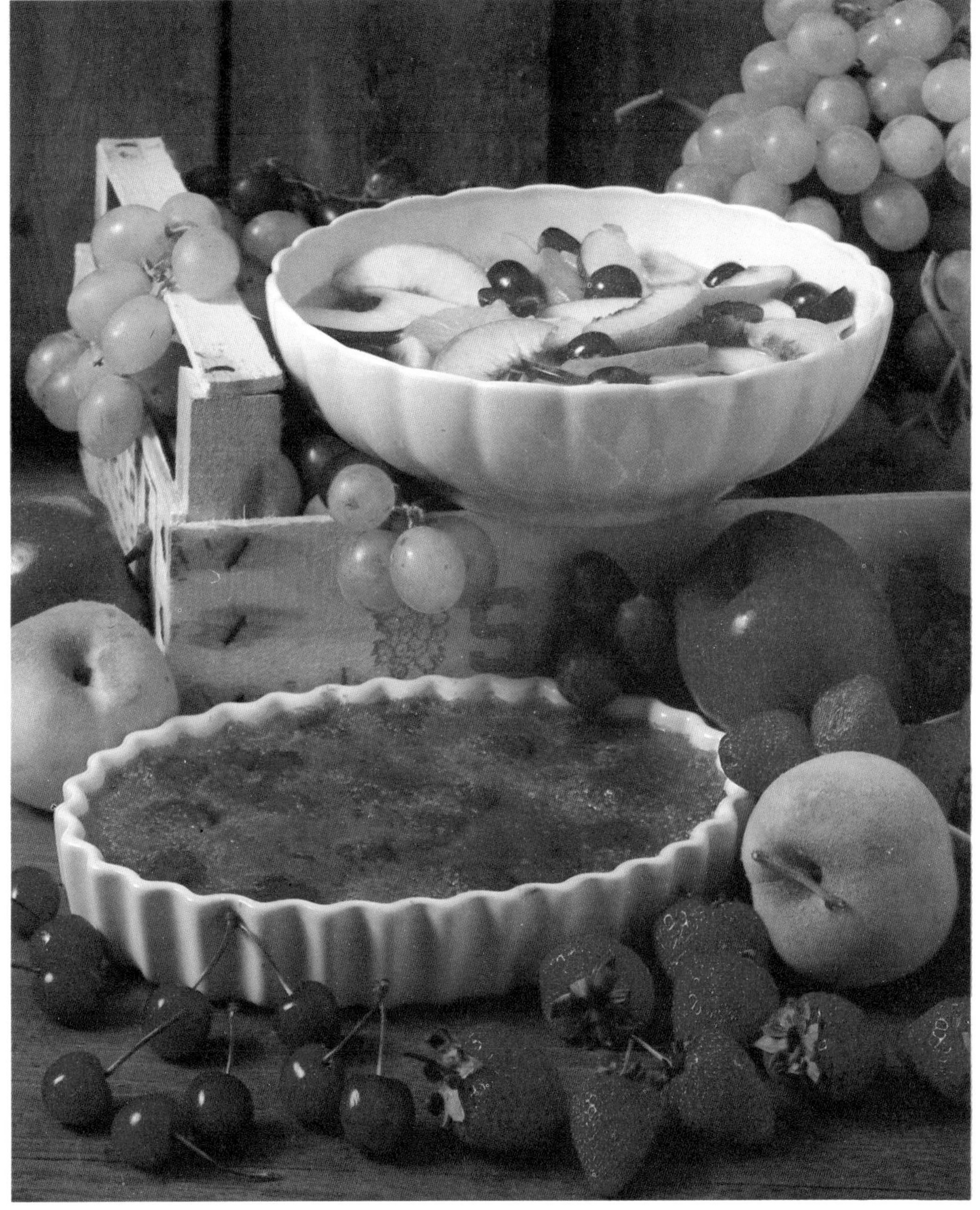

ck: Fresh fruit salad
ont: Strawberry crème caramel

Bramble Cream

Preparation time: 15 minutes

2 teaspoons powdered gelatine
2 tablespoons cold water
450 g/1 lb fresh blackberries and about 25 g/1 oz sugar or 2 × 425 g/15 oz cans blackberries, drained
300 ml/½ pint whipping cream, lightly whipped or
150 ml/¼ pint whipping cream, lightly whipped, mixed with 150 ml/¼ pint quantity chilled custard, made with 1 tablespoon custard powder, 25 g/1 oz sugar, 150 ml/¼ pint milk
25 g/1 oz chopped nuts, to decorate (optional)

A light fruit dessert, ideal for a summer party.

1. Sprinkle the gelatine over the water in a small heatproof bowl, then leave until spongy. Place the basin over a saucepan of hot water and dissolve the gelatine, stirring occasionally. Allow to cool.
2. Meanwhile, pass the blackberries through a sieve and sweeten to taste, if using fresh fruit. Stir the dissolved gelatine into the sweetened blackberry purée.
3. Stir in the lightly whipped cream, or custard and cream, and pour into a 900 ml/1½ pint wetted jelly mould or a serving dish. Chill until set.
4. Turn out the cream on to a serving dish if made in a jelly mould. Decorate with chopped nuts, if using.

VARIATIONS:

In place of blackberry use strawberry, raspberry and redcurrant or blackcurrant purée.

Continental Cheesecake

Serves 8
Preparation time: 25 minutes
Cooking time: 25 minutes

175 g/6 oz digestive biscuits, finely crushed
75 g/3 oz butter, melted
Filling:
500 g/1¼ lb curd cheese
75 g/3 oz caster sugar
4 eggs, beaten
grated rind of 2 lemons
50 g/2 oz sultanas
25 g/1 oz glacé cherries, chopped
1 tablespoon cornflour
2 tablespoons lemon juice
Topping:
150 ml/5 fl oz soured cream
2 teaspoons caster sugar
½ teaspoon vanilla essence
twists of lemon, to decorate

1. Grease a 23 cm/9 inch loose-bottomed cake tin or spring-release cake tin.
2. Place the biscuit crumbs in a bowl and stir in the melted butter. Spoon the mixture into the cake tin and press it firmly over the base of the tin. Chill in the refrigerator.
3. In a large bowl, beat the curd cheese and sugar together. Add the beaten eggs and continue to beat the mixture until smooth.
4. Stir in the lemon rind, sultanas and cherries. Blend the cornflour with the lemon juice and stir into the cheese mixture.
5. Spoon the mixture over the biscuit base and smooth the surface evenly.
6. Bake in the centre of a preheated oven at 180°C, 350°F, Gas Mark 4 for 20 minutes, until just set.
7. Meanwhile, blend the soured cream with the sugar and vanilla essence.
8. Remove the cheesecake from the oven and spread the soured cream mixture over the surface of the cake.
9. Bake for a further 5 minutes in the oven at the same temperature. Remove from the oven and, when cool, refrigerate for a few hours. Turn out on to a serving plate and decorate with lemon twists.

Vanilla Ice Cream

reparation time: 20 minutes

ɔ0 ml/½ pint milk
vanilla pod
eggs, beaten
5 g/3 oz caster sugar
ɔ0 ml/½ pint whipping cream, lightly whipped

1. Turn the refrigerator to its lowest setting.
2. Heat the milk and vanilla pod in a heavy-based saucepan, then leave to infuse for 20 minutes.
3. Add the eggs and sugar and stir over a low heat until lightly thickened.
4. Leave the custard to cool, then fold in the lightly whipped cream. Pour the mixture into a freezing tray and place in the freezer or ice-making compartment of the refrigerator overnight.

VARIATIONS:

Coffee Ice Cream: Add 4 teaspoons powdered coffee, dissolved in 2 teaspoons hot water.

Strawberry or Raspberry Ice Cream: Add 300 ml/½ pint fruit purée.

Chocolate Ice Cream: Add 75 g/3 oz melted chocolate.

Hazelnut Ice Cream: Add 100 g/4 oz chopped hazelnuts.

Orange Sorbet

reparation time: 25 minutes,
'us 5 minutes
'ooking time: 10 minutes

nely grated rind and juice of 3 oranges
nely grated rind and juice of 1 lemon
75 g/6 oz granulated sugar
)0 ml/1 pint water
egg white

1. Place the orange and lemon rind in a large saucepan with the sugar and water. Dissolve the sugar slowly, then bring to the boil and boil for 10 minutes.
2. Remove the saucepan from the heat and allow the syrup to cool completely.
3. Add the strained fruit juices and pour into a suitable container. Cover and place in the freezer or ice-making part of the refrigerator, until the mixture is thick and slushy.
4. Beat the egg white and fold it into the fruit mixture. Return the mixture to the freezer and freeze until stiff.
5. Remove the sorbet from the freezer 10 minutes before serving.

VARIATIONS:

Lemon Sorbet: Use the rind of 2 lemons and juice of 3.

Raspberry or Strawberry Sorbet: Add 450 ml/¾ pint fruit purée and the juice of ½ lemon to 600 ml/1 pint syrup.

Left: Vanilla ice cream
Right: Orange sorbet

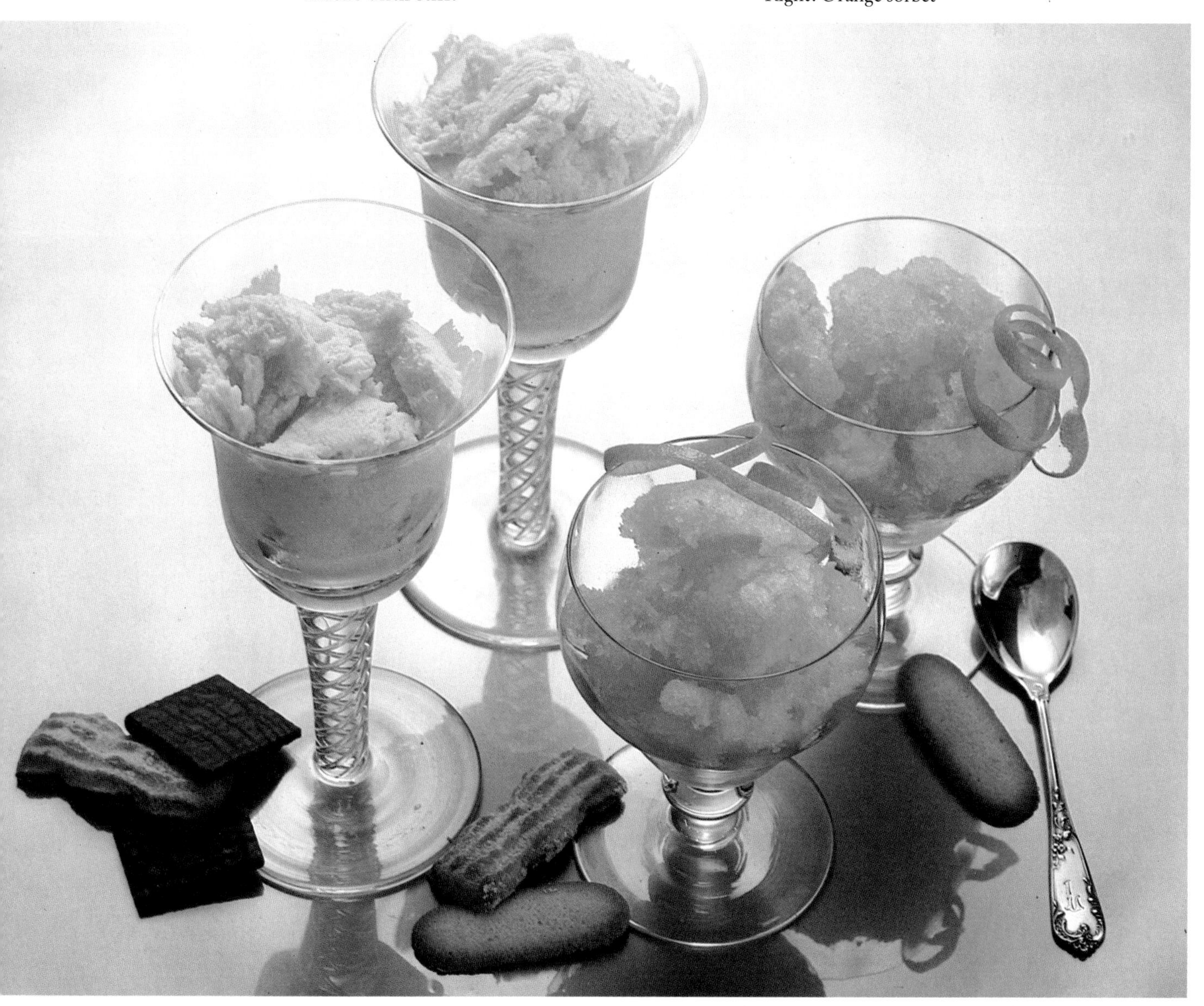

Hot Chocolate Soufflé

Preparation time: 20 minutes
Cooking time: 30–35 minutes

75 g/3 oz dark cooking chocolate
250 ml/8 fl oz milk
40 g/1½ oz butter
40 g/1½ oz plain flour
75 g/3 oz caster sugar
3 egg yolks
4 egg whites

1. Cut a piece of greaseproof paper, folded up 5 cm/2 inches at the bottom long enough to wrap around the outside of a 900 ml/1½ pint soufflé dish and to overlap slightly. The paper must be deep enough to reach from the bottom of the dish to about 7½ cm/3 inches above the top.
2. Grease the top half of the paper and the dish with butter. Secure the paper around the outside with paper clips or string.
3. Break the chocolate into pieces and place them in a bowl with 2 tablespoons of the milk. Place the bowl over a pan of hot water and melt the chocolate.
4. Meanwhile, melt the butter in a large saucepan, stir in the flour and cook for 2 minutes. Allow to cool slightly before adding the milk.
5. Bring slowly to the boil, stirring all the time. Cook for a further 2 minutes, then stir in the sugar and melted chocolate. Allow to cool then beat in the egg yolks.
6. Whisk the egg whites until they just hold their shape.
7. Fold a little of the egg white into the chocolate mixture using a metal spoon, then fold in the rest of the egg white.
8. Pour the mixture into the prepared soufflé dish and bake in the centre of a preheated oven 190°C, 375°F, Gas Mark 5 for 30–35 minutes until well-risen. Quickly remove the greaseproof paper and serve at once.

VARIATIONS:

Orange Soufflé
Put the thinly peeled rind of 2 oranges in the milk and heat to boiling. Cool and leave to infuse for 10 minutes. Separate the oranges into segments and place in a bowl with 3 tablespoons Cointreau or Grand Marnier. Strain the milk and use it to make up the sauce as above. Strain the orange segments and the juices into the sauce. Pour half the soufflé mixture into the prepared dish. Arrange the remaining orange segments on top, then pour over the remaining mixture. Bake as above.

Caramelized Pears with Brandy

Serves 6
Preparation time: 40 minutes
Cooking time: 32 minutes

2 tablespoons lemon juice
6 under-ripe pears, peeled
finely grated rind of 1 lemon
a blade of mace
1 teaspoon ground cinnamon
150 g/5 oz granulated sugar
1–2 tablespoons brandy or few drops of brandy flavouring
1 tablespoon arrowroot
2 tablespoons water
whipping cream, to serve

1. Sprinkle the lemon juice over the peeled pears, then stand them in a large saucepan.
2. Pour in sufficient water to make a depth of 2.5 cm/1 inch in the pan. Add the grated lemon rind, mace and ground cinnamon.
3. Cover and bring to the boil, then reduce the heat and simmer for 20 minutes.
4. Meanwhile, put the sugar in a heavy-based saucepan and allow to caramelize to a light golden colour over a low heat. Remove the saucepan from the heat and cool slightly.
5. Remove the pears carefully with a perforated spoon and reserve them. Pour the cooking liquid from the pears on to the caramel in the saucepan. Using a wooden spoon, loosen the caramel and dissolve it over a gentle heat.
6. Place the pears in the caramel liquid and add the brandy. Bring to the boil, then reduce the heat. Cover the pan and cook for a further 10 minutes.
7. Remove the pears with a perforated spoon and place them on a serving dish.
8. Blend the arrowroot with the water, then add to the caramel liquid. Bring to the boil, stirring all the time. Simmer for 2 minutes, then pour over the pears and serve at once with whipped cream.

Back: Banana and ginger pancakes
Front left: Caramelized pears with brandy
Front right: Barbados bananas

Banana and Ginger Pancakes

eparation time: 35 minutes
›oking time: 10–20 minutes

0 g/4 oz plain flour
›gg
0 ml/½ pint milk
or lard for frying
lling:
ınder-ripe bananas
non juice
g/2 oz caster sugar
:easpoons ground ginger
g/2 oz butter
serve:
emon, quartered
uring cream

These can be prepared in advance and then baked when needed.

1. To make the pancake batter, sift the flour into a bowl, make a well in the centre and drop in the egg. Beat with a wooden spoon and gradually add half the milk.
2. Bring in the flour from the sides, stirring until well blended and smooth. Stir in the remaining milk.
3. In a lightly-greased 20 cm/8 inch frying pan use the batter to make 8 thin pancakes.
4. Layer the pancakes flat on a plate with a piece of greaseproof paper between each one.
5. To make the filling, peel the bananas and cut them in half lengthwise and widthwise. Dredge the bananas in lemon juice. Mix together the ginger and the sugar. Heat 25 g/1 oz of the butter in a frying pan and lightly fry the bananas until just beginning to brown. Remove them from the pan with a perforated spoon and toss in the sugar and ginger.
6. Divide the bananas equally between the pancakes. Fold over the sides of each pancake and arrange in a buttered ovenproof dish.
7. Melt the remaining butter and pour it over the pancakes. Cover and bake in a preheated oven at 190°C, 375°F, Gas Mark 5 for 20 minutes until heated through.
8. Serve with lemon quarters and cream.

VARIATIONS:

Apple and Cinnamon Pancakes: Fill with 450 g/1 lb sliced cooking apples, fried in butter, then sugar and ground cinnamon added.

Apricot and Almond Pancakes: Fill with 425 g/15 oz can apricots, drained and chopped with 25 g/1 oz toasted, chopped almonds.

Orange Pancakes: Flavour batter with the grated rind of 1 orange and pour the juice over the pancakes to serve.

Peach and Cinnamon Pancakes: Add 1 teaspoon ground cinnamon to the batter and fill the pancakes with puréed peaches.

Barbados Bananas

eparation time: 10 minutes
›oking time: 20–30 minutes

:easpoon rum essence
0 ml/¼ pint fresh orange juice
ınder-ripe bananas
:ablespoon dark brown sugar
:nob of butter
nipped cream or ice cream, to serve

1. Stir the rum essence into the orange juice.
2. Peel the bananas and quarter them. Place them in a shallow ovenproof dish and pour over the orange juice. Sprinkle the brown sugar over the bananas. Top with a knob of butter.
3. Cover the dish with kitchen foil and bake in a preheated oven at 180°C, 350°F, Gas Mark 4 for 20–30 minutes until the bananas are soft.
4. Serve immediately with whipped cream or ice cream.

VARIATION:

Omit the rum essence and use half and half fresh orange juice and medium sherry. Stir in ½ teaspoon ground cloves into the sugar before sprinkling it over the bananas.

Queen of Puddings

Preparation time: 40 minutes
Cooking time: 50 minutes

75 g/3 oz fresh white breadcrumbs
450 ml/¾ pint milk
25 g/1 oz butter
finely grated rind of 1 lemon
2 egg yolks
25 g/1 oz caster sugar
3–4 tablespoons marmalade, jam or lemon curd
Topping:
3 egg whites
175 g/6 oz caster sugar

1. Lightly grease a 1.2 litre/2 pint ovenproof dish. Sprinkle the breadcrumbs over the base.
2. Place the milk in a saucepan with the butter and grated lemon rind and heat gently.
3. Whisk the egg yolks and sugar lightly and add the milk, stirring well. Strain this over the breadcrumbs and leave to stand for 15 minutes.
4. Bake in a preheated oven at 180°C, 350°F, Gas Mark 4 for 25–30 minutes until set.
5. Warm the marmalade and spread it over the pudding.
6. Whisk the egg whites stiffly and gradually beat in the caster sugar, a little at a time. Pile the meringue over the marmalade, sprinkle over a little extra caster sugar and bake for a further 20 minutes at the same temperature until the meringue is lightly browned.

VARIATIONS:

Use jam or lemon curd in place of marmalade.

Chocolate Surprise Pudding

Preparation time: 20 minutes
Cooking time: 1 hour

75 g/3 oz plain cooking chocolate
2 tablespoons milk
100 g/4 oz soft (tub) margarine
100 g/4 oz caster sugar
2 eggs, beaten
175 g/6 oz self-raising flour, sifted
1 tablespoon rum or rum essence
25 g/1 oz hazelnuts, chopped
Chocolate sauce:
2 tablespoons cocoa powder, sifted
50 g/2 oz granulated sugar
300 ml/½ pint water

1. Put the chocolate in a heatproof basin with the milk and place in a preheated oven at 180°C, 350°F, Gas Mark 4 to melt for 10 minutes, then allow to cool slightly.
2. Meanwhile cream the margarine with the sugar until light and fluffy. Gradually beat in the eggs. Stir in the cooled chocolate mixture and fold in the flour.
3. Stir in the rum or rum essence and the nuts. Spoon into a greased 1.2 litre/2 pint pie dish, spreading the mixture evenly. Bake in the oven for about 1 hour until risen and firm.
4. To make the sauce, put the cocoa, sugar and water into a saucepan and bring to the boil stirring. Continue to boil for about 10 minutes, until of a pouring consistency. Serve separately.

Damson and Pear Oaty Crumble

Preparation time: 20 minutes
Cooking time: 30–40 minutes

100 g/4 oz plain flour
½ teaspoon ground cinnamon
75 g/3 oz hard margarine
75 g/3 oz demerara sugar
40 g/1½ oz rolled oats
Filling:
450 g/1 lb fresh damsons, washed and trimmed or 425 g/15 oz can damsons, drained
1 medium pear, peeled, cored and sliced
finely grated rind of ½ orange
25–50g/1–2 oz granulated sugar

The rolled oat topping makes an interesting and delicious change to a plain crumble mixture.

1. For the topping, sift the flour and cinnamon together into a mixing bowl.
2. Cut the margarine into pieces and rub into the mixture until it resembles fine breadcrumbs. Stir in the demerara sugar and oats.
3. Put the damsons and pear into a 1.2 litre/2 pint pie dish. Stir in the grated orange rind and sugar. Spoon over the crumble topping and bake in the oven at 190°C, 375°F, or Gas Mark 5 for 30–35 minutes until the filling is soft when tested with a skewer.
4. Serve with a custard sauce.

VARIATIONS:

Use chopped walnuts, crushed cornflakes or crushed ginger biscuits in place of rolled oats for the topping.
Use fruits such as rhubarb and apple, plum, apricot and ginger.

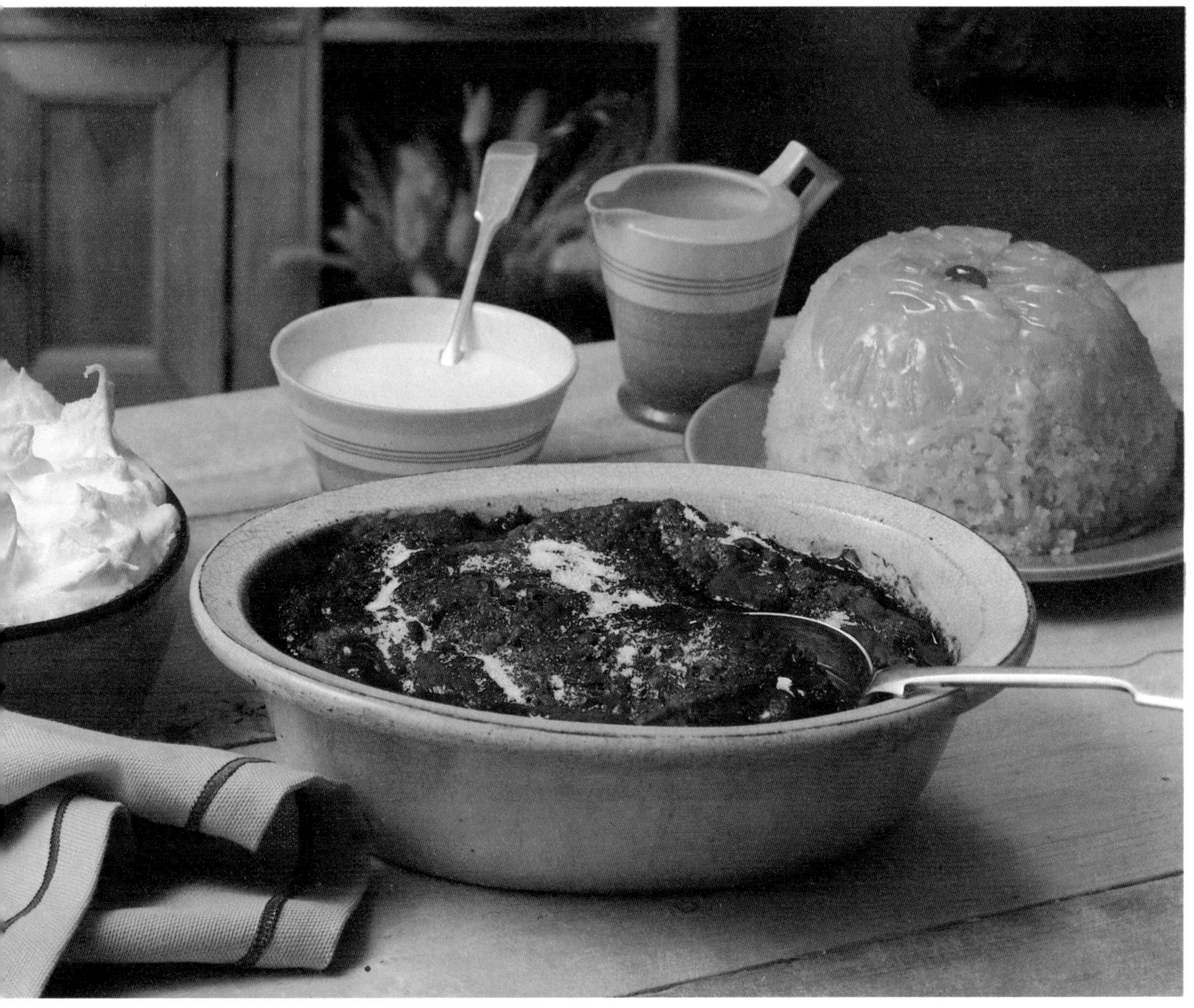

Pineapple Sponge Pudding and Sauce

eparation time: 20 minutes
ooking time: 1½ hours

ablespoon golden syrup
5 g/8 oz can pineapple slices, drained and juice retained
glacé cherry
0 g/4 oz margarine
0 g/4 oz caster sugar
ggs
5 g/6 oz self-raising flour
w drops of almond essence
uce:
easpoons arrowroot powder
g/1oz granulated sugar

ove left to right: Queen of dings; Chocolate surprise ding; Pineapple sponge ding and sauce

1. Lightly grease a 900 ml/1½ pint pudding basin and a piece of foil to use as a lid. Prepare a steamer.
2. Spoon the golden syrup into the base of the pudding basin and arrange 3 pineapple rings and the glacé cherry around the base.
3. Cream the margarine and sugar together until light and fluffy. Beat in the eggs, one at a time, then stir in the flour and almond essence with any remaining pineapple, cut into small pieces.
4. Spoon the creamed mixture into the pudding basin.
5. Cover the basin with the greased foil, making a pleat in the centre to allow the pudding to rise. Secure well then place in a steamer or a large saucepan with sufficient boiling water to reach half way up the basin. Cover and allow to cook for 1½ hours. Top up the steamer, or saucepan, with boiling water, if necessary.
6. To make the sauce, blend the arrowroot with a little water and add to the fruit juice made up to 300 ml/½ pint with water.
7. Stir in the sugar, then pour the mixture into a saucepan and bring to the boil stirring all the time.
8. To serve the pudding, allow it to stand in the basin for 5 minutes then turn it out on to a heated serving plate. Serve the sauce separately.

VARIATIONS:

Jam Pudding: Put 2 tablespoons jam at the bottom of the greased basin. Serve with a custard sauce.

Lemon or Orange Pudding: Add the finely grated rind of 1 orange or lemon when creaming the fat and sugar.
Serve with a lemon or orange sauce.

Chocolate Pudding: Dissolve 25 g/1 oz cocoa powder in 1 tablespoon warm water and add gradually to the creamed fat and sugar.

Fruit Pudding: Put a layer of any canned or stewed fruit in the bottom of the basin.

Grapefruit Meringue Pie

Preparation time: 35 minutes
Cooking time: 10 minutes

175 g/6 oz ginger biscuits, finely crushed
75 g/3 oz butter, melted
Filling:
40 g/1½ oz cornflour
150 ml/¼ pint water
5 tablespoons grapefruit juice
1–2 tablespoons caster sugar
finely grated rind of 1 grapefruit
2 egg yolks
Topping:
2 egg whites
75 g/3 oz caster sugar

This is a refreshing change from a lemon pie and the ginger biscuit base complements the grapefruit flavour.

1. Mix the crushed ginger biscuits into the melted butter and line a 20 cm/8 inch fluted flan dish with the mixture. Chill in the refrigerator for 10 minutes.
2. Meanwhile, blend the cornflour with a little of the water in a basin then stir in the rest of the water and grapefruit juice and pour into a saucepan. Stir in the sugar and grated rind and bring slowly to the boil, stirring all the time. Simmer for 2 minutes.
3. Allow the mixture to cool slightly before beating in the egg yolks. Spoon the filling into the chilled ginger nut base.
4. Beat the egg whites until they hold their shape. Beat in the caster sugar a little at a time until it is all incorporated. Top the grapefruit filling with meringue and bake in a preheated oven at 190°C, 375°F, Gas Mark 5 for 10 minutes. Serve immediately.

VARIATION:

Use the finely grated rind of 1 lemon and the juice of two, for filling. Make a shortcrust pastry base instead of a biscuit base.

Spicy Raisin Tart

Serves 6
Preparation time: 30 minutes
Cooking time: 40 minutes

150 g/5 oz seedless raisins
150 g/5 oz Pâte Brisée, made with 150 g/5 oz plain flour, pinch of salt, 100 g/4 oz chilled butter, 1 teaspoon sugar, water to bind (page 178)
25–50 g/1–2 oz caster sugar
1 tablespoon plain flour
1 teaspoon ground mace
1 teaspoon ground mixed spice
150 ml/5 fl oz soured cream
2 egg yolks, beaten
25 g/1 oz butter, melted
To decorate:
150 ml/¼ pint whipping cream, lightly whipped

1. Put the raisins in a bowl, cover them with warm water and leave for 20 minutes.
2. Line a 24 cm/9½ inch pie plate with a deep bottom or a fluted flan dish with the pâte brisée. Use the trimmings for decoration.
3. Drain the raisins and place them in a bowl. Stir in the sugar, flour, spices and soured cream, then beat in the egg yolks and butter.
4. Pour the mixture into the prepared pastry case and bake in the centre of a preheated oven at 200°C, 400°F, Gas Mark 6 for 10 minutes.
5. Reduce the oven temperature to 190°C, 375°F, Gas Mark 5 for a further 25–30 minutes until the filling is set.
6. Decorate with whipped cream and serve hot or cold.

VARIATIONS:

Flan pastry or basic shortcrust may be used instead of pâte brisée.

Apple and Apricot Pie

reparation time: 10 minutes,
'us 1 hour (for pastry) 15 minutes
o complete pie)
'ooking time: 35 minutes

50 g/6 oz Quick Flaky Pastry, made with 150 g/6 oz flour, pinch of salt, 100 g/4 oz hard margarine, 6 tablespoons cold water (page 179)
medium cooking apples, peeled, cored and sliced
25 g/15 oz can apricots, drained
5 g/1 oz granulated sugar
teaspoon ground mixed spice
eaten egg, to glaze

1. Chill the pastry in the refrigerator for 1 hour after making.
2. Put the sliced apples into a pie dish and mix in the apricots. Combine together the sugar and mixed spice in a bowl and sprinkle them over the fruit.
3. Roll out the pastry into an oblong shape 2.5 cm/1 inch larger than the dish. Cut a strip of pastry 5 mm/½ inch wide off the outer edge to extend around the rim of the pie dish. Wet the rim, then place the pastry strip in position.
4. Damp the pastry strip with water and top the pie with the remaining pastry, sealing edges well together.
5. Flute the edges with fingers or crimp with a fork. Glaze with beaten egg. Make a slit in the centre to allow the steam to escape.
6. Bake on a baking sheet in a preheated oven at 220°C, 425°F, Gas Mark 7 for 15 minutes. Reduce the heat to 180°C, 350°F, Gas Mark 4 for a further 20 minutes to cook the filling thoroughly. If necessary cover the pie with greaseproof paper to prevent it getting too browned.
7. Serve with pouring cream or ice cream.

VARIATION:

Replace the apple and apricot with canned cherries and use shortcrust pastry.

Blackberry and Apple Cobbler

reparation time: 25 minutes
'ooking time: 10–15 minutes

50 g/1½ lb cooking apples, peeled, cored and sliced
-2 tablespoons granulated sugar
tablespoons water
25 g/8 oz blackberries
opping:
25 g/8 oz self-raising flour
nch of salt
) g/2 oz hard margarine, cut into pieces
5 g/1 oz caster sugar
50 ml/¼ pint milk
ilk, to glaze

1. Place the apples in a saucepan with the sugar and water. Poach until softened, then add the blackberries and cook for a further 3 minutes.
2. Pour the cooked fruit into a 1.2 litre/2 pint pie dish.
3. Sift the flour and salt together into a mixing bowl and rub in the fat, until the mixture resembles fine breadcrumbs. Stir in the sugar and enough milk to bind the mixture together.
4. Turn the dough on to a lightly floured board and roll out to a thickness of 1 cm/½ inch. Cut out rounds with a 4 cm/1½ inch fluted cutter.
5. Arrange the scone rounds overlapping round the edge of the dish and glaze with a little milk.
6. Bake near the top of a preheated oven at 220°C, 425°F, Gas Mark 7 for 10–15 minutes until the topping is golden brown.
7. Serve with a lemon flavoured custard.

VARIATIONS:

Use cooked fruits such as plums, gooseberries, apples and raspberries or apricots.

Breads, Cakes and Biscuits

BREAD

White Bread and Rolls

Preparation time: 40 minutes, plus rising time, *see page 183*
Cooking time: 15–20 minutes for rolls, 30 minutes for a loaf

15 g/½ oz fresh yeast or 2 teaspoons dried yeast
450 ml/¾ pint tepid water
725 g/1 lb 10 oz strong flour
1 teaspoon salt
15 g/½ oz lard
To glaze:
1 egg, beaten with a pinch of salt
poppy seeds

1. Grease a 1 kg/2 lb loaf tin, or two 450 g/1 lb loaf tins, and a baking sheet.
2. Blend the fresh yeast with a little of the tepid water. (Reconstitute the dried yeast by putting a little of the measured tepid water and a pinch of sugar in a small bowl. Sprinkle the yeast granules over, stir, then leave in a warm place for 15 minutes, until a frothy head appears. Whisk the yeast mixture well.)
3. Sift the flour and salt into a large, warm, mixing bowl and rub in the lard.
4. Stir in the yeast liquid and water to give a soft dough.
5. Turn out on to a floured board and knead the dough for 10 minutes until it is smooth and elastic. Place the dough in an oiled plastic bag or in a greased bowl covered with a damp cloth and leave it to rise in a warm place until doubled in size, 1–1½ hours.
6. Knead the dough on a floured surface for 2 more minutes, then shape three quarters of the dough into an oblong and place it in a 1 kg/2 lb loaf tin or divide the dough into two oblongs and fit into the two 450 g/1 lb loaf tins.
7. Shape the remaining dough into even-sized round rolls. Place them on a greased baking sheet.
8. Cover the bread and the rolls with an oiled plastic bag and leave in a warm place to rise again until doubled in size, about 45 minutes. Brush the surfaces with the beaten egg glaze and sprinkle poppy seeds over the rolls. Bake in a preheated oven at 230°C, 450°F, Gas Mark 8 for 15–20 minutes.
9. Remove the rolls and cool them on a wire rack. Reduce the oven temperature to 180°C, 350°F, Gas Mark 4 for a further 10–15 minutes until the loaf is golden brown and sounds hollow when tapped with knuckles on the bottom. Cool on a wire rack.

Fruit Bread

eparation time: 40 minutes,
us rising time, see page 183
ooking time: 45 minutes

g/½ oz fresh yeast or 2 teaspoons dried yeast
0 ml/8 fl oz tepid water
0 g/1 lb strong flour
teaspoon salt
teaspoon mixed spice
teaspoon ground cinnamon
g/1 oz caster sugar
0 g/12 oz mixed dried fruit
ated rind of 1 lemon
egg, beaten
tablespoons lemon juice
o glaze:
teaspoons sugar
tablespoons water

1. Grease a 1 kg/2 lb loaf tin or two 450 g/1 lb tins.
2. Blend the yeast with the water, as described in step 3 for Malt Bread (below).
3. Sift together the flour, salt, and spices in a large warm mixing bowl. Stir in the sugar, dried fruit and lemon rind.
4. Pour the yeast mixture, beaten egg, and lemon juice into the dry ingredients and mix well with a wooden spoon.
5. Knead the dough on a lightly floured board for 10 minutes until firm and elastic. Place the dough in a greased polythene bag or a greased bowl covered with a damp cloth and leave to rise in a warm place until doubled in size, about 1½ hours at room temperature or 40 minutes in a warm kitchen.
6. Turn the dough on to a floured board and knead for 2 minutes, then shape to fit into the loaf tin(s). Leave the dough to rise, covered with oiled cling film, until doubled in size.
7. Dissolve the sugar in the water and brush the surface of the loaf, then bake in the centre of a preheated oven at 200°C, 400°F, Gas Mark 6 for 45 minutes for the large loaf, or 30–35 minutes for the smaller loaves.
8. Remove from the tins and cool on a wire rack.

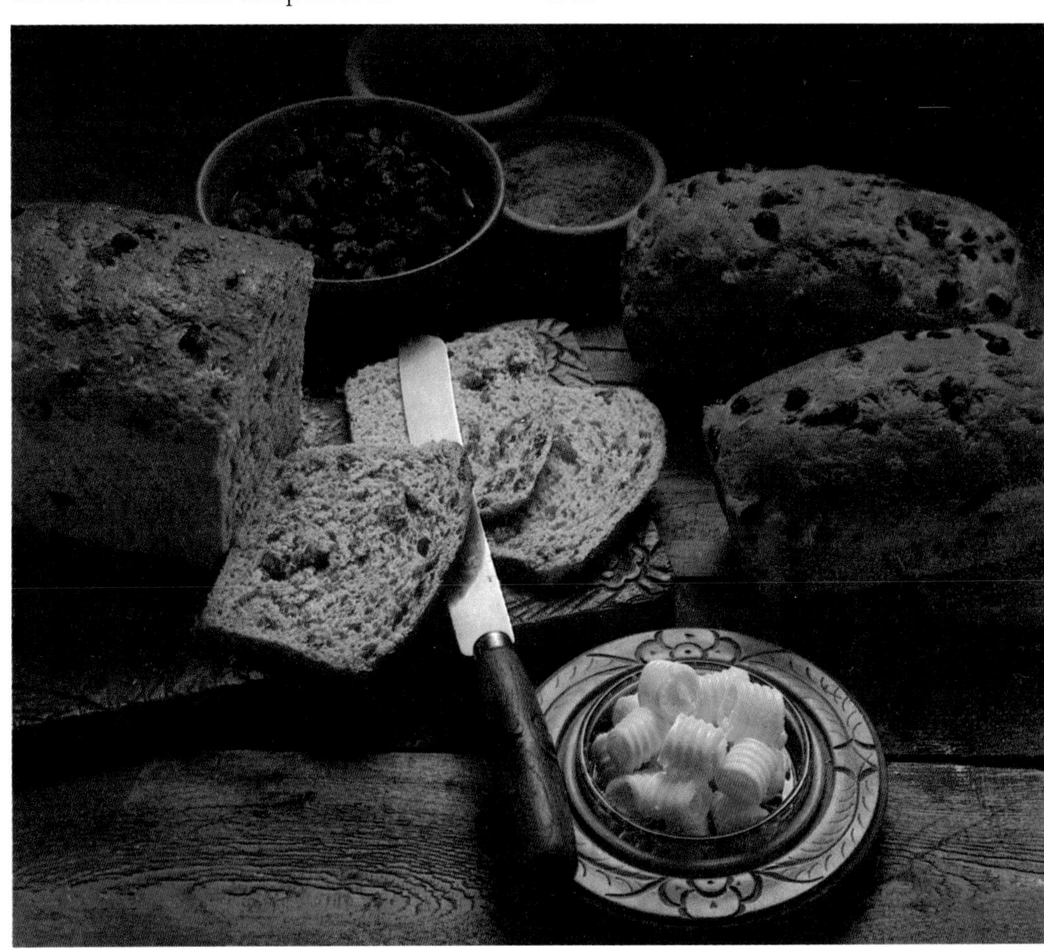

Left: Malt bread
Right: Fruit bread

Malt Bread

eparation time: 30 minutes,
us rising time, see page 183
ooking time: 30–40 minutes

5 g/8 oz plain flour
5 g/8 oz wholewheat strong flour
teaspoon salt
g/1 oz hard margarine
5 g/6 oz sultanas
g/1 oz fresh yeast or 15 g/½ oz dried yeast
0 ml/8 fl oz tepid water
tablespoons malt extract
o glaze:
teaspoons sugar
tablespoons water

1. Grease a 1 kg/2 lb loaf tin or two 450 g/1 lb loaf tins.
2. Sift the flours together in a large warm mixing bowl with the salt. Rub in the fat, then stir in the sultanas.
3. Blend the fresh yeast with a little of the water, then stir in the remaining water. Reconstitute the dried yeast by putting a little of the measured water and a pinch of sugar in a small bowl. Sprinkle in the yeast granules. Stir, then leave in a warm place for 15 minutes until a frothy head appears. Stir in the remaining water. Add the yeast mixture to the dry ingredients with the malt extract, mixing with a wooden spoon.
4. Knead the dough on a lightly floured board for 5–10 minutes, until smooth and elastic.
5. Place the dough in an oiled plastic bag or a greased bowl covered with a damp cloth and leave in a warm place until the dough has doubled in size, about 1 hour.
6. Knead the dough again for 2 minutes. Shape the dough into 1 large or 2 small loaves and fit into the tins. Cover the tins with greased cling film and leave the dough to rise in a warm place until doubled in size.
7. Dissolve the sugar in the water and use to glaze the surface of the loaf. Bake in a preheated oven at 200°C, 400°F, Gas Mark 6 for 40 minutes for a large loaf, or 30 minutes for the smaller loaves.
8. Turn out of the tins and cool on a wire rack. To serve, slice and spread with butter.

Poppy Seed Plait

Preparation time: 50 minutes, plus rising time, *see page 183*
Cooking time: 30–35 minutes

375 g/13 oz strong flour
1 teaspoon caster sugar
15 g/½ oz fresh yeast or 1½ teaspoons dried yeast
200 ml/⅓ pint tepid milk
1 teaspoon salt
75 g/3 oz butter, cut into pieces
1 egg (size 6/small) beaten
To finish:
1 egg, beaten with a pinch of salt
poppy seeds

1. Lightly flour a baking sheet.
2. Sift 100 g/4 oz of the flour into a mixing bowl with the sugar. Make a well in the centre and crumble in the fresh yeast. (Reconstitute the dried yeast by putting a little of the measured tepid milk and a pinch of sugar in a small bowl. Sprinkle the yeast granules over, stir, then leave in a warm place for 15 minutes, until a frothy head appears.)
3. Gradually add the warmed milk and mix the ingredients together, using a wooden spoon.
4. Cover the bowl with cling film and leave in a warm place for 30 minutes, until the batter is frothy.
5. Sift together the rest of the flour and salt and rub in the butter.
6. Stir the beaten egg into the frothing yeast mixture together with the dry ingredients. Mix well and knead the dough for about 10 minutes until smooth and elastic.
7. Place the dough in an oiled plastic bag or a greased bowl covered with a damp cloth and leave to rise in a warm place until doubled in size, about 1 hour.
8. Knead the dough for 4–5 minutes, then divide the dough into three equal portions.
9. Roll each piece into a long thin roll and place side by side. Gather the three ends together and form a plait tucking in the ends neatly.
10. Place the plait on a floured baking sheet, cover with an oiled plastic bag and leave to rise in a warm place, until it has doubled in size.
11. Brush the plait with the beaten egg and sprinkle with poppy seeds. Place the plait in the centre of a preheated oven at 220°C, 425°F, Gas Mark 7 for 30 minutes until browned and risen. Cool on a wire rack.

Apricot Brioche

Preparation time: 45 minutes, plus rising time, *see page 183*
Cooking time: 15–20 minutes

225 g/8 oz strong flour
pinch of salt
15 g/½ oz caster sugar
15 g/½ oz fresh yeast or 2 teaspoons dried yeast
1½ tablespoons tepid water
2 eggs, beaten
50 g/2 oz butter, melted
1 egg, beaten, to glaze
Filling:
1 × 425 g/15 oz can apricot halves, drained and juice retained
3 tablespoons Kirsch
300 ml/½ pint whipping or double cream, lightly whipped

1. Grease a 1.2 litre/2 pint brioche mould.
2. Sift together the flour, salt and sugar into a warm mixing bowl. Blend the yeast with a little of the water. (Reconstitute the dried yeast by putting a little of the measured tepid water and a pinch of sugar in a small bowl. Sprinkle the yeast granules over, stir, then leave in a warm place for 15 minutes, until a frothy head appears.)
3. Pour the dissolved yeast mixture and the remaining water into the dry ingredients, with the eggs and melted butter. Work into a soft dough and knead well for 5 minutes.
4. Place the dough in an oiled plastic bag or a greased bowl covered with a damp cloth and leave to rise in a warm place, until the dough has doubled in size, about 1 hour.
5. Knead the dough for 2–3 minutes and shape three quarters of it into a ball. Place it in the base of the mould.
6. Make a hollow in the centre and place the remaining piece of dough in the middle. Cover the dough with oiled cling film and leave to rise until warm and puffy.
7. Brush the brioche with beaten egg and bak in a preheated oven at 230°C, 450°F, Gas Mark 8 for 15–20 minutes until golden browr Turn out and cool on a wire rack.
8. Cut the top off to use as a lid, and scoop out some of the crumbs.
9. Mix 3 tablespoons of the apricot juice with the Kirsch. Spoon this over the inside of the brioche and leave to soak.
10. Fold all but 6 apricots into most of the whipped cream and spoon into the brioche. Decorate with the rest of the cream, top with the 6 reserved apricots and replace the lid.

Hot Cross Buns

lakes 12
reparation time: 40 minutes,
'us rising time, page 183
'ooking time: 20–25 minutes

50 g/1 lb strong flour
5 g/1 oz fresh yeast or 1 tablespoon dried yeast
teaspoon caster sugar
00 ml/½ pint milk
2 teaspoon ground cinnamon
2 teaspoon mixed spice
teaspoon salt
0 g/2 oz caster sugar
00 g/4 oz currants
5 g/1 oz mixed peel
0 g/2 oz butter, melted
egg, beaten
'o finish:
0 g/2 oz Shortcrust Pastry (page 177)
5 g/1 oz caster sugar
tablespoons water

1. Grease a baking sheet.
2. Sift 100 g/4 oz of the flour into a large mixing bowl and add the yeast and 1 teaspoon sugar.
3. Warm the milk to bloodheat, add the milk to the flour and mix well. Leave in a warm place for 20 minutes if using fresh yeast and 30 minutes for dried yeast, until it becomes frothy.
4. Sift the remaining flour, spices and salt together into a bowl and stir in the sugar.
5. Pour the butter and egg into the batter and stir well, then add the spiced flour and mixed fruit and combine well together.
6. Turn the soft dough on to a floured board and knead until smooth. Place the dough in a lightly greased plastic bag or a greased bowl covered with a damp cloth and leave to rise at room temperature until it has doubled in size.
7. Turn the risen dough on to the board and knead for a further 2 minutes.
8. Shape the dough into a long roll and cut into 12 pieces. Shape the dough into buns, using the palm of the hand.
9. Put the buns on the baking sheet and cover with oiled cling film. Leave the buns to rise in a warm place until doubled in size.
10. Roll out the pastry into a long strip and cut into 5 mm/¼ inch strips.
11. Top each bun with the pastry strips in the shape of a cross, securing them with water. Alternatively, make slashes with a sharp knife to make a cross.
12. Bake just above the centre of the oven at 190°C, 375°F, Gas Mark 5 for 20–25 minutes.
13. Dissolve the sugar in the water and use to glaze the buns when they are removed from the oven and are still hot. Allow them to cool on a wire rack.

Above left: Poppy seed plait
Above centre: Apricot brioche
Above right: Hot cross buns

Rich Fruit Cake

Preparation time: 35 minutes
Cooking time: 3½–4 hours

225 g/8 oz plain flour
1 teaspoon ground mace
1 teaspoon ground mixed spice
225 g/8 oz butter
200 g/7 oz dark brown sugar
1 tablespoon black treacle
4 eggs
225 g/8 oz raisins
225 g/8 oz currants
225 g/8 oz sultanas
100 g/4 oz glacé cherries, quartered
100 g/4 oz mixed peel
finely grated rind of 1 lemon
25 g/1 oz angelica, chopped
During storage:
3–4 tablespoons brandy

To royal ice the cake, it is necessary to almond paste it first; 750 g/1¾ lb almond paste is sufficient for this size cake, and 1 kg/2 lb of royal icing will be needed.

1. Grease and line a 20 cm/8 inch round, or 18 cm/7 inch square, cake tin with greaseproof paper.
2. Place all the prepared fruit in a large bowl.
3. Sift the flour and spices together on to a sheet of greaseproof paper.
4. Cream the butter, sugar and treacle together until light and fluffy, using a wooden spoon.
5. Beat in the eggs one at a time, then stir in the flour and spices using a metal spoon. Stir in the fruit.
6. Turn the mixture into the prepared cake tin. Wrap a band of brown paper or newspaper around the outside of the tin.
7. Bake just below the centre of a preheated oven at 150°C, 300°F, Gas Mark 2 for the first 2 hours. Reduce the oven temperature to 140°C, 275°F, Gas Mark 1 for a further 1½–2 hours.
8 Test to see if the cake is cooked through by inserting a skewer or fine knitting needle into the centre of the cake. If the skewer comes out clean, the cake is cooked. Otherwise cook the cake for a further 20–30 minutes.
9. Allow the cake to cool for 15 minutes in the tin. Turn out on to a wire rack to cool.
10. When completely cold, wrap the cake in aluminium foil. The cake will store for up to 3 months wrapped in this way, in a cool, dry place.
11. During storage, prick the surface of the cake with a fine skewer and pour the brandy over the cake.

Country Fruit Cake

eparation time: 15 minutes
ooking time: 1–1¼ hours

0 g/9 oz self-raising flour
teaspoon mixed spice
teaspoon bicarbonate of soda
g/3 oz hard margarine, cut into pieces
0 g/4 oz caster sugar
0 g/4 oz raisins
0 g/4 oz sultanas
g/1 oz mixed peel
egg, beaten
0 ml/¼ pint milk
sugar cubes

1. Grease and line a 15 cm/6 inch round cake tin, or a 22 × 11 × 6 cm/8½ × 4½× 2½ inch loaf tin.
2. Sift the flour, spices and bicarbonate of soda together into a large bowl.
3. Rub in the margarine.
4. Stir in the sugar, fruit and mixed peel. Pour in the beaten egg and mix well. Stir in the milk to give the mixture a soft consistency.
5. Spoon the mixture into the prepared cake tin. Roughly crush the sugar cubes with the end of a rolling pin and scatter them over the cake.
6. Bake in the centre of a preheated oven at 180°C, 350°F, Gas Mark 4 for about 1–1¼ hours until golden brown.
7. Cool slightly before turning out on to a wire rack.

Honey and Nut Cake

eparation time: 20 minutes
ooking time: 45 minutes

75 g/6 oz soft (tub) margarine or butter
75 g/6 oz caster sugar
eggs
½ tablespoons clear honey
00 g/4 oz ground almonds
50 g/5 oz plain flour
o decorate:
–2 tablespoons clear honey
5 g/1 oz flaked almonds, toasted

1. Grease a 20 cm/8 inch sandwich tin and cut a piece of greaseproof paper long enough to extend around the inside of the tin, and 2.5 cm/1 inch above the rim of the tin.
2. Cream the margarine or butter and sugar together until light and fluffy, using a wooden spoon.
3. Beat in the eggs one at a time, then beat in the honey. Lightly fold in the ground almonds and flour.
4. Spoon the mixture into the prepared tin, and bake in the centre of a preheated oven at 180°C, 350°F, Gas Mark 4 for about 45 minutes. Leave for 5 minutes before turning out carefully on to a wire rack.
5. Allow to cool completely, then brush the surface with honey and sprinkle the toasted almonds over the top.

Sticky Orange and Almond Gingerbread

reparation time: 30 minutes
ooking time: 1 hour

75 g/10 oz plain flour
teaspoon bicarbonate of soda
teaspoons ground ginger
teaspoon mixed spice
75 g/6 oz margarine
00 g/14 oz golden syrup
0 g/2 oz caster sugar
eggs
20 ml/4 fl oz milk
tablespoons fresh orange juice
0 g/2 oz nibbed almonds
nely grated rind of 1 orange
o glaze:
–3 tablespoons golden syrup
rips of orange peel, finely cut

1. Well grease and flour a 23 cm/9 inch round cake tin.
2. Sift together the flour, soda, ginger and mixed spice into a large bowl.
3. Warm the margarine, syrup and sugar in a saucepan over a low heat.
4. Beat together the eggs and milk.
5. Make a well in the centre of the dry ingredients and add the milk mixture and orange juice. Gradually incorporate the flour from the sides to the centre.
6. Pour in the syrup mixture a little at a time, beating well. Stir in the almonds and orange rind.
7. Pour the mixture into the prepared tin, and bake in the centre of a preheated oven at 180°C, 350°F, Gas Mark 4 for about 1 hour. Leave to cool for a few minutes in the tin, then turn out on to a wire rack.
8. Heat the syrup in a saucepan and brush it over the surface of the cake. Sprinkle with the strips of orange peel.

Date and Walnut Squares

Preparation time: 20 minutes
Cooking time: 40 minutes

100 g/4 oz Shortcrust Pastry, made with 100 g/4 oz plain flour, pinch of salt, 50 g/2 oz fat, 1–2 tablespoons cold water (page 177)
225 g/8 oz caster sugar
100 g/4 oz ground almonds
150 g/5 oz dates, chopped
50 g/2 oz walnuts, chopped
2 eggs, beaten
To decorate:
50 g/2 oz icing sugar, sifted
1 tablespoon warm water

1. Grease a shallow 18 cm /7 inch square tin.
2. Roll out the pastry thinly on a lightly floured surface and use to line the base and sides of the tin. Trim off the edges with a sharp knife.
3. Combine the sugar, ground almonds, dates and walnuts together in a mixing bowl. Add the beaten eggs and mix well.
4. Spread the mixture into the lined tin and bake in a preheated oven at 200°C, 400°F, Gas Mark 6 for 20 minutes, then reduce the temperature to 190°C, 375°F, Gas Mark 5 for a further 20 minutes. Cool in the tin before turning out on to a wire rack to ice.
5. Blend the icing sugar with the water, spread the glacé icing over the top, and cut into squares when the icing has set.

Victoria Sandwich

Preparation time: 15 minutes
Cooking time: 20–25 minutes

100 g/4 oz hard margarine or butter
100 g/4 oz caster sugar
2 eggs
100 g/4 oz self-raising flour, sifted
Filling:
2–3 tablespoons raspberry or apricot jam
sifted icing sugar

1. Grease and flour two 15 cm/6 inch sandwich tins.
2. Cream the margarine and caster sugar together in a mixing bowl until light and fluffy, using a wooden spoon.
3. Beat in the eggs one at a time and then stir in the flour, using a metal spoon.
4. Divide the mixture between 2 sandwich tins and bake in a preheated oven at 190°C, 375°F, Gas Mark 5 for 20–25 minutes.
5. Allow the cakes to cool slightly then turn them out on to a wire rack.
6. Spread the jam evenly over one cake and place the remaining cake on top. Sprinkle the top with sifted icing sugar.

VARIATIONS:

Chocolate Sandwich: Substitute 25 g/1 oz sifted cocoa powder for the flour.

Coffee Sandwich: Add 1 tablespoon coffee essence to the creamed mixture.

Slab Cake: Double the ingredients and turn into a shallow rectangular 23 × 34 cm/ 9 × 13½ inch tin. Bake for 30–35 minutes.

Above: Date and walnut squares
Below left: Crunch-topped spice cake
Below centre: Victoria sandwich
Below right: Oven-baked scones

Crunch-topped Spice Cake

reparation time: 20 minutes
ooking time: 1 hour–1 hour 40 inutes

25 g/8 oz self-raising flour
teaspoon ground cinnamon
teaspoon mixed spice
2 teaspoon ground coriander
75 g/6 oz butter or hard margarine
75 g/6 oz caster sugar
eggs
00 g/4 oz glacé cherries, quartered
0 g/2 oz mixed peel
0 g/2 oz cornflakes, crushed
tablespoons golden syrup, slightly warmed

1. Grease and flour a 23 cm/9 inch spring-release cake tin fitted with a tubular base, or a 20 cm/8 inch round cake tin. Line the sides with a greased piece of greaseproof paper.
2. Sift the flour and spices together into a mixing bowl.
3. Cream the fat and sugar together in a mixing bowl until light and fluffy using a wooden spoon.
4. Beat in the eggs one at a time, then stir in the sifted flour and spices until completely mixed. Stir in the cherries and the mixed peel.
5. Spoon the mixture into the prepared tin and spread evenly. Stir the cornflakes into the syrup and carefully spread the mixture over the cake.
6. Bake in a preheated oven at 180°C, 350°F, Gas Mark 4 for 30 minutes, then reduce the oven temperature to 160°C, 325°F, Gas Mark 3 for a further 30 minutes for the spring-release tin, or 40 minutes for the round cake tin, until well-risen and firm to the touch.
7. Allow the cake to cool in the tin for a few minutes, then remove the sides of the tin and invert the cake on to a rack, to remove the base. Turn the cake over and cool it completely.

Oven-baked Scones

reparation time: 10 minutes
ooking time: 7–10 minutes

25 g/8 oz self-raising flour
0 g/2 oz butter or hard margarine, cut into pieces
5 g/1 oz caster sugar
egg
ilk
o glaze:
eaten egg
anulated sugar

1. Grease a baking sheet.
2. Sift the flour into a large bowl. Rub the fat into the flour and stir in the sugar.
3. Beat the egg in a measuring jug and add enough milk to make the liquid up to 150 ml/¼ pint.
4. Bind the flour mixture together with the egg and milk to form a soft dough.
5. Lightly flour the work surface and toss the scone dough lightly in the flour. Roll out lightly to 1 cm/½ inch thickness.
6. Using a 5 cm/2 inch fluted cutter, cut out 8 scones. Glaze the scones with beaten egg and sprinkle sugar over the top.
7. Bake near the top of a preheated oven at 220°C, 425°F, Gas Mark 7 for 7–10 minutes.

VARIATIONS:

Fruit Scones: Stir in 25 g/1 oz sultanas to the dry ingredients.

Cheese Scones: Stir in 75 g/3 oz grated Cheddar cheese and 1 teaspoon of dry English mustard powder to the dry ingredients, and omit all the sugar.

Chocolate Battenberg

Preparation time: 45 minutes
Cooking time: 30–35 minutes

175 g/6 oz hard margarine
175 g/6 oz caster sugar
3 eggs
175 g/6 oz self-raising flour
25 g/1 oz cocoa, sifted
10 tablespoons apricot jam
2 × 225 g/8 oz packets almond paste

Below left: Chocolate battenberg
Below right: Chocolate and orange gâteau

1. Grease a 20 cm/8 inch square cake tin and divide the tin in half by lining the base with foil and making a pleat in the centre. Place a piece of cardboard inside the pleat for better support.
2. Cream the fat and sugar together in a mixing bowl until light and fluffy, using a wooden spoon.
3. Beat in the eggs one at a time, then stir in the flour using a metal spoon.
4. Divide the mixture in half and add the sifted cocoa to one half, mixing well, and keep the other half plain.
5. Spoon the chocolate flavoured mixture into one side of the tin, and the plain mixture into the other half.
6. Bake in a preheated oven at 180°C, 350°F, Gas Mark 4 for about 30–35 minutes. Turn out on to a cooling rack.
7. Trim each piece of cake and cut in half lengthwise. Sandwich two alternate layers together with half the jam. Measure the cake lengthwise and the two ends.
8. Add the total of all the sides and cut out a piece of non-stick paper to the measurements.
9. Roll out the almond paste on top of the paper to just fit.
10. Spread the rest of the jam over the almond paste and wrap closely round the battenberg. Flute the top edges with fingers and make diagonal lines over the top surface with a knife.

Chocolate and Orange Gâteau

Preparation time: 45 minutes
Cooking time: 40 minutes

4 eggs
175 g/6 oz caster sugar
100 g/4 oz plain flour
20 g/¾ oz cocoa powder
Filling:
150 ml/¼ pint milk
100 g/4 oz caster sugar
3 egg yolks
225 g/8 oz butter
finely grated rind of 2 oranges
2 tablespoons orange juice
1 tablespoon orange curaçao
3 tablespoons apricot jam
To decorate:
50 g/2 oz mixed chopped nuts
50 g/2 oz cooking chocolate, grated

1. Grease and line the base of a 20 cm/8 inch round cake tin.
2. Place the eggs and sugar together in a large bowl and whisk over a saucepan of hot water until thick and creamy.
3. Sift the flour and cocoa over the egg mixture and fold in using a large metal spoon.
4. Turn the mixture into the prepared cake tin and bake in a preheated oven at 190°C, 375°F, Gas Mark 5 for about 40 minutes. Turn out on to a wire rack.
5. Meanwhile make the filling. Warm the milk, then remove from the heat. Cream the sugar and egg yolks together until thick and creamy. Add the warmed milk and place over a pan of hot water, stirring until thick enough to coat the back of a spoon, but do not boil. Cool.
6. Cream the butter until light and fluffy and gradually beat in the cooled egg mixture. Beat in the orange rind and juice and orange liqueur until well incorporated.
7. Split the cake in half and sandwich together with the apricot jam. Spread some of the filling over the sides of the cake, and decorate with chopped nuts.
8. Spread the remaining filling over the top of the cake and sprinkle grated chocolate over the surface.

Walnut Refrigerator Biscuits

akes 24
reparation time: 10 minutes
ooking time: 10–12 minutes

- 0 g/3½ oz hard margarine or butter
- 0 g/1½ oz caster sugar
- 0 g/2 oz walnuts, finely chopped
- 5 g/5½ oz plain flour, sifted
- teaspoon coffee essence
- few glacé cherries, quartered

1. Grease a baking sheet.
2. Cream the margarine or butter and sugar together in a mixing bowl until light and fluffy, using a wooden spoon.
3. Stir in chopped walnuts and then the flour until thoroughly mixed. Add the coffee essence and work well into the mixture, until evenly blended.
4. Place the mixture on non stick paper or on a piece of oiled foil, and shape the mixture into a long thin rectangle.
5. Wrap the paper (or foil) around, and place in the refrigerator until firm enough to slice, or until required. The mixture can be stored in the refrigerator for up to 2 weeks.
6. Using a sharp knife, cut the dough into 5 mm/¾ inch slices and place the slices on the greased baking sheet. Top each with a quartered glacé cherry.
7. Bake in a preheated oven at 190°C, 375°F, Gas Mark 5 for 12 minutes. Cool on a wire rack.

Below left: Walnut refrigerator biscuits
Below right: Coffee creams

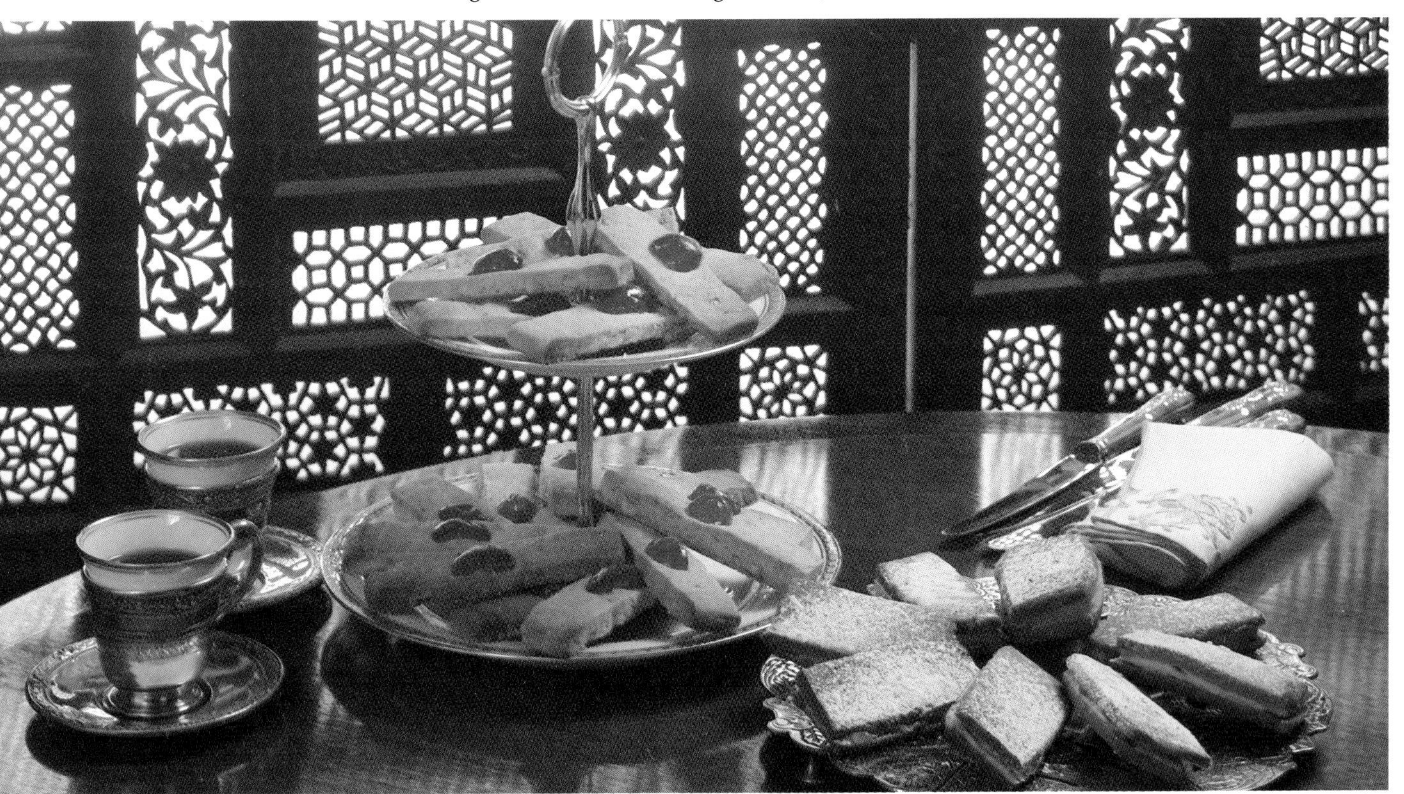

Coffee Creams

reparation time: 15 minutes
ooking time: 15–20 minutes

- 0 g/4 oz plain flour
- teaspoon baking powder
- 0 g/2 oz butter
- 0 g/2 oz caster sugar
- tablespoon golden syrup
- teaspoon coffee essence

lling:

- 0 g/1½ oz icing sugar
- 0 g/¾ oz butter
- tablespoon caster sugar
- tablespoon coffee essence
- ted icing sugar, to decorate

1. Grease two baking sheets.
2. Sift together the flour and baking powder into a mixing bowl.
3. Cream the butter and sugar in a mixing bowl until soft and light, using a wooden spoon. Beat in the syrup and coffee essence.
4. Stir in half the flour mixture and mix until smooth, then stir in the rest of the flour to make a soft dough.
5. Chill the dough in the refrigerator for 10 minutes.
6. Sprinkle a little caster sugar over the dough, then roll out thinly to 5mm/¼ inch on a sheet of greaseproof paper.
7. Cut the dough into 28 oblongs, 2.5 cm/1 inch wide, and 6 cm/2½ inches long. Carefully lift the oblongs on to the greased baking sheets.
8. Prick each biscuit with a fork 3 or 4 times, then bake in the centre of a preheated oven at 160°C, 325°F, Gas Mark 3, for 15–20 minutes. Cool on a wire rack.
9. To make the cream filling, sift the icing sugar in a basin. Put the butter, caster sugar and coffee essence into a saucepan.
10. Dissolve the sugar over a low heat then bring contents to the boil. Pour the mixture into the sifted icing sugar and mix well. Allow the mixture to cool until it is of coating consistency.
11. Sandwich the biscuits in pairs with the icing. Dredge with sifted icing sugar.

Gingernuts

Makes 30
Preparation time: 15 minutes
Cooking time: 15–20 minutes

225 g/8 oz plain flour
½ teaspoon bicarbonate of soda
2 teaspoons ground ginger
100 g/4 oz hard margarine, cut into pieces
225 g/8 oz soft brown sugar
1 egg
1 tablespoon golden syrup

1. Grease 2–3 baking sheets.
2. Sift the flour, bicarbonate of soda and ground ginger into a mixing bowl. Rub the margarine into the flour until the mixture resembles fine breadcrumbs. Stir in the sugar.
3. Make a well in the centre of the mixture and drop in the egg and golden syrup. Beat the mixture thoroughly to incorporate all the ingredients. The mixture will now resemble a crumbly dough.
4. Roll the dough into walnut-sized pieces and place on baking sheets, 5 cm/2 inches apart. Flatten the pieces gently with fingers.
5. Bake in a preheated oven at 180°C, 350°F, Gas Mark 4 for 15–20 minutes.
6. Leave the biscuits on the sheets for some minutes, then carefully transfer them to a cooling rack, where they will harden.

Chocolate Drops

Makes 25
Preparation time: 10 minutes
Cooking time: 15 minutes

75 g/3 oz hard margarine or butter
100 g/4 oz caster sugar
2 tablespoons fresh orange juice
50 g/2 oz nibbed almonds
65 g/2½ oz self-raising flour
15 g/½ oz cocoa powder

1. Grease 2–3 baking sheets.
2. Cream the margarine, or butter and sugar together in a mixing bowl until soft and fluffy, using a wooden spoon. Stir in the orange juice and almonds and mix well.
3. Sift the flour and cocoa over and fold into the mixture.
4. Drop heaped teaspoonfuls of the mixture well apart to allow for spreading on the baking sheets during cooking.
5. Bake in a preheated oven at 180°C, 350°F, Gas Mark 4 for about 15 minutes.
6. Leave to cool for a few minutes on the sheets, then transfer to a wire rack.

Lemon Meltaways

Makes 25–30
Preparation time: 10–15 minutes
Cooking time: 25 minutes

225 g/8 oz hard margarine or butter
50 g/2 oz icing sugar, sifted
grated rind of 1 lemon
225 g/8 oz plain flour
For the icing:
4 tablespoons icing sugar
4 teaspoons lemon juice

1. Grease 2 baking sheets.
2. Cream the margarine and icing sugar together in a mixing bowl, using a wooden spoon. Stir in the lemon rind and flour.
3. Spoon the mixture into a forcing bag fitted with a 1 cm/½ inch large star nozzle. Pipe rosettes and shell shapes on to the baking sheets, then chill in the refrigerator for 20 minutes.
4. Bake in a preheated oven at 160°C, 325°F, Gas Mark 3 for 25 minutes. Transfer the biscuits to a cooling rack.
5. To make icing, blend the icing sugar with the lemon juice in a mixing bowl until a smooth paste of a coating consistency is formed. Spoon a little icing over each biscuit. Allow to set.

Left: Lemon meltaways
Right: Brandy snaps

Orange Shortbread

akes 14
eparation time: 15 minutes
oking time: 15–20 minutes

5 g/6 oz plain flour
g/2 oz caster sugar
ely grated rind of 1 orange
0 g/4 oz unsalted butter, cut
into pieces

1. Grease 2 baking sheets.
2. Sift the flour into a mixing bowl. Stir in the sugar and grated orange rind.
3. Rub in the butter, using fingertips, then blend the ingredients together with the hands to form a smooth dough.
4. Lightly flour a cool work surface and roll out the dough to 5 mm/¼ inch thick. Using a 6 cm/2½ inch fluted cutter, cut out biscuits carefully and place them on the baking sheets.
5. Prick the biscuits with a fork and bake in the centre of a preheated oven at 160°C, 325°F, Gas Mark 3 for 15–20 minutes.
6. Allow the biscuits to cool slightly then transfer to a wire rack to cool.

Brandy Snaps

akes 15
paration time: 20 minutes
oking time: 8–10 minutes

g/2 oz plain flour
easpoon ground ginger
g/2 oz butter
g/2 oz caster sugar
g/2 oz golden syrup
easpoon brandy
decorate:
) ml/¼ pint double cream,
ightly whipped

1. Line 2 baking sheets with non-stick paper and grease the handles of several wooden spoons.
2. Sift the flour and ginger together into a mixing bowl.
3. Put the butter, sugar and golden syrup in a saucepan and heat slowly until the butter is melted.
4. Remove the saucepan from the heat and stir in the sifted flour, ginger and the brandy.
5. Spoon teaspoons of the mixture on to the baking sheets spacing them well apart. (It is best to cook only 4 brandy snaps at a time.)
6. Bake in a preheated oven at 180°C, 350°F, Gas Mark 4 for 8–10 minutes until they are golden brown.
7. Allow to cool for 1–2 minutes then lift the brandy snaps with a palette knife and roll them round the wooden spoon handles, with the top side of the brandy snap at the top.
8. When the biscuits have hardened, slip them off the spoon handles on to a cooling rack.
9. Fill the brandy snaps with whipped cream.

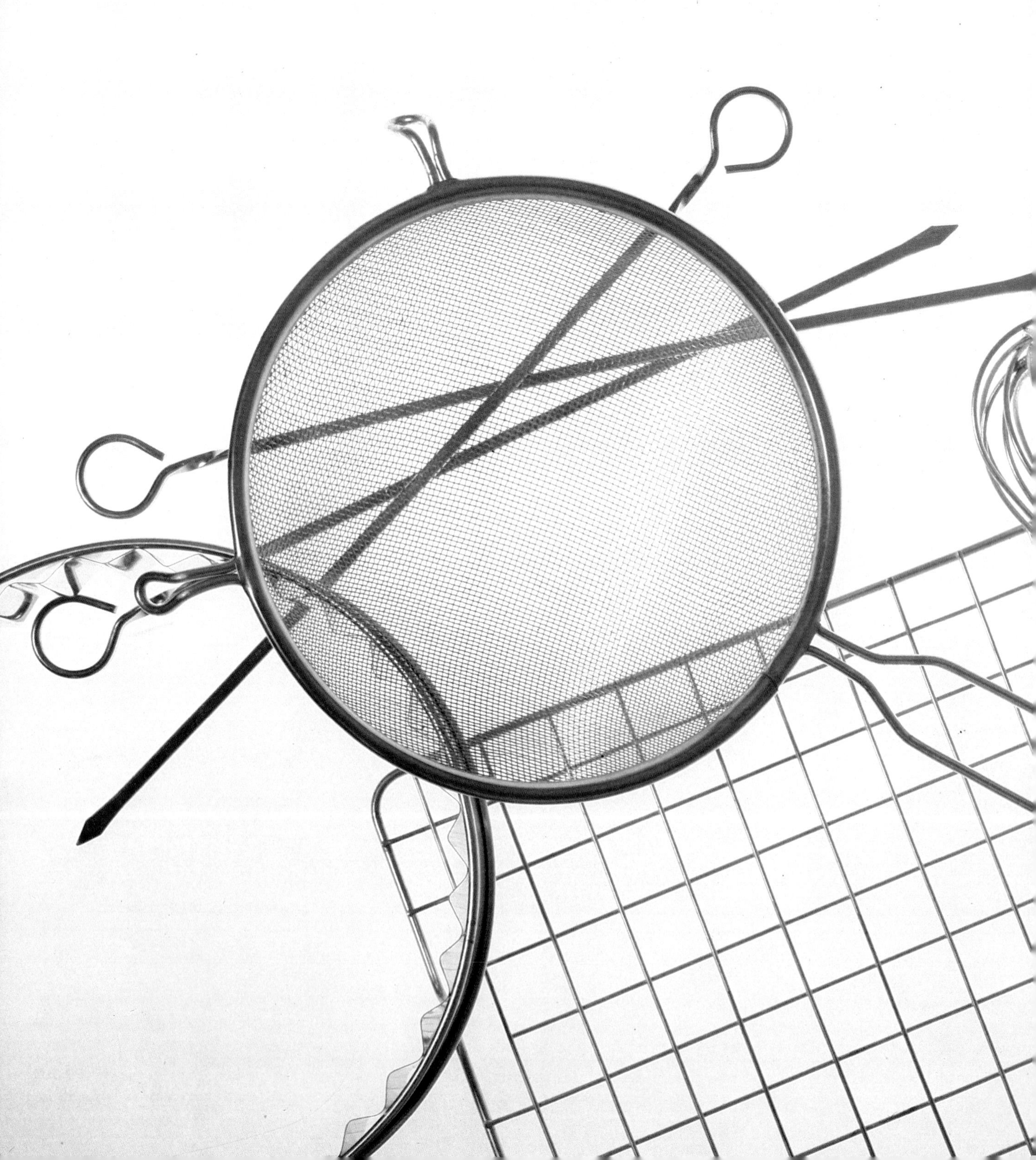

REFERENCE SECTION

ie basic skills of cookery are important to every cook who wants to achieve
e best results. This section provides the background knowledge on cookery
chniques. Basic cooking methods for every type of food are given and there
information on preparing and cooking food as well as the type of food to
oose for each particular method. There are also some useful recipes for
eryday use including eggs, pastries, sauces, dressings and savoury butters.

SOUPS AND STOCKS

Soups are a basic food all over the world, originating from the Latin word 'suppa'. Home-made soups are very satisfying, and easy to make. The most important ingredient is good home-made stock as a base.

Soup is basically water or stock in which other foods have been cooked for a long time to extract the flavour, such as meat, fish, poultry, vegetables, cereals, fruits. Soups can be divided into two types – thin and thick.

They can be served as a starter or main course, either hot or cold.

THIN SOUPS

A thin soup is either a consommé, a clear clarified stock; or a broth, a semi-clear soup consisting of stock with the addition of meat, vegetables and cereals.

THICK SOUPS

There are several ways of thickening a soup: either by liquidizing, or rubbing through a sieve, the cooked ingredients, such as vegetables, pulses, meats, with the stock to make a purée; thickening the liquid with flou or cornflour, making a thin sauce; or enrichi the soup with a liaison of egg yolks and crean

GARNISHES

The appearance, colour, texture and flavour most soups are improved with a garnish adde just before serving: croûtons of fried bread o toast, dumplings, chopped, shredded or slice vegetables (raw and cooked), lemon or orang slices, sprigs or chopped herbs, grated cheese swirls of yogurt, cream or soured cream.

STOCK

Stock is made by long slow cooking of raw or cooked bones with vegetables and flavourings (ask the butcher to chop the bones into manageable pieces as this is difficult to do at home).

A pressure cooker is extremely useful. It cuts down the cooking time and also reduces the smell which can be rather overpowering when the stockpot is simmering for 4 hours.

Follow the manufacturer's instructions, but basically use half to three-quarters the amount of water so that the cooker is no more than two-thirds full. Bring to the boil and remove the scum before covering and bringing to high (15 lb) pressure. Maintain the pressure for 1 hour.

The stock is strained after cooking, discarding the bones and vegetables. When cool, the stock must be skimmed of the fat, which rises to a layer on the top, with a spoon and/or absorbent paper.

Keeping Stock

Home-made stock will keep for up to 4 days the refrigerator, covered, or in a cool place an boiled up every day.

Stock can also be kept in the freezer for up 3 months. Concentrate the stock by boiling rapidly to reduce it by half, leave to cool then pour into rigid containers, seal, label and freeze. It is also very useful to freeze the concentrated stock in ice cube trays and store in polythene bags in the freezer – ideal when only a small quantity of stock is required, or enrich a bland soup.

White Stock

Makes 1–1.5 litres/2–2½ pints
Preparation time: 5 minutes
Cooking time: 4¼ hours

¾–1 kg/1½–2 lb veal bones, chopped
2.25 litres/4 pints cold water
1 onion, peeled and roughly chopped
1 carrot, sliced
1 celery stick, sliced
strip of lemon rind
1 bouquet garni, or bay leaf, sprig of parsley and thyme
½ teaspoon salt
6 white peppercorns

Use for pale-coloured and delicately flavoured soups, sauces and casseroles.

1. Place the bones in a large saucepan and cover with the water. Bring to the boil and skim off any scum that rises.
2. Add the remaining ingredients, bring back to the boil, cover and simmer for about 4 hours.
3. Remove the saucepan from the heat and strain the stock, discarding the bones and the vegetables.
4. Leave the stock to cool, then skim off the fat with a spoon or absorbent kitchen paper.
5. Use immediately or store in the refrigerator for up to 4 days.

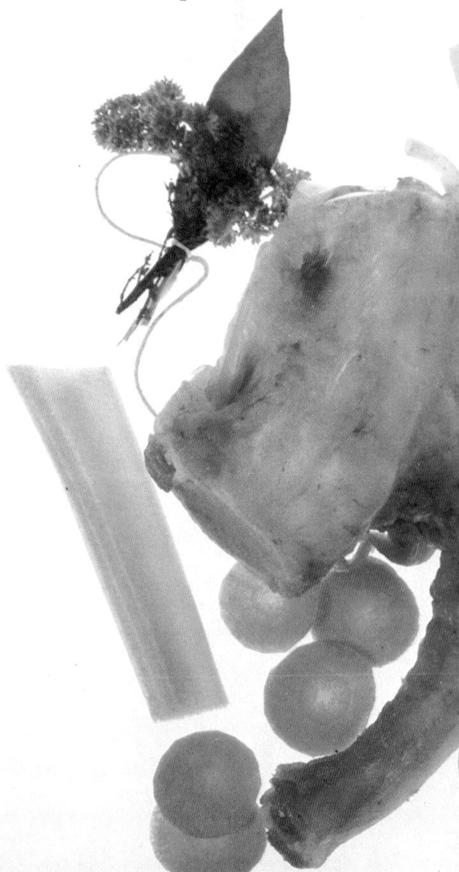

Brown Stock

ikes 1–1.5 litres/1¾–2½ pints
eparation time: 5 minutes
oking time: 5 hours

-1 kg/1½–2 lb beef bones
shin/marrow), chopped
nion, peeled and roughly
chopped
arrot, sliced
elery stick, sliced
nushroom or few stalks,
chopped
5 litres/4 pints cold water
ouquet garni, or bay leaf,
prig of parsley and thyme
teaspoon salt
lack peppercorns

Use this beef stock for meat and vegetable soups, consommé, casseroles and gravies.

1. Trim away any fat from the bones and place the fat and the bones in a large saucepan.
2. Fry over a gentle heat for 15 minutes, turning the bones occasionally, to render down so that the fat runs.
3. Add the vegetables and continue to fry for 30 minutes, turning occasionally until the bones and vegetables are browned.
4. Add the water and flavourings and bring to the boil. Skim off any scum that rises, cover and simmer for about 4 hours.
5. Remove the saucepan from the heat and strain the liquid, discarding the bones and vegetables. Leave the stock to cool, then skim off the fat with a spoon or absorbent kitchen paper.
6. Use immediately or store in the refrigerator for up to 4 days.

Poultry or Game Stock

ikes 1–1.5 litres/1¾–2½ pints
eparation time: 5 minutes
oking time: 3¼–4¼ hours

hicken carcass (or turkey,
luck, game birds)
lets
tres/2½ pints cold water
nion, peeled and roughly
chopped
arrot, sliced
nushroom or few stalks,
chopped
ouquet garni, or bay leaf,
prig of parsley and thyme
ted rind and juice ½ lemon
teaspoon salt
vhite peppercorns

Use for poultry and vegetable soups and casseroles.

1. Place the bones and the giblets in a large saucepan and pour over the water. Bring to the boil and skim off any scum that rises.
2. Add the remaining ingredients, bring back to the boil, cover and simmer for 3 to 4 hours.
3. Remove the saucepan from the heat and strain the stock, discarding the bones and vegetables. Leave the stock to cool, then skim off the fat with a spoon or absorbent kitchen paper.
4. Use immediately or store in the refrigerator for up to 4 days.

Fish Stock

ikes 900 ml–1 litre/1½–1¾
ts
eparation time: 5 minutes
oking time: 1 hour

) g/1 lb white fish trimmings
head, bones, tails of cod,
naddock, whiting and plaice)
litres/2 pints cold water
nion, peeled and roughly
chopped
elery stick, sliced
ouquet garni, or bay leaf,
prig of parsley and thyme
ip of lemon rind
teaspoon salt
vhite peppercorns

This stock may be used immediately after straining as there is no fat to skim off. Use for fish soups, casseroles and sauces.

1. Place the fish trimmings in a colander and rinse them under running cold water. Place them in a saucepan and cover with the water. Bring to the boil and skim off the scum.
2. Add the remaining ingredients, bring back to the boil, cover and simmer for 45 minutes, skimming occasionally if necessary.
3. Remove the saucepan from the heat and strain the stock, discarding the bones and vegetables.
4. Use immediately or cool, then chill in the refrigerator and use the same or the next day.

SAUCES, DRESSINGS AND SAVOURY BUTTERS

The purpose of a sauce, dressing or savoury butter is to enhance the food it accompanies by providing contrasting or complementary flavours or textures. A good sauce raises the status of almost any dish and can positively transform bland foods or leftovers. A baked jacket potato enlivened with a pat of chive butter is a good example.

Sauces are often much easier and quicker to prepare than you may think; many sauces need no cooking at all, simply mixing or blending. Even cooked sauces are simple once you have mastered the basic techniques, and from a few 'parent' sauces many variations can be made to enrich and widen your cookery repertoire.

HINTS FOR EASIER SAUCE MAKING

Keeping sauces hot
There is no need for a last minute rush to make a sauce at dishing up time because most sauces benefit from being made in advance and kept hot – the extra cooking helps to blend and mellow the flavours. Simply stand the saucepan or basin containing the sauce in a larger saucepan or deep baking dish with gently simmering water to reach half way up the container. Keep the sauce covered and stir it from time to time.

Reducing and concentrating thin sauces
Boil the sauce rapidly in an uncovered pan, stirring continuously, until it reduces to the desired consistency and flavour.

Thinning a too thick sauce
Beat milk, stock or thin cream, 1 tablespoon a a time, into the simmering sauce until a suitab consistency is reached.

Smoothing a lumpy sauce
Beat briskly with a small wire whisk (provide this will not injure a non-stick pan surface). Alternatively, liquidize in an electric blender o press the sauce through a fine wire sieve then reheat it.

Preventing a skin forming
Float a very thin film of water, stock or milk, or press a piece of wet greaseproof paper, ove the entire surface of the sauce. Set the sauce aside to cool, or keep hot as above.

Rescuing a curdled mayonnaise
This is unlikely to happen if you follow the directions on Page 149, but if it does, put eith 1 teaspoon made French mustard or 1 egg yol into a dry warm bowl and gradually beat in th curdled mayonnaise no more than 1 tablespoo at a time.

ROUX-BASED SAUCES

Basic White Sauce

Makes 300–450 ml/½–¾ pint
Preparation time: 2 minutes
Cooking time: about 8 minutes

25 g/1 oz butter
25 g/1 oz plain flour
300–450 ml/½–¾ pint hot liquid
salt
freshly ground white pepper

PROPORTIONS
Thick or coating sauce:
25 g/1 oz each fat and flour to 300 ml/½ pint liquid.
Medium pouring sauce:
25 g/1 oz each fat and flour to 450 ml/¾ pint liquid.

This simple sauce thickened with a white roux (that is to say a mixture of butter and flour cooked slowly together without colouring before any liquid is added) is the parent sauce of a great many variations. The consistency is controlled by the proportion of flour to liquid, and the liquid can be milk; fish, veal or poultry stock; or a mixture of milk and stock. Variations can include white wine, cream or egg yolks, as well as flavouring ingredients.

If you adopt the chef's trick of using a small wire whisk instead of a wooden spoon the sauce is quickly made. And provided the initial roux is cooked enough (for at least 2 minutes to eliminate any raw starch flavour) it does not need long cooking.

1. Melt the butter in a small heavy based saucepan, but avoid a non-stick pan if using a whisk.
2. Add the flour and cook for 2 minutes over a low heat without colouring it, stirring constantly.
3. Add the hot liquid all at once and whisk briskly until the sauce thickens and boils. Lower the heat, add salt and pepper to taste and simmer very gently for 5 minutes, stirrin occasionally.

Speedy all-in-one method:
The Basic White Sauce may be made in a different way which excludes the roux-makin process, and is very easy to do. This method i perhaps best used when the sauce is to be fairl strongly flavoured (e.g. Sauce Mornay), as th flavour may not be quite so rich and good as when made by the traditional method. Put all the ingredients into a small pan, set it over a moderate heat, stirring continuously with a wooden spoon or wire whisk until the sauce thickens and boils. Simmer for 4–5 minutes, stirring frequently.
Makes 300–450 ml/½–¾ pint

VARIATIONS:

Béchamel Sauce
If the sauce is to be served plain, give it a more interesting taste by making it with flavoured milk. In advance, put a generous 300 ml/½ pint milk into a saucepan with a sliced small onion, carrot and celery stick, and a bayleaf, blade of mace, and 6 black peppercorns. Bring slowly to boiling point, then cover and leave to infuse off the heat for at least 30 minutes (it can be left all day). Strain before using.

Sauce Velouté
For fish or chicken dishes. Use a well flavoured fish or chicken stock instead of milk.

Sauce Crème
For fish, chicken, egg or vegetable dishes. Gradually beat 4–5 tablespoons double cream into 300 ml/½ pint of thick white sauce and simmer for a few minutes. Add a few drops of lemon juice.

Sauce Mornay
For vegetable, egg, fish, poultry and pasta dishes. Off the heat, stir in 25–50 g/1–2 oz grated cheese (either dry Cheddar or a mixture of Parmesan and Gruyère) with a little grated nutmeg and a little cayenne pepper.

Sauce Soubise
For eggs, vegetables, poultry, veal or mutton. Drain, chop and sieve or liquidize 225 g/8 oz freshly boiled onions. Stir into 300 ml/½ pint thick white sauce with 2 tablespoons cream and salt and pepper to taste.

Prawn or Shrimp Sauce
For fish. Stir 50 g/2 oz shelled prawns or shrimps into a thick white sauce made with part milk and part fish stock. Season to taste with lemon juice or anchovy essence.

Mustard Sauce
For herring or mackerel. Stir 1–2 tablespoons prepared strong French or English mustard into 300 ml/½ pint thick white sauce, adding 1 tablespoon wine vinegar and 1 teaspoon sugar. Simmer for 2–3 minutes.

Parsley Sauce
For fish, boiled chicken or ham. Stir 2–3 tablespoons finely chopped fresh parsley into a medium pouring sauce and simmer for 1–2 minutes.

Espagnole Sauce (Basic Brown Sauce)

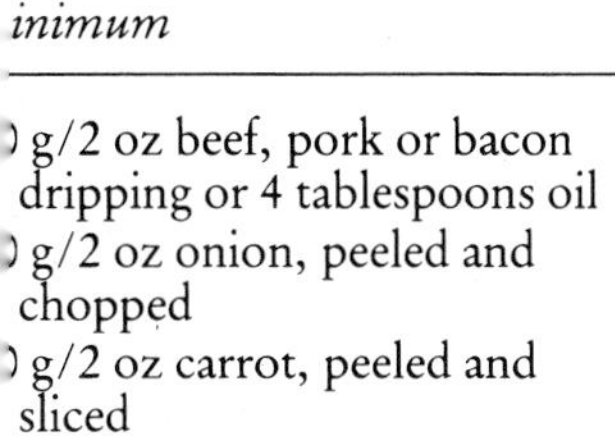

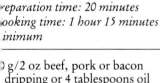

akes about 450 ml/¾ pint
eparation time: 20 minutes
ooking time: 1 hour 15 minutes
inimum

- g/2 oz beef, pork or bacon dripping or 4 tablespoons oil
- g/2 oz onion, peeled and chopped
- g/2 oz carrot, peeled and sliced
- celery stick, sliced
- g/3 oz cooked lean ham or bacon scraps, diced
- tablespoons plain flour
- 0 ml/1 pint good meat stock
- teaspoons tomato purée
- rig of parsley, rig of thyme, small bay leaf } tied together
- lt
- eshly ground black pepper

This sauce thickened with a brown roux (that is to say fat and flour cooked slowly together until the flour turns an even nut brown) forms the basis of many of the classic brown sauces. Although quite simple to make, both the initial preparation and the cooking need considerable time, so it is worth making the sauce in double or even treble quantities and freezing the surplus.

1. Heat the fat in a heavy based saucepan, add the onion, carrot, celery and bacon and cook together gently, stirring occasionally, for 10 minutes.
2. Stir in the flour, and continue cooking over a moderately low heat, stirring frequently, until the flour turns to a nut brown colour.
3. Add the stock, tomato purée, herb bouquet and a little salt and pepper.
4. Bring to the boil, cover and simmer for 1 hour and preferably longer (the longer a brown sauce cooks the finer the flavour). From time to time skim off any scum or fat from the surface.
5. Strain the sauce, pressing the vegetables to extract their juices. Return it to the rinsed pan, reheat and taste and adjust the seasoning. The final consistency should lightly coat the back of a spoon, but if necessary reduce or thin the sauce as described opposite.

VARIATIONS:

Madeira Sauce
For ham, tongue, veal, beef and egg dishes. Add 4–5 tablespoons Madeira to the basic sauce about half way through the cooking, allowing time for the wine to reduce and mellow. Just before serving beat in 25 g/1 oz softened butter.

Sauce Piquante
For pork, tongue, boiled beef or meat leftovers. Fry 50 g/2 oz chopped shallots gently in 25 g/1 oz butter, then add 2 tablespoons wine vinegar and boil until reduced to 1 tablespoon. Add to the basic sauce with 1 tablespoon each finely chopped gherkins and pickles, ½ teaspoon French mustard and a little cayenne pepper. Heat together for a few minutes and finish with 2 tablespoons chopped fresh parsley.

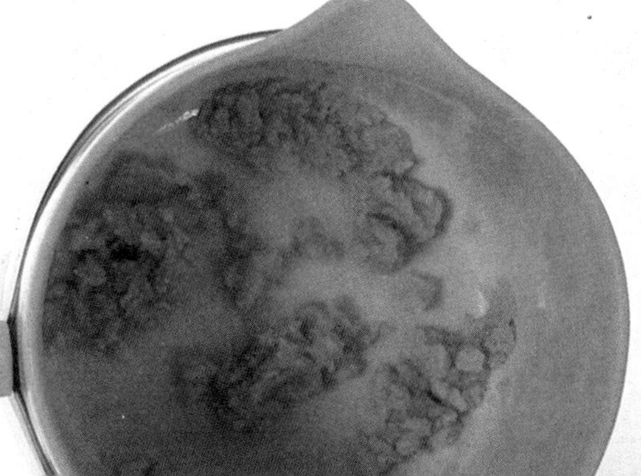

Hollandaise

Makes a generous 400 ml/½ pint
Serves 4–6
Preparation time: 10 minutes
Cooking time: 10 minutes

3 egg yolks
1 tablespoon lemon juice
1 tablespoon cold water
salt
white pepper
175 g/6 oz unsalted butter, at warm room temperature

Beating to a smooth cream

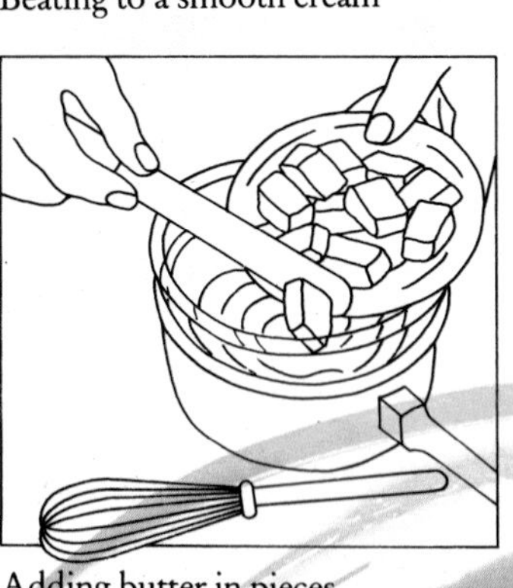

Adding butter in pieces

This famous thick, rich and golden sauce is a perfect partner for poached fish, eggs or chicken, and for delicate vegetables such as asparagus or broccoli spears. Success depends upon heating the egg yolks *slowly*, so that they thicken to a smooth cream which is capable of absorbing a large amount of butter. The butter must be added in small pieces, and each thoroughly incorporated before the next is added.

1. Put the egg yolks, lemon juice, water and a good pinch of salt and pepper into a small basin. Rest the basin over a pan of near boiling water (the basin should not touch the water) and place over a low heat.
2. With a small wire whisk, beat steadily until the mixture thickens to a smooth cream. Immediately remove the pan and basin from the heat, add about 15 g/½ oz of the butter and whisk until completely absorbed.
3. Continue adding the butter in roughly 15 g/½ oz pieces, whisking in each addition until completely absorbed before adding the next. The result should be a creamy sauce of coating consistency, but if too thick, thin it by beating in a few drops of warm water.
4. Adjust the seasoning and serve luke warm. If the sauce is not served immediately, stand the basin containing the sauce in a pan of tepid water. Never allow the sauce to overheat at any stage or it will become thin and may even curdle.

VARIATIONS:

Sauce Mousseline
A light sauce for fish or soufflés. Beat 6 tablespoons double cream until thick but not stiff and fold lightly into the finished sauce.

Sauce Maltaise
For fish or vegetables. Beat the finely grated rind of 1 orange and 2 tablespoons orange juice into the finished sauce.

Sauce Béarnaise
A stronger flavoured sauce to serve with grilled meats, chicken or fish. Instead of flavouring the egg yolks with lemon juice use the following reduction of vinegar and shallots: put 6 tablespoons tarragon vinegar, : crushed peppercorns and 1 tablespoon chopped shallot or spring onion into a small saucepan and boil gently until the liquid has reduced to 2 tablespoons. Strain into a basin and continue exactly as for a Hollandaise Sauce. Finish by stirring in 1 tablespoon chopped fresh tarragon or ½ tablespoon drie tarragon.

Mayonnaise

akes a scant 450 ml/¾ pint
eparation time: 10 minutes in a
ender, 20 minutes by hand

whole egg or 2 egg yolks
teaspoon dry mustard
teaspoon salt
-2 tablespoons wine vinegar or lemon juice
0 ml/½ pint olive oil
:ablespoon boiling water

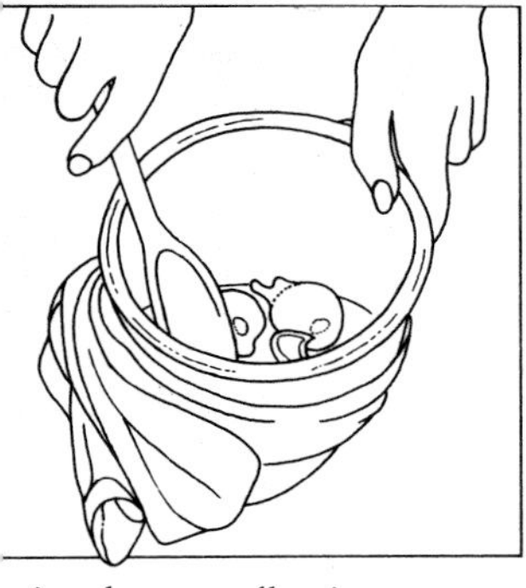

ating the egg yolk mixture

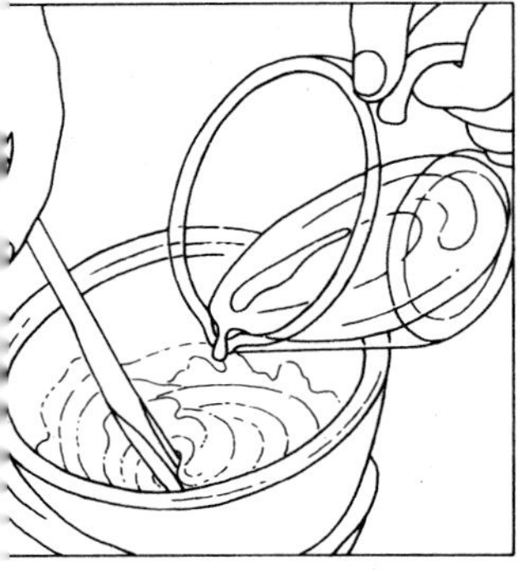

dding the oil, drop by drop

ft: Hollandaise sauce
ght: Half-made and finished
ayonnaise

An exceedingly useful cold sauce with many variations and many different uses. If you do not care for the distinctive flavour of olive oil use ground nut, corn, or a mixture of oils. To store, turn the prepared sauce into a small airtight container, cover tightly and keep in the lower part of the refrigerator for a few days. Should the mayonnaise become thin follow the 'rescue' directions on page 146.

1. If using a blender, put the whole egg into the blender goblet with the mustard, salt, 2 tablespoons vinegar or lemon juice and run the machine until well blended.
2. With the machine still running, remove the small cap in the lid and add the oil in a slow, steady stream, followed by the boiling water, until the mayonnaise is smoothy blended.
3. To make mayonnaise by hand, stand a small mixing bowl on a folded cloth to prevent it slipping.
4. Put the 2 egg yolks into the basin and add the mustard, salt and a few drops of vinegar or lemon juice. Using a small wire whisk, a wooden spoon or a hand-held electric beater, beat thoroughly *before* adding any oil.
5. Still beating all the time, start adding the oil *drop by drop* from a teaspoon and continue until the sauce becomes very thick and half the oil has been incorporated.
6. Add 1 teaspoon of the vinegar or lemon juice and, still beating steadily increase the flow of oil to an intermittent thin stream.
7. When all the oil has been incorporated, and the mayonnaise is thick, beat in the boiling water and season to taste with the remaining vinegar or lemon juice.

VARIATIONS:

Mayonnaise Chantilly
Flavour the basic recipe with lemon juice instead of vinegar and fold 4–5 tablespoons whipped, double cream into the finished mayonnaise.

Sauce Tartare
To the finished mayonnaise add 1–2 tablespoons each of drained and finely chopped gherkins and capers, snipped chives and finely chopped parsley.

Sauce Remoulade
Add 1 teaspoon each of made mustard and anchovy essence to a Sauce Tartare.

Shellfish Cocktail Sauce
Mix 6 tablespoons mayonnaise with 3 tablespoons each of tomato ketchup and soured cream or double cream, and flavour to taste with a few drops of lemon juice and Worcestershire sauce.

Garlic Mayonnaise
Pound 2 peeled garlic cloves to a fine paste and add to the egg yolks when starting a hand mixed mayonnaise. Not recommended for blender mayonnaise.

Bread Sauce

Preparation time: 15 minutes
Cooking time: 10 minutes, plus 30 minutes infusion time

1 medium onion, peeled and quartered
1 small bay leaf
blade of mace
2 cloves
4 black peppercorns
300 ml/½ pint milk
50 g/2 oz fresh white breadcrumbs
15 g/½ oz butter
salt

A traditional accompaniment to roast chicken, turkey and pheasant. For a well flavoured bread sauce allow ample time for the milk to become thoroughly infused with the flavours of the onion and spices.

1. Put the onion, bay leaf, spices and milk into a small saucepan and bring very slowly to boiling point.
2. Cover the pan and leave in a warm place to infuse for at least 30 minutes.
3. Strain the milk and return it to the rinsed saucepan. Add the breadcrumbs and butter and reheat gently, stirring frequently, until the sauce thickens. Add salt to taste and serve hot.

Mint Sauce

Serves 4
Preparation time: 10 minutes

4 tablespoons very finely chopped fresh mint
1 tablespoon caster sugar
3 tablespoons boiling water
4 tablespoons wine vinegar

A traditional sauce to serve with roast lamb or mutton and best made from freshly picked young mint leaves. Brown malt vinegar is often used, but white wine vinegar gives a more subtle flavour.

1. Put the mint and sugar into a small sauce boat and stir in the boiling water.
2. When cool add the vinegar and leave to stand for an hour or so before serving.

Apple Sauce

Serves 4–6
Preparation time: 10 minutes
Cooking time: 10–15 minutes

350 g/12 oz cooking apples, peeled, cored and quartered
2 tablespoons water or cider
15 g/½ oz butter
thin strip of lemon rind (optional)
1–2 tablespoons sugar

A sauce to counteract the richness of roast pork, pork sausages, mackerel and other oily fish. Use tart, well flavoured cooking apples, or add sharpness to insipid apples with cider and lemon rind.

1. Put the apples into a saucepan with the liquid, butter and lemon rind, if used. Simmer gently until the apples are soft, discard the rind and beat to pulp.
2. Add sugar to taste and serve warm or cold.

Cranberry Sauce

rves 6
eparation time: 5 minutes
ooking time: 15 minutes

5 g/6 oz granulated sugar
0 ml/⅓ pint water
5 g/8 oz cranberries, washed
teaspoon finely grated orange rind

For roast turkey, chicken, lamb or mutton, this sauce can be made at any time of the year with frozen cranberries. It is usually served cold.

1. Heat the sugar and water together gently until the sugar dissolves. Add the cranberries and cook fairly rapidly for several minutes until the skins begin to 'pop'.
2. Reduce the heat and simmer gently until the berries are tender but not mushed, about 6–8 minutes. Stir in the orange rind.

Cumberland Sauce

rves 6–8
eparation time: 10 minutes
ooking time: 15 minutes

arge oranges
mall lemon
5 g/8 oz redcurrant jelly
ablespoons tawny port
easpoons made mustard
nch of powdered ginger

Rich in flavour and colour, this is an excellent sauce to serve with all cold meats, especially cured meats such as ham, tongue, pressed beef and brawn.

1. With a potato peeler, pare the rind in strips, very thinly, from the oranges and lemon.
2. Put the rinds into a small pan, cover with cold water, bring to the boil and simmer for 5 minutes. Drain and cut the strips into matchsticks.
3. Meanwhile, squeeze the oranges and put the juice into a saucepan with all the remaining ingredients.
4. Heat gently, stirring until the jelly dissoves and the ingredients blend smoothly. (If the jelly fails to dissolve press the sauce through a sieve and return it to the pan.)
5. Add the shredded rinds and simmer for 5 minutes (the sauce thickens a little on cooling).

Basic Tomato Sauce

akes about 300 ml/½ pint
eparation time: 10 minutes
oking time: 40 minutes

ablespoons oil
mall onion, peeled and very finely chopped
mall garlic clove, crushed
× 400 g/14 oz can peeled tomatoes
ablespoon tomato purée
2 teaspoons sugar
t
shly ground black pepper
ouquet garni

Peeled canned tomatoes make a well flavoured sauce at any time of the year and minimize the preparation time. This sauce has a rough texture but can, if preferred, be made smoother by sieving or blending.

1. Heat the oil in a saucepan and fry the onion very gently for 5 minutes until beginning to soften.
2. Add the garlic and cook for 1 minute, then add the tomatoes and their juice, the tomato purée, and sugar, salt and pepper to taste. Mash with a potato masher or wooden spoon to break up the large pieces of tomato.
3. Bring to the boil, add the bouquet garni, cover and simmer gently for about 40 minutes.
4. Check the seasoning, remove the bouquet garni and use the sauce as required.
5. For a smooth textured sauce press the contents of the pan through a sieve, or liquidize in a blender, and reheat.

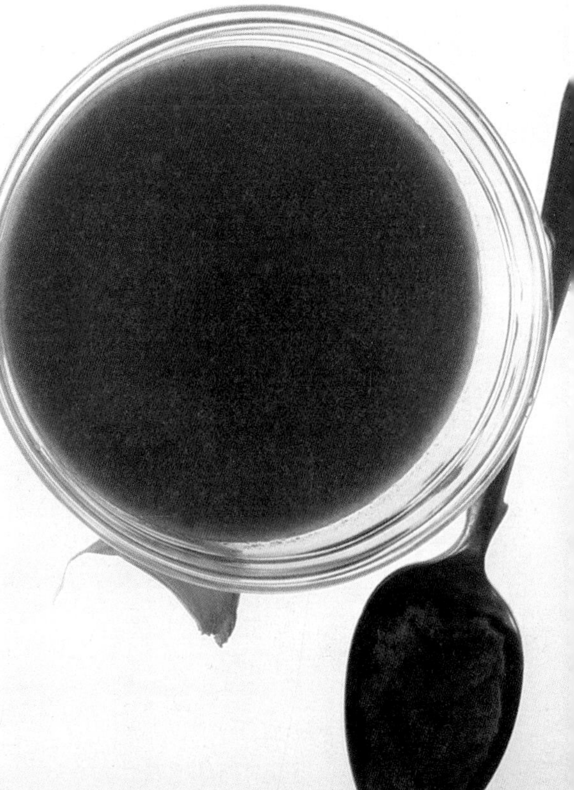

French Dressing (Sauce Vinaigrette)

Makes about 150 ml/¼ pint
Preparation time: 5 minutes

1 tablespoon white wine vinegar
1 tablespoon lemon juice
¼ teaspoon dry mustard
pinch of salt
freshly ground black pepper
7–10 tablespoons olive, ground nut or corn oil

This most widely used of all salad dressings can be varied to suit personal tastes. For a blander basic dressing simply add more oil; for a sharper flavour increase the vinegar, replace it with lemon juice or, best of all, use equal parts of each. For convenience mix and store small quantities of dressing in a screw-top jar.

1. Put all the ingredients into a plastic-lidded screw-top jar and shake vigorously for about half a minute until well blended. Shake again just before using.

VARIATIONS:

Herb Dressing
Just before using stir in 1–2 tablespoons chopped mixed fresh herbs, e.g. chives, parsley, chervil and tarragon.

Garlic Dressing
Stir in 1 finely crushed garlic clove and 2 tablespoons chopped fresh parsley.

Blue Cheese Dressing
Stir in 1 tablespoon finely crumbled Stilton, Danish blue or Roquefort.

Sauce Ravigote
Stir in 1 finely chopped small shallot, 1 teaspoon drained and chopped capers, and 1 tablespoon chopped fresh parsley, plus chervil and tarragon when available.

Note: The simplest variation of all is to use a flavoured wine vinegar such as tarragon or garlic vinegar.

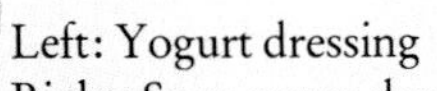

Left: Yogurt dressing
Right: Sour cream dressing

Yogurt Dressing

Serves 4
Preparation time: 10 minutes

1 × 150 g/5 oz carton plain, unsweetened yogurt
1 tablespoon olive oil
1 tablespoon lemon juice or white wine vinegar
salt
white pepper
1–2 tablespoons fresh chopped herbs – chives, parsley, chervil, mint, tarragon or a mixture

A light, low calorie dressing to serve with salads, or a refreshing sauce to accompany grilled or fried fish.

1. Put the yogurt, oil and lemon juice or vinegar into a basin and mix well. Season to taste with salt and pepper and stir in the herbs.
2. Refrigerate until required.

VARIATIONS:

Cucumber and Yogurt Sauce
Cut half a small, unpeeled cucumber into very small dice, put into a colander, sprinkle with 2 teaspoons of salt and leave to drain for 30 minutes. Rinse in cold water and pat dry with kitchen towels. Stir into the basic yogurt sauce flavoured with fresh mint.

Watercress Dressing
Omit the herbs and stir in 2–3 tablespoons finely chopped fresh watercress.

Sour Cream Dressing

Serves 4–6
Preparation time: 10 minutes

1 × 150 g/5 oz carton soured cream
1 tablespoon lemon juice or wine vinegar
1 tablespoon milk (or more if required)
salt
white pepper
2 tablespoons chopped fresh parsley or chives (optional)

A richer dressing for green salads, and good with potato, egg, fish and poultry salads.

1. Beat the soured cream, the lemon juice or vinegar and the milk together in a basin. Season to taste with salt and pepper and stir in the chopped herbs if used.
2. If a thinner dressing is preferred, stir in a little extra milk.
3. Leave to blend in the refrigerator for 20 minutes before serving.

VARIATION:

Horseradish Sauce
Omit the lemon juice or vinegar and the milk. Stir in about 2 tablespoons grated fresh horseradish or 3–4 tablespoons prepared horseradish relish, and salt and pepper to taste.

SAVOURY BUTTERS

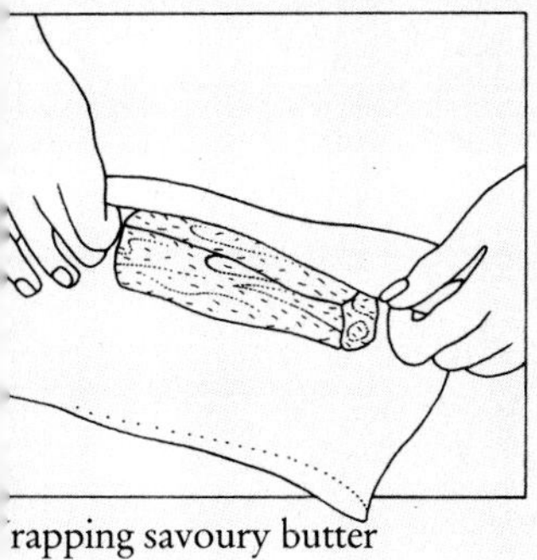
rapping savoury butter

An effective garnish that adds extra flavour and succulence to plain grilled foods such as steaks, chops or fish. Savoury butters make excellent 'toppings' for cooked vegetables and can be used to flavour stuffed hard-boiled eggs, to dress pasta or to enrich a plain soup.

For garnishing, chill the butters in the refrigerator and top each portion of food with a pat of butter immediately before serving. Savoury butters will keep in the refrigerator for up to 2 weeks.

Maitre d'Hotel Butter

akes toppings for 12–16 rtions
eparation time: 10 minutes

0 g/4 oz unsalted butter
3 tablespoons finely chopped fresh parsley
easpoons lemon juice
t
shly ground black pepper

Cream the butter until light and fluffy then beat in all the other ingredients. Turn on to greaseproof paper, form into a 2.5 cm/1 inch diameter roll, wrap the paper around the roll, overwrap in foil and chill for several hours until firm. To use, cut into slices.

VARIATIONS:

Herb Butters
Add 1–2 tablespoons chopped fresh tarragon, mint, or chives.

Orange Butter
Omit the parsley and add 1 tablespoon of finely grated orange rind, ¼ teaspoon ground coriander and a large pinch of paprika.

Mustard Butter
Add 2 tablespoons French mustard.

Garlic Butter
Add 2 tablespoons finely grated shallot and 2 garlic cloves, finely crushed.

Anchovy Butter
Omit the salt and parsley. Add 6–8 canned anchovy fillets, previously pounded to a paste.

OTHER ACCOMPANIMENTS

Bread, garlic and herb breads, toast, melba toast or crispbread make excellent accompaniments to soups, pâtés and stews.

For Garlic or Herb Bread: follow the recipe for Maitre d'Hotel Butter (above) using 175 g/6 oz butter and substituting 1 tablespoon dried mixed herbs or 2 crushed garlic cloves for the fresh herbs. Slice a long French loaf diagonally at 2.5 cm/1 inch intervals close to the base without cutting through, then spread the slices generously with the flavoured butter. Spread any left over on the top. Wrap loosely in foil and put in a preheated oven at 180°C, 350°F, Gas Mark 4 for 25 minutes. Open the foil wrapping, increase the heat to 230°C, 450°F, Gas Mark 8 for a further 10 minutes until crisp.

For Melba Toast: toast medium slices of white or brown bread on both sides. Trim off and discard the crusts and cut carefully through the untoasted centres. Grill the untoasted surfaces until brown and the edges of the toast curl up.

EGGS

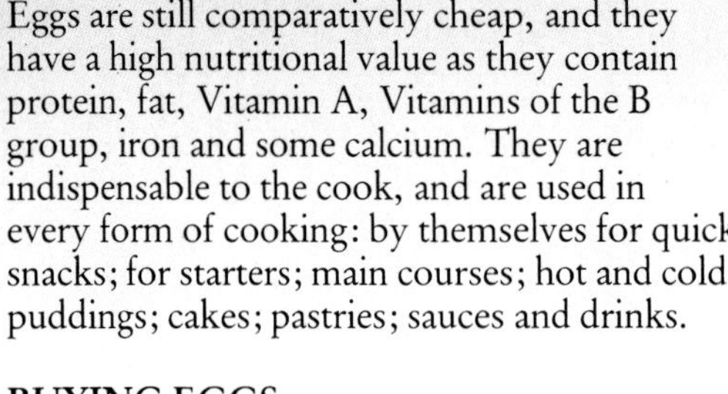

Eggs are still comparatively cheap, and they have a high nutritional value as they contain protein, fat, Vitamin A, Vitamins of the B group, iron and some calcium. They are indispensable to the cook, and are used in every form of cooking: by themselves for quick snacks; for starters; main courses; hot and cold puddings; cakes; pastries; sauces and drinks.

BUYING EGGS

Egg sizes are now graded by numbers indicating their weight, rather than by their old description: small, medium, standard and large. They are sold in the following way:

Size 1: 70 g (2½ oz) and over
Size 2: 65 g–70 g (2¼ oz–2½ oz)
Size 3: 60 g–65 g (2 oz–2¼ oz)
Size 4: 55 g–60 g (1⅞ oz–2 oz)
Size 5: 50 g–55 g (1¾ oz–1⅞ oz)
Size 6: 45 g–50 g (1½ oz–1¾ oz)
Size 7: under 45 g (under 1½ oz)

Sizes 1–2 are best to use for cake making and meringues because they provide a greater volume. Sizes 3–4 and 5–6 are perfectly suitable for ordinary cooking.

The colour of the egg shell varies according to the breed of chicken, and both brown and white eggs have exactly the same food value and flavour.

Duck's eggs

These need to be well cooked to be safe to eat, so should be boiled for at least 10 minutes. They can be used in cakes and puddings, but not in meringues or short-baked dishes, as the cooking time is not long enough and the temperature too low for them to be safe to eat. They should not be preserved or stored, and must be eaten when completely fresh.

Turkey and goose eggs

These are similar to hen's eggs and can be used for all purposes. They need 7 minutes for soft boiling as they are much larger.

STORING EGGS

Egg shells are porous and they will absorb flavours from other foods, so they should be left in their containers if stored in the refrigerator, away from strong smelling foods such as fish, cheese or onions. Eggs are best stored in a cool, rather than very cold place (i.e. not the refrigerator), otherwise they crack when boiled, and are difficult to whisk.

There is little need to preserve eggs these days for long-term storage because they are sc readily available and relatively cheap all year round. However, if you keep your own hens, you can preserve eggs in waterglass according to the instructions provided on the container. Eggs will store for up to 2–3 weeks in the refrigerator, or a month if completely fresh, slightly less in a cool place.

Testing for freshness

Eggs have an air space inside the shell which increases in size with age. To test an egg for freshness, place it in a tumbler of cold salted water. If it lies flat at the bottom, it is very fresh. If it tilts slightly it is not fresh enough fc boiling, but suitable for using in cakes and puddings. If it floats it is bad and should be discarded. You can also break the eggs, one at time, into a cup and if they smell slightly unpleasant they are not fresh.

HOW TO BOIL EGGS

Soft-boiled eggs: Eggs should be simmered and not boiled. The base of the egg may be pricked with a small pin or commercially mad egg-pricker to prevent it cracking. Lower them into boiling water, reduce the heat and simmer for 3 minutes for soft eggs, 4½ minut for a medium set. Alternatively, put them intc cold water and bring slowly to the boil. Remove from the water, and they will be read

Hard-boiled eggs: Place the eggs into boiling or cold water. Bring to the boil and allow to simmer for 12–15 minutes, depending on the method used. Plunge the eggs into cold water immediately and leave until cold. This preven a dark rim forming around the yolk, and the shell is easier to remove. Crack the egg all round by tapping on the work surface, then peel the shell away.

HOW TO CODDLE EGGS

Place the eggs in boiling water and boil for 1 minute. Remove the pan from the heat and leave for 5 minutes. The egg will be very light set. Take out and serve as for boiled eggs. Thi method is particularly suitable for invalids anc children, as the egg is more digestible.

HOW TO SCRAMBLE EGGS

Allow 2 eggs per person. Crack the eggs into a bowl, add salt and pepper and beat with a fork. (Add 2 tablespoons milk, if liked, though this is not strictly necessary.) Melt 15 g/½ oz butter in a heavy-based pan, pour in the eggs and cook over a moderate heat. Stir occasionally then more rapidly as the eggs begin to set. Cook for a further ½ minute if necessary, but do not overcook. The eggs should be soft and creamy. Serve immediately on hot buttered toast.

VARIATIONS:

Add to a 4-egg mixture any of the following:
50 g/2 oz lightly fried mushrooms.
2 rashers bacon, rinded, chopped and fried.
50 g/2 oz chopped ham, tongue or other cooked meat.
50 g/2 oz smoked fish, skinned, boned and flaked.
50 g/2 oz grated cheese.
50 g/2 oz peeled prawns, squeeze of lemon juice and ½ tablespoon chopped fresh parsley.
1 tablespoon chopped mixed fresh herbs.

HOW TO FRY EGGS

Heat some dripping, bacon fat, lard or oil in a frying pan. Check each egg for freshness, and when the fat is hot drop the egg gently into the pan. Cook gently until set, basting the surface with fat occasionally, using a spoon. Remove the eggs from the pan using a fish slice or palette knife.

HOW TO POACH EGGS

Eggs must be completely fresh for poaching. Fill a medium-sized saucepan two thirds full of water and add a few drops of vinegar. This helps the eggs to keep their shape. Bring to the boil, then reduce to a simmer. Stir the water with a spoon and, when gently swirling, drop the egg into the centre, and increase the heat. The movement of the water will draw the white over the yolk. Remove when just set, with a slotted spoon. Serve on hot buttered toast. Do not attempt to poach more than 2 eggs at a time in this way.

If using an egg poacher, half fill the lower container with water. Add a knob of butter to each cup and place over the heat. When the water is boiling, break the eggs into the cups, season lightly and cover the pan with the lid. Simmer until the eggs are set. Loosen gently with a knife to remove.

HOW TO BAKE EGGS

Grease individual ovenproof or cocotte dishes and add salt and pepper. Place in a roasting tin and pour in sufficient water to reach half way up the sides of the dishes. Break an egg into each dish and bake in the centre of a preheated oven at 180°C, 350°F, Gas Mark 4 for 6–7 minutes until the whites are barely set and the yolks soft. Garnish with chopped fresh herbs and serve at once.

POINTS TO REMEMBER WHEN COOKING WITH EGGS

The foundation of a hot soufflé is a panada, which is a very thick white sauce. The panada must be smoothly blended and the egg yolks well beaten into this mixture, otherwise the soufflé will be leathery. It is best to use a large saucepan to make the panada, as the beaten egg whites have to be folded into the mixture in the saucepan.

When beating egg whites for folding into soufflés or mousses, they need to be only lightly whisked until just beginning to hold their shape. Stir in a small quantity with a metal spoon to the panada before the main bulk is added. This softens the mixture, so that when the rest of the egg white is added, the soufflé will be light and fluffy.

Serve the soufflé immediately as it will sink in minutes.

When whisking egg whites for meringues, choose a large grease-free bowl and whisk the egg whites until very stiff and standing in peaks, before adding any sugar.

Any mixture of egg and milk will curdle if allowed to overheat, so use a bain-marie (a roasting tin half-filled with hot water) for baking a custard in the oven. For a pouring custard made with eggs, use a double saucepan with hot water in the lower pan, or cook very gently in a heavy based saucepan.

VEGETABLES

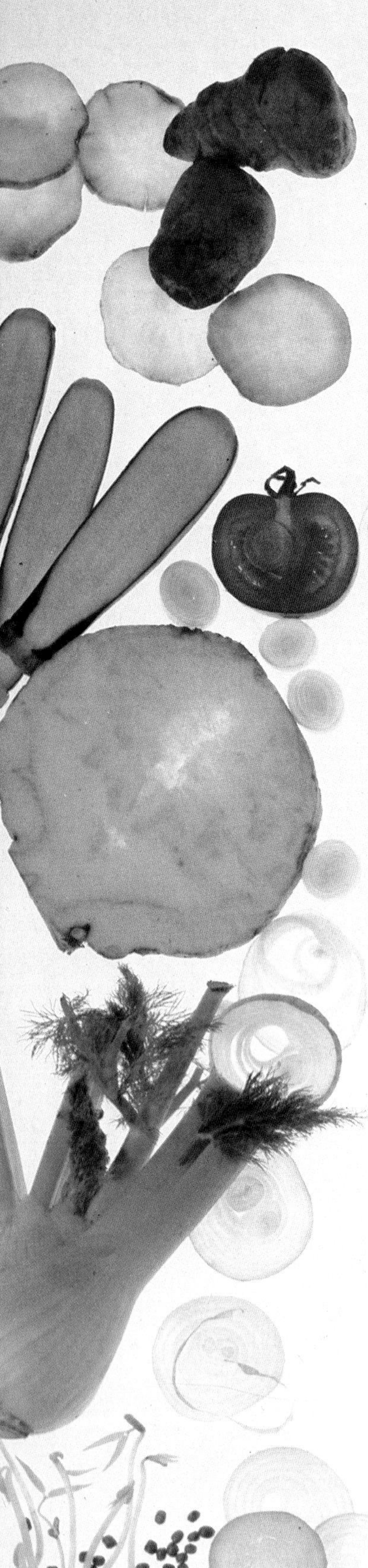

Vegetables can be used in many different ways from starters, salads, main course and vegetarian meals and snacks, to accompaniments to other foods such as meat and fish.

The abundance of fresh vegetables available throughout the year gives a very wide variety to choose from.

Use vegetables as soon as possible – if they must be stored, keep them in a cool airy place or covered in the vegetable compartment of the refrigerator.

PREPARATION

Vegetables should be prepared and cooked carefully to ensure that they are appetizing and to retain as much of their goodness as possible. Often the tastiest and most nutritious parts of vegetables are thrown away, the skins for example. Many vegetables, such as potatoes, carrots and mushrooms, may be just washed or scrubbed instead of peeling.

The stalks of green vegetables can be chopped and cooked with the leaves; the green tops of leeks are very tasty and sweet; and cauliflower leaves can be cooked with the cauliflower. Very young peas and broad beans can be cooked in their pods, as well as mange-tout peas.

COOKING

The most important thing to remember is to cook vegetables as little as possible to retain the best flavour, texture, colour and nutritive value. The simplest way to cook vegetables is to add them to the minimum amount of boiling water. This inactivates an enzyme present in the vegetables which destroys vitamin C. Cover the pan so the vegetables will cook more quickly, and the ones at the top cook in the steam. Alternatively, the vegetables may be steamed over boiling water, which takes longer but because the vegetables never come into contact with the water, their nutritive value is preserved. Root vegetables need longer cooking in more water. Add them to cold water not hot. Never add bicarbonate of soda to improve the colour as this destroys the vitamin C. Vegetables must also be served as soon as possible after cooking as keeping them warm also reduces the vitamin C content and destroys the vividness of the colour.

From the top: sliced Jerusalem artichoke, courgettes, tomato, leeks, celeriac, onions, Florence fennel, beansprouts, whole aubergine, whole salsify, cabbage leaves, chicory leaves, green pepper. Top right: carrots, globe artichoke, sliced mushrooms

GARNISHES

A knob of butter or sprigs of chopped fresh herbs such as parsley, watercress, mint, thym chives and oregano make simple and effectiv garnishes. Grate a little nutmeg or grind blac peppercorns over before serving.

GROWING BEANSPROUTS

It is also possible to produce beansprouts fro dried beans which have not been split. The beansprouts will contain vitamin C.

The easiest and most common beans to sprout are the green mung beans and the sma alfalfa seeds.

Place the beans in a large jar (about half ful as they swell considerably). Pour over warm water, cover the jar with damp muslin, and leave the beans to swell for a few hours or overnight.

Drain and rinse the beans several times a day, keeping them dry between rinses. They should sprout in 3–6 days depending on the type of bean. Store the beansprouts in the refrigerator.

CATEGORIES OF VEGETABLES

Onions and leeks

Vegetable fruits:
Tomato, aubergine, marrow, courgette, peppers, pumpkin, cucumber, avocado pear.

Stalks and shoots:
Fennel, asparagus, celery, artichoke, seakale, cardoon.

Brassicas and leaves:
Brussels sprouts, spinach, red and green cabbages, broccoli, cauliflower.

Tubers:
Potato, sweet potato, Jerusalem artichoke.

Root vegetables:
Carrot, turnip, swede, parsnip, salsify, celeriac, beetroot, kohlrabi.

Pods and seeds:
Peas, beans (runner, French, broad), sweetcorn, okra, mange-tout peas.

Mushrooms

Salads:
Lettuce, chicory, endive, cress, celtuce, corn salad (lamb's lettuce), radicchio, dandelion leaves.

ooking methods

ethod	How to cook	Suitable vegetables
oiling	Root vegetables: place prepared vegetable in a saucepan, just cover with cold salted water, cover the pan and bring to the boil. Simmer until just tender.	Root vegetables Tubers
	Other vegetables: bring the minimum amount of salted water to the boil in a saucepan, add the prepared vegetables and return to the boil. Cover and simmer until just tender but still crisp and a bright colour.	Onions and leeks Vegetable fruits Brassicas and leaves Pods and seeds Mushrooms
	Drain off the water and use it for soups, stocks, or reduce by boiling rapidly and use to glaze vegetables.	
eaming	Place the prepared vegetables in a steamer or a colander over rapidly boiling water. Sprinkle lightly with salt, cover the pan and steam until just tender but still crisp and a bright colour. (This takes a few minutes longer than boiling.)	Root vegetables Tubers
raising	Fry the prepared vegetables in oil or butter without browning. Add the minimum amount of stock or water, add salt and pepper. Cover the pan and simmer until just tender and most of the liquid has evaporated. Alternatively, after frying, place the vegetables in a casserole with the liquid, cover and bake in a moderate oven until tender.	Root vegetables Tubers
hallow frying/sauté	Fry tender vegetables in oil or butter, uncovered, turning until golden brown all over and cooked through. They can be dusted in seasoned flour before cooking.	Onions Vegetable fruits (aubergine, courgette) Leaves (spinach) Mushrooms
	Firmer vegetables must be par-boiled and thoroughly drained before frying.	Root vegetables Tubers
eep frying	Except for chipped potatoes, vegetables are usually coated in flour or batter, or egg and breadcrumbs. Fill a deep heavy saucepan less than half full with oil and heat to 180°C/350°F (or until a cube of bread browns in one minute). Place the prepared vegetables in a frying basket and lower into the hot fat. Cook until golden brown and cooked through.	Onions, potatoes Vegetable fruits (aubergine, courgette pepper) Brassicas (cauliflower) Mushrooms
aking	Place the prepared vegetables in an ovenproof dish, covered or uncovered. Bake in a moderate oven until tender. Some vegetables may be stuffed.	Onions and leeks Vegetable fruits Brassicas (red and green cabbage) Root vegetables Tubers Mushrooms
oasting	Place the prepared vegetables in hot fat in a roasting tin and bake in a hot oven for about 1 hour until golden brown, crisp and tender. Alternatively, par-boil before roasting.	Root vegetables Tubers
rilling	Brush the prepared vegetables with oil, season and place under a moderate grill until browned and cooked, turning. Firmer vegetables may be par-boiled first.	Vegetable fruits (tomato, courgette, peppers, aubergines) Onions

RICE, PASTA AND PULSES

RICE

Rice, which is the staple diet of Eastern countries, is also widely used in the West as a vegetable accompaniment and as the basis for more substantial meals such as risotto, paella, kedgeree, stuffings and sweet dishes.

TYPES OF RICE

There are numerous varieties of rice, which fall into two categories. Firstly, the brown unpolished rice and the white polished rice which may be sold raw, par-boiled or fully cooked (instant rice). Secondly wild rice, which is not a cereal, but long black seeds from a wild grass. It is very expensive and usually served with poultry and game birds.

SHAPES OF RICE

Rice also comes in 3 different shapes: long grain rice, which is usually used in savoury dishes and for plain boiling as the grains separate on cooking; medium and short grain rice, which are moister and stick together on cooking and are therefore more suitable for risottos, stuffings, moulds and sweet dishes; ground rice and rice flour, which are used as thickening agents and for baking.

COOKING RICE

There are several methods of cooking rice, the most common is to boil it in salted water in a pan, but rice can also be cooked in the oven. Allow 50 g/2 oz uncooked rice per person.

BOILED RICE

Method 1: add the rice to a large pan of boilin salted water and boil, uncovered, for 10–15 minutes until the rice is tender and there is no hard core left in the centre. Drain the rice well *Method 2:* measure the rice and water into a saucepan in the proportion of twice as much water as rice, for example, 600 ml/1 pint wate and ½ teaspoon salt to 225 g/8 oz rice.

Bring the water to the boil, add the salt, rice cover the pan and simmer for about 15 minute until the rice is tender and the water is absorbed

OVEN-COOKED RICE

Measure the rice into an ovenproof dish and pour over boiling water and salt (proportions as for boiled rice, method 2). Cover and bake in a preheated oven at 180°C, 350°F, Gas Mar 4 for 30–45 minutes until the rice is tender anc all the water has been absorbed.

Brown rice is cooked in exactly the same way but takes twice as long to cook.

PULSES

Pulses are the dried seeds of vegetables such as peas and beans. For centuries they have been the staple winter diet of many countries as they store well and are very nutritious. They are especially rich in protein, minerals and vitamins, but unlike other vegetables do not contain vitamin C.

They can be used as vegetable accompaniments, starters and salads as well as main course and vegetarian dishes. However, they do have to be reconstituted with water and then cooked, which is a lengthy process.

SOAKING AND COOKING

Beans may be soaked in several ways, depending on the time available. Pick over the beans and wash them, removing any grit. Soak them in the proportion of 225 g/8 oz beans to 600 ml/1 pint water. They will absorb a lot of water and should double in size and weight.

Long soaking

Soak in cold water for 8 to 12 hours.

Short soaking

a) Pour over boiling water, soak for 2 hours.
b) Pour over cold water in a pan, bring to the boil, cook for 2 minutes, then soak for 1 hour.

Drain the beans and make up the soaking water to 600 ml/1 pint with water. Add 1 teaspoon salt to every 225 g/8 oz beans, bring to the boil, cover and simmer for 30 minutes to 3 hours. See the chart for specific cooking times.

COOKING TIMES FOR PULSES

The most common pulses are listed here. Cooking time depends on the type and quality of the bean, as well as the length of soaking, sc use this chart as a guide and test the beans frequently towards the end of the cooking time. Beans taking longer to cook may need more water during cooking to prevent them boiling dry.

Type of bean	*Long soaking*	*Short soaking*
Black eye peas	½–¾ hr	¾–1 hr
Broad beans	1½ hr	2 hr
Butter beans	¾ hr	1 hr
Chick peas	1 hr	1½ hr
Dried peas	1 hr	1½ hr
Flageolet beans	¾ hr	1 hr
Haricot beans	1 hr	1½ hr
Red kidney beans	1 hr	1½ hr
Soya beans	2 hr	2½ hr

The following beans do not need soaking before cooking, but soaking will shorten the cooking time.

Type of bean	*Short soaking*	*Unsoaked*
Green lentils	15 mins	¾–1 hr
Split peas	20–30 mins	¾–1 hr
Split red lentils	10 mins	30–40 mins

Pasta is a dough made from flour, salt and water, usually enriched with eggs. The addition of chopped spinach or spinach juice makes a delicious green pasta. Wholewheat flour can be used to give a brown pasta.

Pasta is available in a large variety of shapes and sizes. The most common are spaghetti, macaroni, tagliatelle (noodles), cannelloni, lasagne, and fancy shapes such as shells, wheels, butterflies and letters.

Pasta can also be made at home and is not nearly as difficult as it may seem. Only the simple, flat shapes can be made at home, as the others require a special machine.

COOKING PASTA

All pasta is cooked in a large pan of boiling, salted water, uncovered. The time varies from 5–20 minutes, depending on whether the pasta is fresh, dried or stuffed, and according to the shape and size of the pasta. A little oil added to the cooking water helps to prevent the pasta from sticking together. It should be cooked until just tender, but still firm *(al dente)*, then drained well.

The Italians allow 75 to 100 g/3–4 oz pasta per person, but 50 g/2 oz is usually enough for British taste.

Home-made Pasta

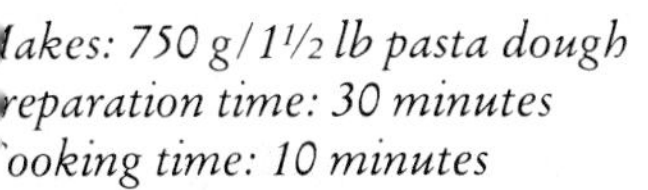

lakes: 750 g/1½ lb pasta dough
reparation time: 30 minutes
ooking time: 10 minutes

50 g/1 lb plain flour
teaspoon salt
eggs
tablespoons water
0 g/2 oz butter
5–50 g/1–2 oz Parmesan
cheese, grated

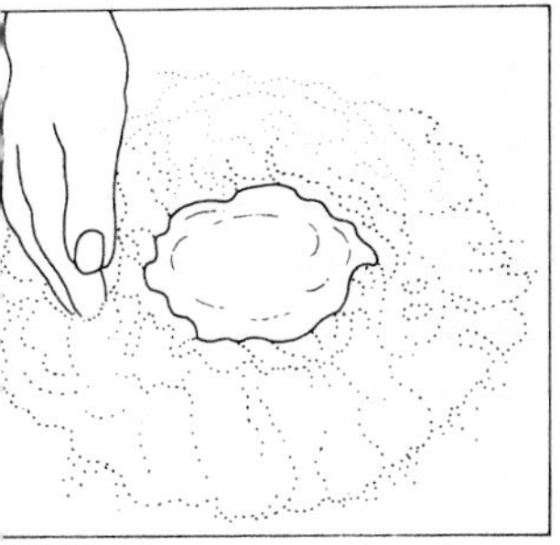

aw flour into the centre

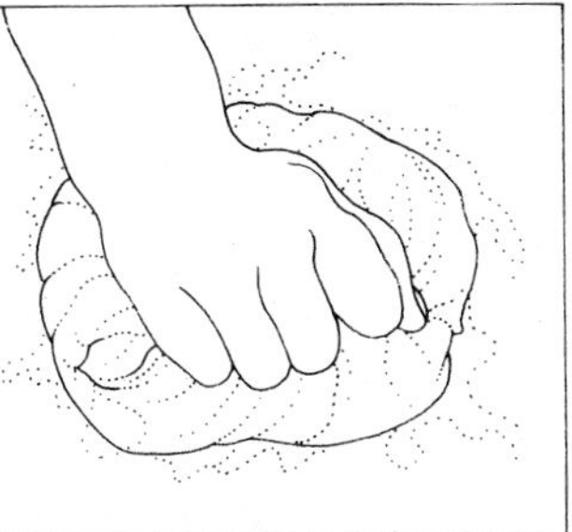

ıead the pasta dough

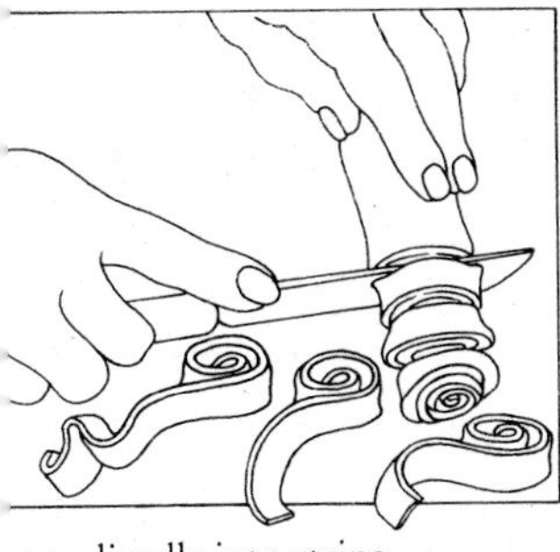

ıt tagliatelle into strips

About 225 g/8 oz pasta dough will serve 4 people. Any remaining dough may be refrigerated or frozen before rolling out. It will keep for 1 day if kept covered in the refrigerator, or 2–3 months if wrapped and frozen. In both cases bring the dough back to room temperature before rolling out.

1. Mix the flour and salt together on a large board or on a cool working surface. Make a well in the centre of the flour. Lightly beat the eggs and water and pour the mixture into the well.
2. Using your fingers, gradually draw the flour into the egg mixture until a stiff dough is formed. Knead the dough vigorously for 10 minutes with the heels of the hands until the dough is smooth and elastic.
3. (Alternatively, an electric mixer with a dough hook attachment may be used. Place all the ingredients in a mixer bowl and mix on a low speed for about 5 minutes.)
4. Divide the dough into 3 equal pieces. Roll out the first piece on a lightly floured surface, stretching the dough as much as possible without tearing it, until it is very thin and almost transparent. It should be pliable.
5. Lift the rolled dough and lay it on a clean tea towel over the back of a chair. Leave the dough to rest for 15 minutes. Roll out the other two pieces in the same way.
6. Cut the dough as required, then leave it to dry for 10 minutes before cooking.
7. For lasagne cut the dough into strips about 5 cm/2 inches wide and for cannelloni 10 cm/4 inches wide.
8. For tagliatelle, roll up the dough loosely like a Swiss roll, cut across at 5 mm/¼ inch intervals, then unroll the strips.
9. To cook, place in a large pan of boiling salted water and boil for 3–5 minutes until tender, but still slightly firm — *al dente*.
10. Drain, return the pasta to the pan and stir in the butter. Serve hot with grated Parmesan cheese; or make into other pasta recipes.

FISH

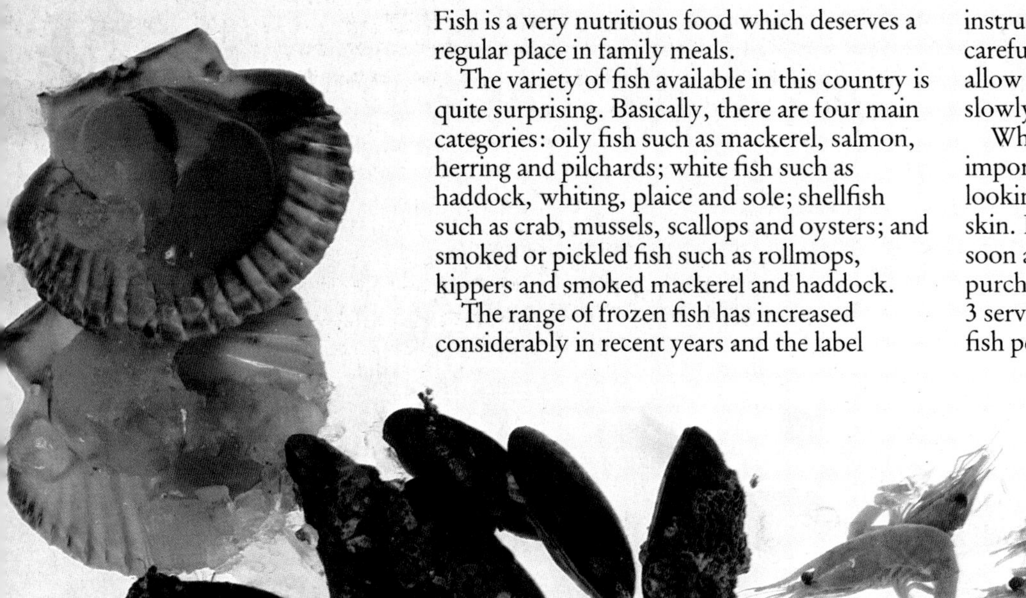

Fish is a very nutritious food which deserves a regular place in family meals.

The variety of fish available in this country is quite surprising. Basically, there are four main categories: oily fish such as mackerel, salmon, herring and pilchards; white fish such as haddock, whiting, plaice and sole; shellfish such as crab, mussels, scallops and oysters; and smoked or pickled fish such as rollmops, kippers and smoked mackerel and haddock.

The range of frozen fish has increased considerably in recent years and the label instructions should always be followed carefully. If cooking the fish from frozen, allow half as long again and cook the fish mor slowly than usual.

When buying wet fish, freshness is all important. The fish should be firm and bright looking with no flabbiness, sunken eyes or du skin. It should always be cooked and eaten as soon as possible, preferably on the day of purchase. Allow 450 g/1 lb of boneless fish fc 3 servings, and 225–350 g/8–12 oz of whole fish per portion.

PREPARATION OF FISH

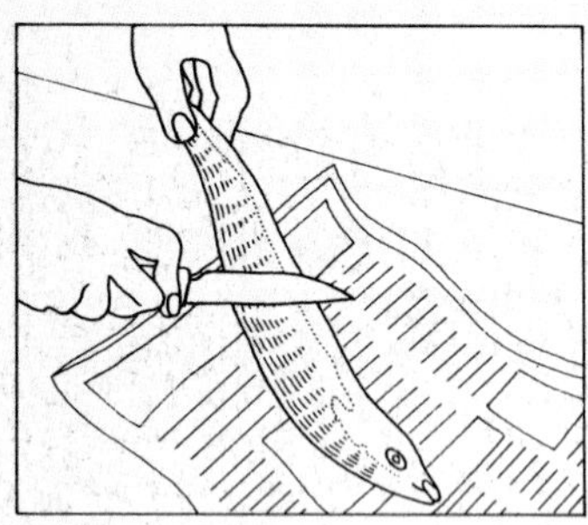

Scaling fish

Most fishmongers will clean and fillet fish ready for cooking. However, it is not a difficult job to do at home, all you need is a thin sharp knife, running cold water and some newspaper.

SCALING

This is only necessary for fish which have very scaly skins, e.g. herring, mullet, pilchards.

1. Lay the fish on newspaper and hold it by the tail.
2. Push the scales from the tail towards the head with the blunt side of a knife.
3. Rinse the fish under cold water.

CLEANING

This simply involves removing the gut. In round fish this is found in the belly, but in flat fish it is found in the cavity immediately below the head.

Round fish e.g. cod, haddock, mackerel, trout, whiting.

1. Cut off the head just below the gills, and discard it.
2. Slit the belly open and scrape out all the entrails.
3. Rinse the cavity under running cold water.
4. Gently scrape away any black membrane attached to the cavity walls and rinse again.
5. Cut off all the fins with scissors.

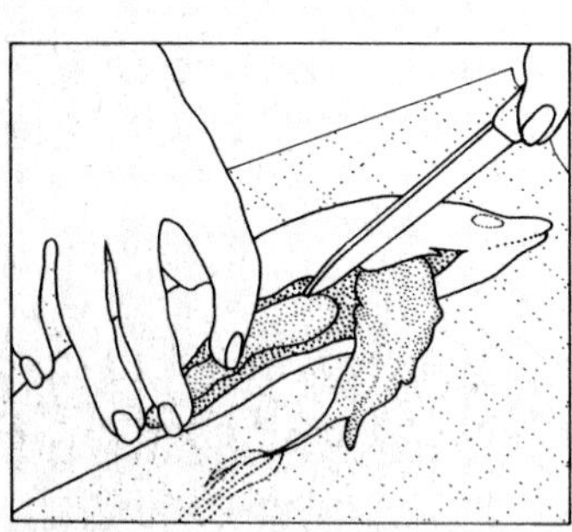

Cleaning round fish

Flat fish e.g. plaice, sole, dab, turbot, brill.

1. Make a semi-circular cut just below the head on the dark skin-side; cut off the head.
2. Scrape out all the entrails from the cavity.
3. Wash under running cold water.
4. Cut off all the fins with scissors.

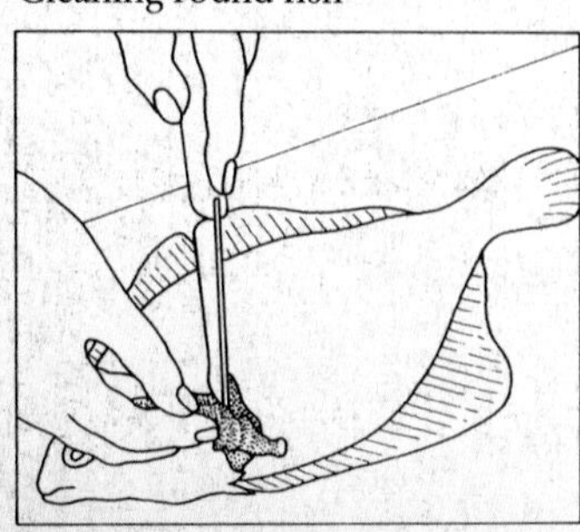

Cleaning flat fish

FILLETING

Round fish of 450 g/1 lb or over give 2 fillets, one from either side of the backbone.

1. Lay the beheaded and cleaned fish flat and place your left hand on top to steady it.
2. Slanting the knife blade towards the bone, ease the flesh from the bone with short slicing movements, working from head to tail, until the whole top fillet is freed. Cut off at the tail.
3. Lift the backbone and pull it away from th underfillet, from head to tail. Cut off at the ta

Flat fish

There are two methods of filleting, depending on the size of the fish.

Cross-cut fillets (for cutting one fillet from either side of small fish of about 450 g/1 lb).

1. Lay the cleaned and beheaded fish flat witl the head facing to the right.
2. Working from the head end, insert the kni against the bone and with a sawing movemen free the whole upper fillet from the bone.
3. Lift the bone and with a sawing movemen free the bone from the under fillet.

Quarter-cut fillets (for cutting fillets from fisl weighing 750 g–1 kg/1½–2 lb).

1. Lay the cleaned and beheaded fish flat, da skin uppermost, with the tail facing you. Cut off the tail.
2. Starting at the head end, make an incision along the length of the backbone.
3. Work the knife under the cut, and, keepin it pressed against the bone, ease the fish off tl bone until a quarter fillet is freed.
4. Turn the fish around and repeat to remov the second fillet.
5. Turn the fish over, cut down the backbon and remove the last two fillets in the same wa

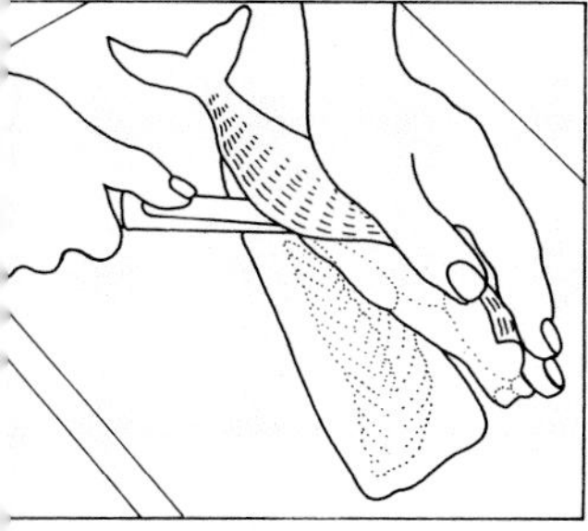

illeting round fish

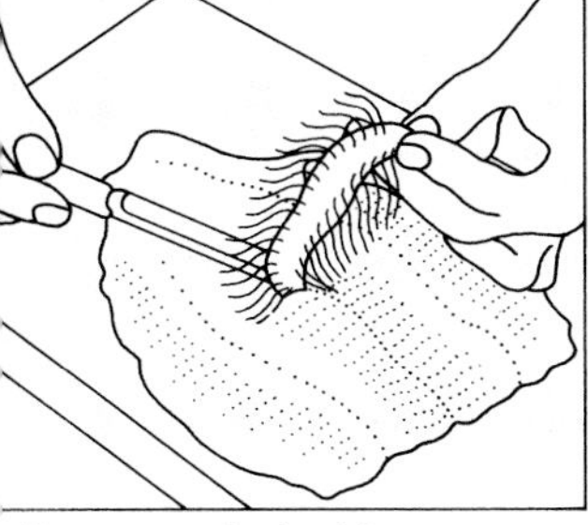

ulling away the backbone

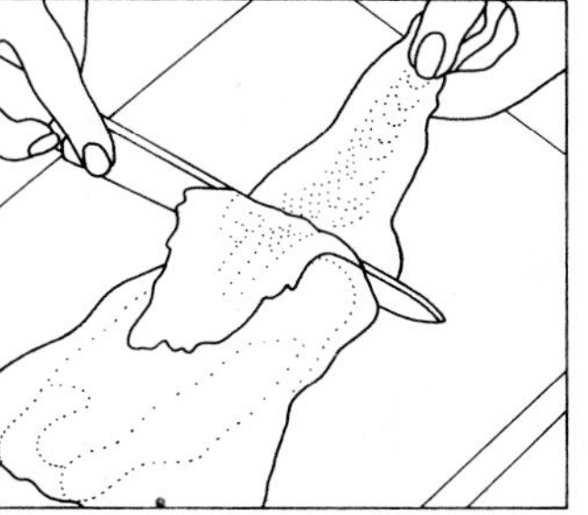

kinning fillets of flat fish

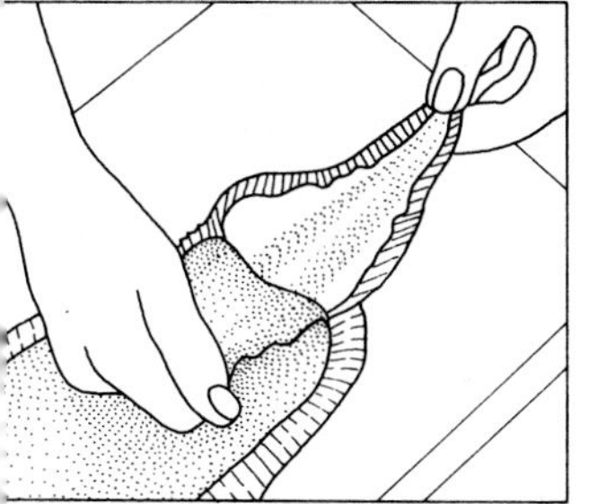

kinning Dover sole

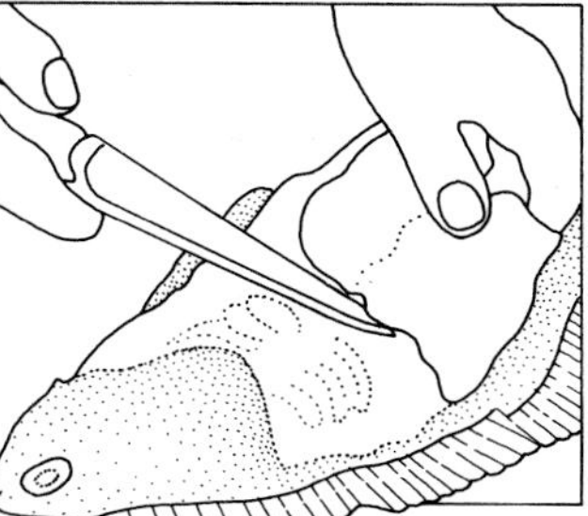

laking quarter-cut fillets

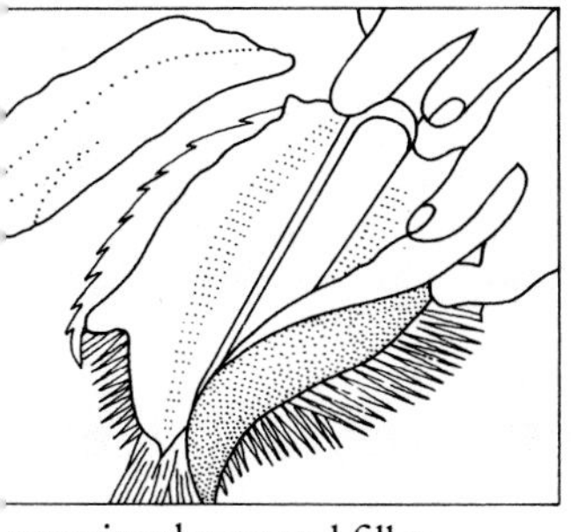

emoving the second fillet

SKINNING

It is not essential to skin fish but many people like to remove the dark coloured skin.

Fillets

1. Lay the fillet skin-side down on a board with the tail towards you.
2. Cut through the flesh about 1 cm/½ inch from the tail end, and hold this firmly in one hand with fingers dipped in salt to give a good firm grip.
3. Using a sharp knife, push the flesh forward towards the head until completely freed.

Whole fish

This is a job best left to the fishmonger except in the case of Dover sole.

1. Lay the sole flat and dark side uppermost.
2. Make a slit through the skin at the tail end.
3. Grip the skin with fingers dipped in salt and pull sharply from tail to head. It should come away in one piece.

BONING A MACKEREL OR HERRING

1. Cut off the head, tail and all the fins.
2. Slit the fish open along the belly.
3. Lay the fish flesh-side down on a board, and with your thumbs press heavily downwards all along the backbone.
4. Turn the fish flesh-side up, and pull away the loosened backbone with most of the smaller bones attached.

SEASONING FISH

After cleaning and preparing the fish sprinkle it well with salt and pepper, then cover the fish and refrigerate until ready to cook. Seasoning the fish at least 1 hour in advance greatly improves the flavour.

Left: scallops, mussels, prawns
Right: from the top: 2 herring, trout, whole plaice and fillet, kipper, smoked haddock

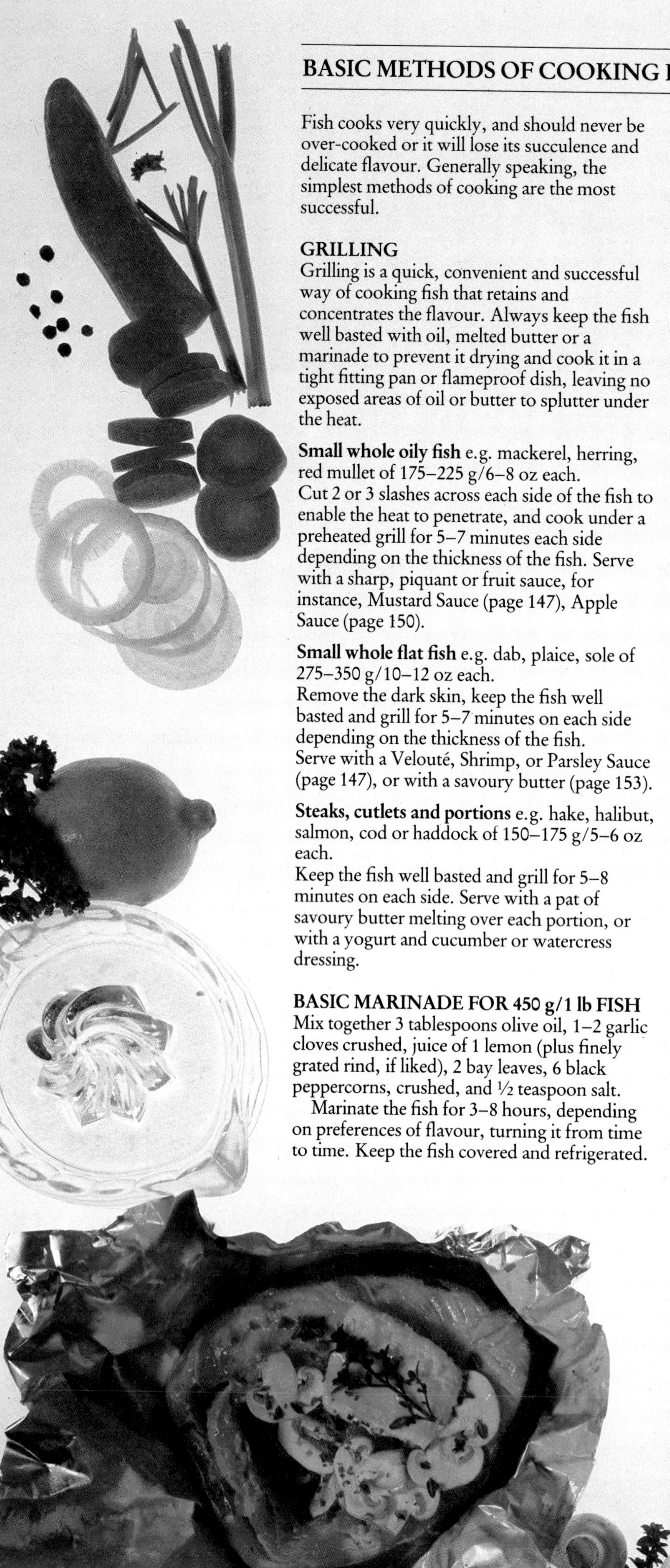

BASIC METHODS OF COOKING FISH

Fish cooks very quickly, and should never be over-cooked or it will lose its succulence and delicate flavour. Generally speaking, the simplest methods of cooking are the most successful.

GRILLING

Grilling is a quick, convenient and successful way of cooking fish that retains and concentrates the flavour. Always keep the fish well basted with oil, melted butter or a marinade to prevent it drying and cook it in a tight fitting pan or flameproof dish, leaving no exposed areas of oil or butter to splutter under the heat.

Small whole oily fish e.g. mackerel, herring, red mullet of 175–225 g/6–8 oz each.
Cut 2 or 3 slashes across each side of the fish to enable the heat to penetrate, and cook under a preheated grill for 5–7 minutes each side depending on the thickness of the fish. Serve with a sharp, piquant or fruit sauce, for instance, Mustard Sauce (page 147), Apple Sauce (page 150).

Small whole flat fish e.g. dab, plaice, sole of 275–350 g/10–12 oz each.
Remove the dark skin, keep the fish well basted and grill for 5–7 minutes on each side depending on the thickness of the fish.
Serve with a Velouté, Shrimp, or Parsley Sauce (page 147), or with a savoury butter (page 153).

Steaks, cutlets and portions e.g. hake, halibut, salmon, cod or haddock of 150–175 g/5–6 oz each.
Keep the fish well basted and grill for 5–8 minutes on each side. Serve with a pat of savoury butter melting over each portion, or with a yogurt and cucumber or watercress dressing.

BASIC MARINADE FOR 450 g/1 lb FISH

Mix together 3 tablespoons olive oil, 1–2 garlic cloves crushed, juice of 1 lemon (plus finely grated rind, if liked), 2 bay leaves, 6 black peppercorns, crushed, and ½ teaspoon salt.

Marinate the fish for 3–8 hours, depending on preferences of flavour, turning it from time to time. Keep the fish covered and refrigerated.

STEAMING

Steaming is a good and economical way of cooking, provided the fish is totally enclosed that the juices are retained for adding to an accompanying sauce.
Steaming on a plate: ideal for small amounts folded thin fillets or thin steaks.

Set the fish on a buttered plate, cover with buttered paper and a pan lid, set the plate ove a pan of boiling water and steam for 15–20 minutes.
Steaming in a parcel: for larger portions or whole fish.

Wrap the fish loosely but securely in buttered foil and cook in a perforated steame over boiling water. Allow 12–15 minutes per 450 g/1 lb plus 12 – 15 minutes, depending on the thickness of the fish. Serve with a Shrimp, or Parsley Sauce (page 147).

POACHING

Poaching is a method of cooking in barely enough liquid to cover the fish. The water temperature must be kept well below boiling point so that it 'quivers' rather than bubbles.

Poach thin fish for 5–10 minutes, larger fis for 8–12 minutes, depending on thickness. If serving the fish cold, poach for 2–3 minutes, then remove from the heat, allowing the fish t cool in the covered pan.

Poach smoked cod or haddock in milk and water; shellfish or early season salmon in plai salted water; and skate, trout, late season salmon or mackerel in court-bouillon.

Simple court-bouillon
Put 1.2 litres/2 pints water into a saucepan an add a peeled and sliced onion and carrot, 8 crushed black peppercorns, a few parsley stalks, 2 tablespoons white wine vinegar and 2 teaspoons salt. Simmer, uncovered, for 30 minutes, then strain and use as required.
Large whole fish: if no large fish kettle is available, bake in foil in the oven (see Salmon Trout en Bellevue, page 76).

BAKING

There are many ways of cooking fish in the oven such as braising, poaching, sousing and pickling, stuffing and baking whole, and fillets gratinée (see Fillets of Whiting Gratinée, page 74). The method described below is particularly useful for retaining the flavour and juices and for minimizing any cooking smells.
Baked fish in foil parcels: (ideal for small, whol fish such as red mullet or mackerel; or portion such as salmon, halibut or turbot steaks).

Butter oval pieces of foil large enough to enclose the fish loosely. Lay the seasoned fish in the centre, sprinkle the fish with lemon juice, chopped fresh herbs, sliced mushrooms (if liked) and a nut of butter. Seal the parcel securely, set on a baking sheet and cook in a preheated oven at 190°C, 375°F, Gas Mark 5 for 20–25 minutes. Serve in the opened foil parcel, complete with juices.

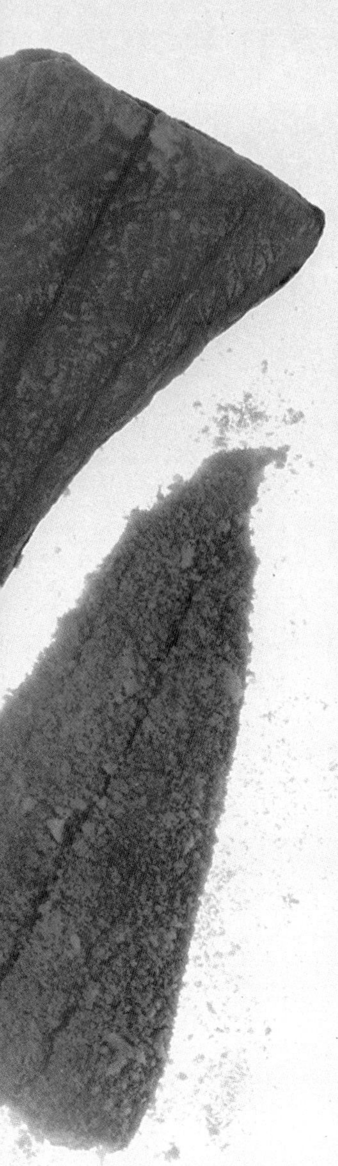

FRYING IN DEEP FAT

This is a quick method of cooking 2.5 cm/1 inch thick fish to crisp, golden perfection, but one that needs constant vigilance because a pan of hot fat is a potential fire hazard. Use a deep pan, fitted with a frying basket, and a thermometer.

General method

1. Prepare the fish by coating in flour, then egg, beaten with 1 teaspoon cold water, and finally a coating of fine, dry white breadcrumbs; or dip the fish in batter (see below).
2. Half fill a frying pan with vegetable oil and heat slowly, with the frying basket in position, until the thermometer registers 180°C, 195°C–350°F, 380°F, the higher temperature is for very small pieces of fish that cook quickly.
3. Raise the basket, put in the fish (a small quantity at a time as large amounts reduce the temperature too much) and lower gently into the fat. (Do not use a frying basket when frying fish coated in batter, as it tends to stick.)
4. Fry until the coating is crisp and golden and the fish cooked through. This will take from 1½–5 minutes, depending on the thickness of the pieces. Turn once.
5. Lift out in the basket (or with a perforated spoon if the fish is battered), drain for a second or two, then turn on to a baking sheet lined with crumpled kitchen paper. Keep hot in the oven until ready to serve.
6. Cool the oil, then strain it into a storage jar ready for the next time.

SHALLOW FRYING À la meunière

This is a quick and attractive method of frying flour-coated fish to a crisp golden finish in butter. Use for small whole fish such as dab, plaice, trout, small mackerel, herring, sole, sprats and sardines or for thin fillets of sole, plaice, dab or John Dory. Clarify the butter before using it to prevent it burning. To do this, bring the butter slowly to the boil, let it settle for a few minutes, then pour it slowly through a damp muslin-lined strainer so that the salty white solids are left behind. Alternatively, fry the fish in a mixture of oil and unsalted butter.

1. Season the cleaned fish with salt and pepper.
2. Coat the fish evenly in flour, shaking off the excess.
3. Heat enough oil and unsalted butter (half and half) to cover the base of a shallow frying pan to a depth of about 3 mm/1/8th inch.
4. Heat until the butter ceases to foam then put in the fish in a single, uncrowded layer.
5. Fry over a moderate heat, turning once, until the fish is golden brown on both sides. Allow a total of 6–8 minutes for fillets, 8–12 minutes for whole fish.
6. Lift the fish on to a hot serving dish and keep hot.
7. If the fat is overbrowned, wipe out the pan.
8. Melt about 50 g/2 oz of salted butter in the pan and heat rapidly until it turns golden and begins to smell 'nutty'. Immediately pour it over the fish, followed by a sprinkling of lemon juice or wine vinegar, and some chopped fresh parsley. Serve immediately.

Batter Coating

akes about 300 ml/½ pint tter (enough for 4 portions of h).

0 g/4 oz plain flour, sifted with a large pinch of salt
ablespoons oil
0 ml/¼ pint cold water
(size 1 or 2) egg whites

This is a light, very crisp batter, suitable only for portions of boneless fish to be deep fried. Dip the fish in the batter immediately before frying.

1. Put the flour into a basin, make a well in the centre and pour the oil and water into it. Gradually mix in the flour from the sides with a small wire whisk, and beat until smooth batter is formed. Leave to rest, or not, as convenient.
2. Just before using the batter, whisk the egg whites until stiff but not dry, and fold them gently into the batter. Use immediately.

MEAT

Cuts of meat differ in their muscular structure and it is vital, if you want tender meat, to choose a cooking method suitable to the cut. Although only prime cuts can be grilled, roasted at high temperatures or fried in an open frying pan, other cuts make excellent dishes if cooked by slow, moist methods.

Fresh meat is a perishable food and should not be kept for any length of time. Always transfer meat to a refrigerator within 2–3 hours of purchase and follow any label directions about storing and keeping. If there are none, remove the meat from its plastic wrappings and cover it loosely with foil or film so that air can circulate around it. Cook minced meats and offal on the day of purchase, small cuts within 2 days and joints within 3 days if kept in the refrigerator.

For longer storage, buy frozen meat and store it in your freezer. Remember that frozen meat is best allowed to thaw and come to room temperature before cooking. The exception is steaks and chops which can, if necessary, be cooked while frozen, provided the cooking is gentle and allows time for thawing as well as cooking. Once thawed, all meat should be treated as fresh.

How much meat to allow depends on appetites and personal inclinations, but in general allow 90–175 g/3½–6 oz boneless meat per person, or about 225 g/8 oz meat on the bone.

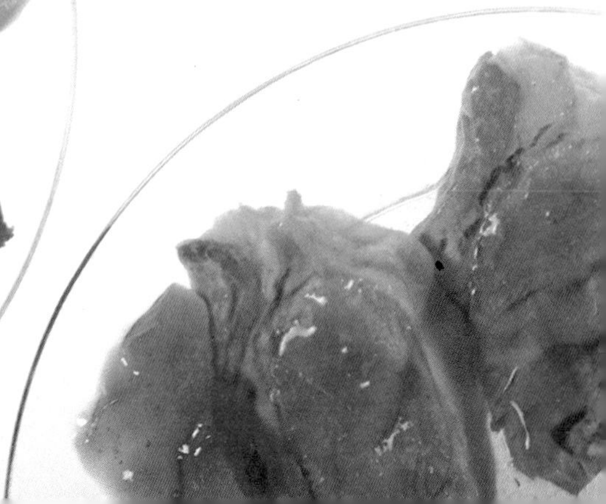

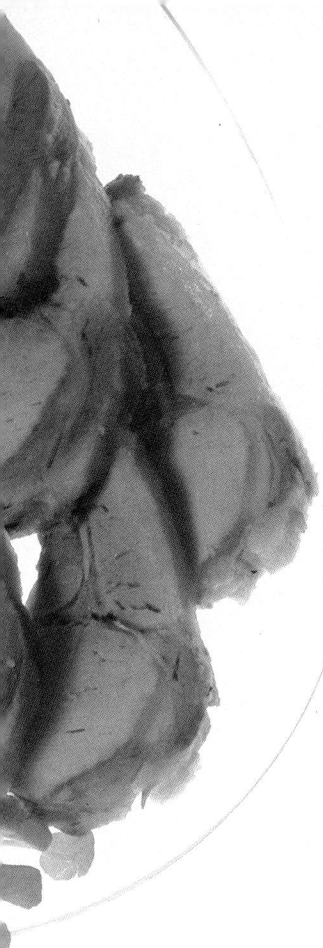

BASIC METHODS OF COOKING MEAT

ROASTING

The dry heat circulating around the joint while roasting gradually penetrates and cooks the meat from the outside inwards, so the centre is always rarer than the outside. The hotter the oven and the shorter the roasting time the greater this differential will be.

Slow roasting is recommended for small joints because the cooking is more even and the weight loss from shrinkage and evaporation appreciably less. Even so, joints of under 1 kg/2 lb in weight are better cooked by a moist method such as pot roasting, braising, cooking in a 'roasting' bag or wrapped loosely in foil.

Cuts to use

Beef: sirloin, rump, wing rib, fore rib, fillet, aitchbone, top rump.
Lamb: leg, shoulder, loin, best end of neck, stuffed breast.
Pork: any joint of young pork is suitable for slow roasting.
Veal: only prime cuts of veal, such as leg fillet and loin, are suitable for roasting, and these should always be covered with a thin layer of pork fat or fat bacon to prevent drying. Pot roasting or braising are the best methods for cooking joints of veal.

Method

1. Preheat the oven to 180°C, 350°F, Gas Mark 4.
2. Wipe the meat with a damp paper towel and season with salt and pepper. If required, stuff the meat and tie or skewer into a neat shape.
3. Weigh the joint, including any stuffing, and calculate the cooking time.
4. Put the meat into a roasting tin, preferably standing on a rack so that the heat can circulate all around it. If using a meat thermometer insert it into the centre of the thickest part of the joint, making sure that the tip is not touching a bone.
5. If the joint has no covering of natural fat, spread about 1 tablespoon dripping or oil or butter over the top surface, more if vegetables are to be baked around the joint.
6. Roast the joint for the calculated time.
7. Lift it on to a hot dish, remove any trussing and leave to stand while making the gravy and dishing up the rest of the meal.
8. Pour any surplus fat from the roasting tin and make gravy in the tin, stirring and scraping up the browned and savoury meat juices from the base of the tin.

Timing the cooking

The chart below is a useful guide but remember that bone is a good heat conductor, so joints on the bone cook in less time than boneless meat. Similarly, thin cuts of meat or large joints over 2¼ kg/5 lb in weight need less time. For any one of these factors reduce the following times by 4–5 minutes per 450 g/1 lb.

eat	*Average slow roasting times (oven preheated to 180°C, 350°F, Gas Mark 4)*	*Thermometer reading*	*Classic accompaniments*
ef underdone	25 mins per 450 g/1 lb plus 25 mins	60°C/140°F	Yorkshire or herb pudding, horseradish sauce, English or French mustard, thin gravy
medium cooked	30 mins per 450 g/1 lb plus 30 mins	71°C/160°F	
well done	35 mins per 450 g/1 lb plus 35 mins	77°C/170°F	
mb medium to well done	30 mins per 450 g/1 lb plus 30 mins	80°C/175°F	Redcurrant or mint jelly, mint sauce or onion sauce
rk well done	35 mins per 450 g/1 lb plus 30 mins	82°C/180°F	Sage and onion or fruit stuffing, apple sauce
eal medium to well done	30 mins per 450 g/1 lb plus 30 mins	77°C/170°F	Lemon and herb stuffing, bacon rolls

GRILLING

Grilling under a gas or electric grill, or over glowing charcoal, is a fierce method of cooking small, very tender cuts of prime quality meat, and is not recommended for very thin cuts.

Although speedy, this method needs the full attention of the cook because, to prevent drying, the meat needs frequent basting.

Cuts to use for grilling	*Average cooking time*	*Special points*
Beef Fillet steak 2.5 cm/1 inch thick Rump steak 2.5 cm/1 inch thick Ground beef patties 2.5 cm/1 inch thick	7 mins for rare 10 mins for medium 12 mins for well done	Brush steaks with oil before grilling. Turn at half time. Top with chilled Herb, Mustard or Maître d'Hôtel butter on completion of cooking, or serve with Béarnaise Sauce (see pages 148 or 153).
Lamb Loin or chump chops 2–2.5 cm/¾–1 inch thick Best end cutlets 2–2.5 cm/¾–1 inch thick Shoulder chops 2–2.5 cm/¾–1 inch thick	10–15 mins 7–10 mins 12–18 mins	Brush with oil or savoury butter and turn at half-time. Serve with a Mint, Soubise or Tomato Sauce (see Sauces pages 146–151).
Kidneys	8–10 mins	Best grilled with a frequently applied sauce baste. Cut in halves, skewer open, keep well basted with oil or melted butter.
Pork Loin chops 2–2.5 cm/¾–1 inch thick Shoulder chops 2–2.5 cm/¾–1 inch thick Gammon steaks, Bacon chops	12–16 mins 14–20 mins 10–12 mins	Brush with oil and baste with pan juices. Serve with apple sauce. Keep well basted with a barbecue sauce. Brush with melted butter and turn at half-time.

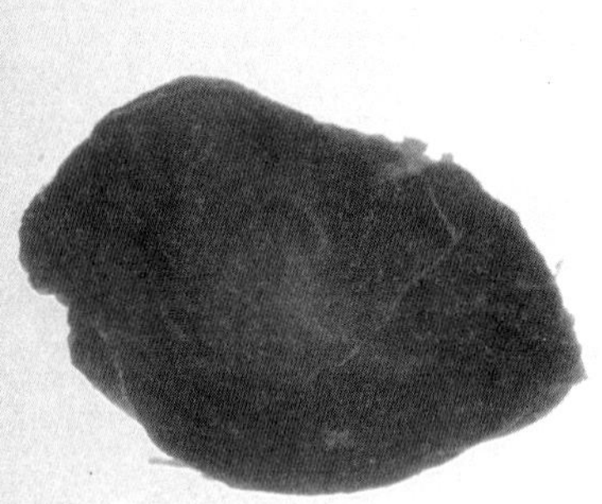

General method for grilling

1. Preheat the grill until hot. Brush the grill rack with oil to prevent the meat sticking.
2. Wipe the meat with a damp paper towel. To prevent curling during cooking, snip any fat border at 2 cm/¾ inch intervals with scissors. Brush both sides of the meat with oil or melted butter and sprinkle with black pepper. (Salt tends to draw out the meat juices and is therefore best added after cooking.)
3. Lay the meat flat on the rack and grill, close to the heat, for 1–2 minutes each side to lightly brown the surfaces.
4. Then, depending on the type of grill, either reposition the grill pan to its lowest position or reduce the heat and continue cooking gently, turning and basting the meat every few minutes, until cooked to your liking.

Above: Veal escalopes, plain and coated with egg and breadcrumb for frying

SHALLOW FRYING

This is a fast method of cooking slices or small pieces of tender prime quality meat. It is ideally suited to steaks (up to 2.5 cm/1 inch thick), chops and escalopes.

Use a heavy-based frying pan to distribute the heat evenly, and control the heat carefully so that the fat is very hot initially to sear the surface of the meat on each side, then adjust the heat according to the type and thickness of the meat. Have all the accompanying foods and garnishes ready, and the plates hot, before you begin to fry.

Open frying: suitable for all thin cut steaks, chops and escalopes up to a maximum thickness of 2.5 cm/1 inch. When frying uncoated meat, heat sufficient fat to cover the base of the pan to a depth of 3 mm/⅛ inch. Double the amount of fat when frying meat coated in egg and breadcrumbs (e.g. veal escalopes), which absorb more fat. Use the pan juices as a base for a sauce.

Dry frying: when frying fatty meat such as slices of belly pork or bacon rashers it is only necessary to grease the heated pan with oil before putting in the meat.

Covered frying: this is a rather slower and moister method of frying, and is ideal for slightly less tender cuts of meat as it helps to tenderize them. After the initial browning, simply cover the pan with a lid and allow the meat to cook through over a moderate heat. For extra moisture and flavour, add a little cider, wine, stock or cream to the cooking juices to form a sauce to serve with the meat.

Preparing the meat

Wipe the meat with a damp paper towel. Beat boneless steak or veal escalopes to flatten and help tenderize them (see chicken breasts). A light coating of seasoned flour, applied immediately before frying, absorbs any surface moisture and enables the meat to brown attractively. Heavier coatings such as egg and crumbs protect soft textured meats and provide a golden, crisp and crunchy surface. Extra flavourings such as dried herbs, grated cheese or dry mustard can be added to the bread-crumbs used for coating. If uncoated, pat the meat dry with kitchen paper just before frying, as wet surfaces do not brown well.

:uts to use for frying	Method and total cooking time	Special points
eef		
illet steak 2–2.5 cm/¾–1 inch thick	open fry 6–8 mins	All times are for medium cooked steaks, i.e. pink and juicy inside. If preferred well done, increase cooking time by 2–4 minutes. Top steaks with a savoury butter, or pour over a pan sauce.
ump steak 2–2.5 cm/¾–1 inch thick	covered fry 8–10 mins	
irloin steak 2–2.5 cm/¾–1 inch thick	open fry 8–10 mins	
linced beef patties 2–2.5 cm/¾–1 inch thick	open fry 8–10 mins	
linute steak 5 mm/¼ inch thick	open fry 4–6 mins	
hin cut steaks 5 mm/¼ inch thick	open fry 3–5 mins	
lash fry steaks 5 mm/¼ inch thick	open fry 2–3 mins	
amb		
oin chops 2–2.5 cm/¾–1 inch thick	covered fry 12–15 mins	After initial browning cook over moderate to low heat. Times are for moderately well cooked lamb. Top with a herb or mustard butter or serve with mint or cranberry sauce or redcurrant jelly.
:hump chops 2–2.5 cm/¾–1 inch thick	covered fry 12–18 mins	
Ieck chops 2–2.5 cm/¾–1 inch thick	covered fry 12–15 mins	
hin chops	open fry 6–8 mins or covered fry 8–10 mins	
ork		
oin chops 2 cm/¾ inch thick	open fry 15–18 mins or covered fry 18–20 mins	Cook thoroughly but do not allow to become dry. Serve with a piquant apple or gooseberry sauce.
houlder chops 2 cm/¾ inch thick	covered fry 18–20 mins	
3elly (streaky) slices 5 mm/⅛ inch thick	dry fry 12–15 mins	Cook until the surfaces are slightly crisp and golden brown. Serve as above.
acon		
;ammon rashers 5 mm–1 cm/¼–½ inch ıick	open fry 8–12 mins	Fry over moderate heat.
acon chops 5 mm–1 cm/⅛–½ inch thick	open fry 8–12 mins	Fry over moderate heat.
acon rashers 3 mm/⅛ inch thick	dry fry 5–6 mins	Overlap rashers with fat part touching the pan.
eal		
:scalopes less than 5 mm/¼ inch thick	open fry 5–6 mins or covered fry 8–10 mins	Cook uncoated or coated in a mixture of oil and butter.
)ffal		
iver slices alf's, lamb's or pig's 5 mm–1 cm/¼–½ inch ıick	open fry 5–8 mins	Avoid over-cooking and drying.
idneys		Cook in oil and butter and turn or stir frequently to cook evenly.
mb's (halved)	open fry 6–8 mins	
alf's (sliced)	open fry 8–10 mins	
weetbreads		Usually coated in egg and crumbs before frying.
mb's	open fry 5–6 mins	
alf's (pressed or sliced)	open fry 6–8 mins	

General method for frying

1. Heat the pan thoroughly and add fat as specified in the recipe. (Vegetable oils which can be heated to high temperatures without burning, are most convenient. For the best flavour use a half and half mixture of oil and butter or clarified dripping.)
2. When sizzling hot (i.e. when a small cube of dry bread browns in 20 seconds) put in the pieces of meat and cook over high heat for 1–2 minutes to sear and brown the surface.
3. Turn and sear the other side.
4. Reduce the heat (add additional ingredients and cover the pan where applicable) and continue frying, turning the meat as necessary, until cooked through. Serve immediately.

CASSEROLING AND STEWING

Both these methods are ways of tenderizing the coarser and more sinewy cuts of meat by means of long and very slow cooking with added moisture. Stewing generally refers to cooking in a saucepan with a really tight fitting lid on top of the stove, and casseroling to cooking, covered, in the oven. Basically, there are two methods of preparing casseroles and stews: the *fry start* method involves frying and browning the meat and vegetables before any liquid is added and can be used for all cuts of meat or poultry, except very tough or bony ones; the *cold start* method is used for tenderizing bony cuts such as leg and shin of beef, and neck and scrag of mutton. The meat is covered with cold stock or water and gradually brought to simmering point. A small amount of strong, full-bodied wine, full-flavoured mild ale, lager or stout, or dry cider may be added for extra flavour.

General fry start method

1. Wipe the meat with damp paper towel and, if necessary, trim away any surplus fat. Cut into pieces and dust with seasoned flour.
2. Prepare the chosen vegetables and slice the onion.
3. Heat a little dripping or oil and butter in a heavy based pan and fry the meat fairly briskly, turning frequently, until lightly browned on all sides. Lift out and reserve.
4. Reduce the heat and fry the onion gently until golden.
5. Stir in the remaining flour and fry gently, stirring, until pale brown. (Spices such as curr powder and paprika are added at this stage.)
6. Stir in the stock, water, cider, beer or wine and continue stirring until it boils. Use a minimum of liquid so that the gravy becomes rich and flavoursome; 300 ml/½ pint per 450 g/1 lb of meat is the maximum. Use less liquic pro rata when increasing the quantity of meat.
7. Add the meat, vegetables, herbs and spices
8. Cover the pan tightly and simmer very gently, either in the oven at a low temperature or on top of the cooker, until tender. If contro is difficult on top of the stove, try an asbestos or wire heat-spreading mat under the pan. Check the rate of cooking from time to time, and add dumplings, if used, half an hour befo serving. Garnish with fresh herbs, croûtons o diced root vegetables and serve with hot herb bread (see page 153).

Reheating casseroles and stews

The flavour of these slowly cooked dishes actually improves if they are cooked ahead an reheated. So it is a worthwhile economy to cook enough for at least two meals, or more i you have freezer space to fill.

Always take great care when planning to reheat meat. Cool the cooked dish as rapidly a possible by standing the pan in cold water; once cold, refrigerate until time to reheat, the bring slowly to the boil and simmer gently fo about 5 minutes.

Cuts to use for casseroling and stewing	*Cooking time*	*Special points*
Beef		
Braising cuts such as chuck, blade, skirt, neck	2½–3 hours	Fry the meat first (dusted in flour if liked) to brown it, thicken the sauce with flour and gravy browning, and add red wine or tomato purée.
Stewing cuts such as leg, shin, ox-tail	3½–4 hours	
Lamb and veal		
Shoulder meat	1½–2 hours	Cook in a light sauce, coloured with paprika, curry spices or tomato.
Breast, middle neck and scrag, hearts	2 hours	
Liver or kidneys	30 minutes	
Pork		
Hand	2 hours	Season well with salt, freshly ground black pepper, herbs and spices.
Streaky	2 hours	

BRAISING AND POT ROASTING

Both these methods combine the processes of frying and steaming, and are particularly suited to the less tender cuts of meat and to very lean meats such as veal or tongue.

In braising, the browned meat is cooked on top of a thick bed of vegetables with liquid added, while pot roasting may not have vegetables added and is usually cooked with very little, if any, liquid.

Top of stove cooking demands a thick, heavy-based saucepan or flameproof casserole dish with a tight fitting lid, as well as additional liquid.

The shape and size of the pan should be such that the meat, plus vegetables, if used, fit fairl snugly into it.

Cuts to use and approximate cooking times

Calculate time from when simmering point is first reached. Note minimum times for small joints under 1¼ kg/2½ lb.

Beef

Joints: brisket, topside, flank, fresh silverside: allow 45 minutes per 450 g/1 lb with a minimum of 2 hours for topside, 3 hours for brisket or silverside.

Thick slices: buttock or braising steak 1½–2 hours.

Lamb and mutton

Joints: leg; boned and rolled shoulder; stuffed breast: allow 40 minutes per 450 g/1 lb with a minimum of 1½ hours.

Thick chops or slices: 45 minutes

Veal

All joints: allow 40 minutes per 450 g/1 lb with a minimum of 1½ hours.

Pork

Not usually cooked by these methods.

Offal

Lamb's, pig's or veal hearts: 2 hours.
Sliced ox heart: 2 hours.

General method for braising

1. Wipe the meat with a damp paper towel and trim away excess fat. Weigh the meat and work out the approximate cooking time.
2. Heat a little oil or dripping to cover very thinly the base of the pan.
3. When hot, put in the meat and fry, turning as necessary, to sear and lightly brown all surfaces. Transfer to a plate.
4. Add the vegetables and fry in the same fat, stirring now and then, until lightly browned. Pour off any excess fat.
5. Add sufficient stock, water, ale, cider or wine almost to cover the vegetables, add a bay leaf or bouquet of herbs and a little salt and ground black pepper.
6. Replace the meat on top of the vegetables and cover with a very tight fitting lid.
7. Simmer very gently on top of the cooker or cook in the centre of a preheated oven at 160°C, 325°F, Gas Mark 3 for the calculated time. Check the rate of cooking occasionally and reduce the heat, if necessary. Add more liquid, if necessary. Serve with separately cooked root vegetables; purée the vegetables from the pan with a little cooking liquid to make a rough-textured sauce.

SIMMERING

This is a method of tenderizing the more muscular cuts of meat by long, slow cooking in gently simmering water, and is the traditional way of cooking bacon joints and pickled and cured meats such as salted silverside and ox tongue. It is a method that uses a minimum of fuel, especially as root vegetables and dumplings can be cooked in the same pan, and is useful when cooking facilities are limited. Another bonus is that the cooking liquid, if it is not over salty, provides a well flavoured stock for soup.

Preparing salted and pickled meat: in the absence of packet instructions, cover the meat with fresh cold water and soak for 2 hours. However, the degree of pickling can vary, so, when possible, ask the butcher how much soaking he advices before the meat is cooked. An alternative to soaking mildly cured bacon is to blanch it–cover the joint with cold water, bring slowly to the boil and then drain the bacon.

General method for simmering

1. Wipe the meat with a damp paper towel, weigh it and calculate the cooking time.
2. Put the meat in a deep pan into which it fits snugly, but allow space for vegetables and dumplings if these are to be added later.
3. Add just enough cold water to cover the meat, and bring slowly to boiling point.
4. Remove any scum from the surface with a perforated spoon.
5. For fresh meat add for each 1.2 litres/2 pints water; 2 × 5 ml spoons/2 teaspoons salt, 1 bay leaf, 6 black peppercorns and 1 tablespoon wine vinegar for red meats, or lemon juice for white meats.
6. For salted or cured meat omit the salt and in addition to the above add 1 tablespoon soft brown sugar.
7. Cover the pan tightly and simmer very gently at about 86°C/185°F, i.e. below boiling point.
8. Add small or roughly chopped root vegetables 1 hour before the cooking time is up, or dumplings 20 minutes before the end.

Serve the drained meat on a hot serving dish surrounded by the vegetables and/or dumplings. Serve some strained and seasoned cooking liquid with the meat, or use some of it for making a Béchamel Sauce variation such as Parsley (for gammon and tongue), Crème (for chicken or veal) or Soubise (for mutton) (see page 147).

Calculate time from when simmering point is reached.

'uts to use for simmering	*Cooking time*	*Special points*
acon joints, salt beef and ickled pork	30 mins per 450 g/1 lb plus 30 mins, with a minimum time of 1½ hours	When bacon is cooked, the meat thermometer should read 71–77°C/160–170°F, depending on preference of taste.
Iutton	20 mins per 450 g/1 lb plus 20 mins, with a minimum time of 1½ hours	
ongues: pickled ox	3½–4½ hours, depending on size	
fresh lamb's	2½–3 hours	
fresh calf's	3–3½ hours	

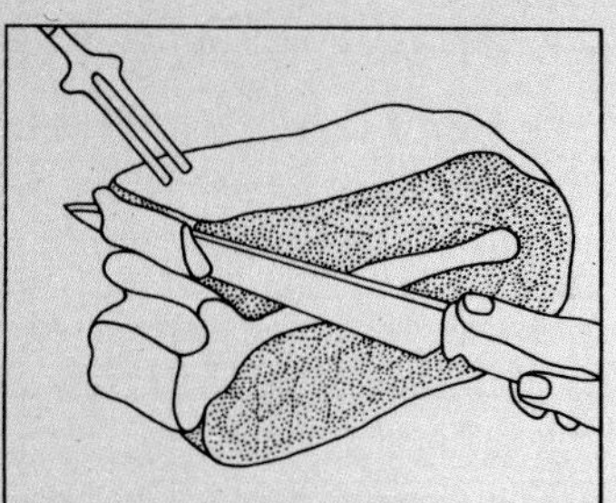
Removing the top bone

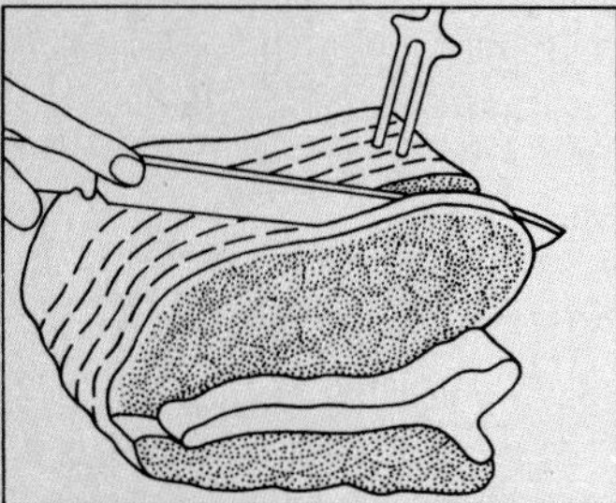
Carving beef sirloin

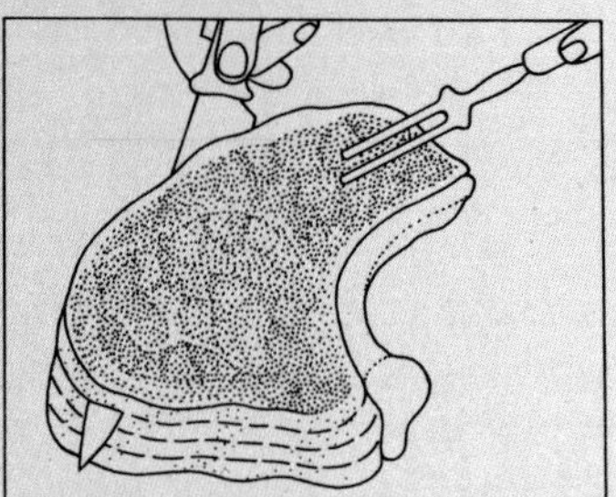
Carving rib roast

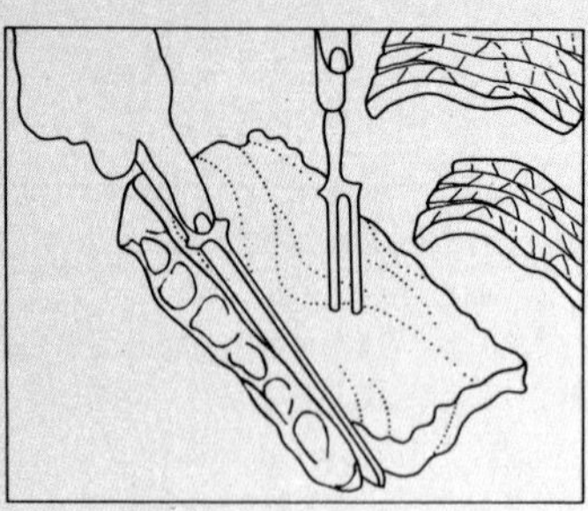
Removing the chine bone

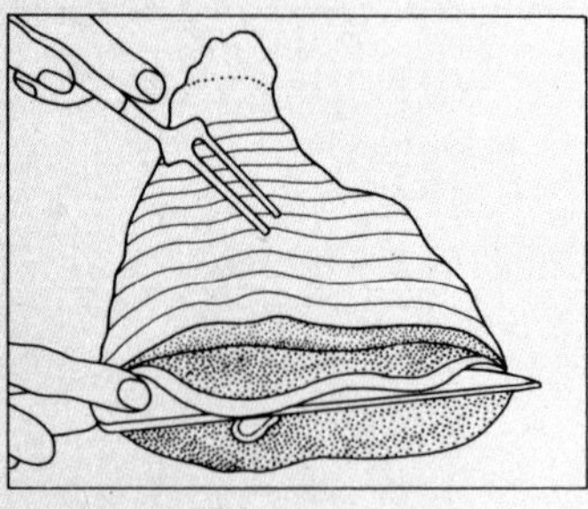
Carving pork loin

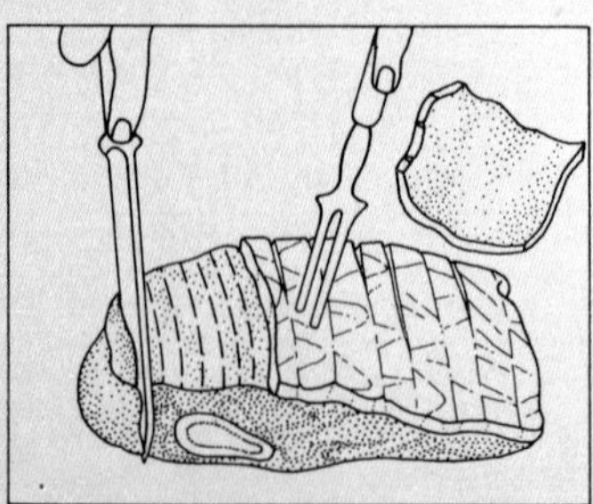
Carving blade of pork

CARVING MEAT

The first essential to good carving is a knife with a keen cutting edge. Flat but spiked carving dishes are useful for holding the joint securely, and they should have grooves to catch the juices. Meat carves more economically if it has been allowed to stand and 'firm up' for 15 minutes before carving begins. If possible, carve across the grain of the meat as short fibres are more tender to eat. Arrange the carved slices overlapping each other on very hot plates, adding a spoonful of stuffing or a portion of crackling if applicable.

Carving beef

Sirloin on the bone:
This joint consists of the uppercut and undercut (or fillet) attached to part of the backbone with rib bones dividing the two sections. (If the fillet has been removed and sold separately ignore stages 3 and 4.)

1. Place the joint with the fat-side uppermost. Press the knife against the backbone and cut downwards right across the joint until the rib bone is reached and the upper part of the back bone can be removed.
2. Turn the joint with the backbone facing away from you, and carve lengthwise and downwards in thin slices, freeing each slice from the rib bone as you cut.
3. Turn the joint over and, pressing the knife against the backbone, cut down and along the rib bone until the fillet portion has been freed completely.
4. Carve the fillet into thin slices. Each portion should consist of a slice each of uppercut and fillet.

Rib roast:
A small joint is best laid flat and carved in horizontal slices towards the bone. A large joint with two bones is best stood on the rib bones with the fat-side uppermost. Then follow stages 1 and 2 for sirloin.

Carving pork

Loin:
1. Slip the knife under the crackling, remove and divide into portions.
2. Free the meat from the chine bone.
3. Carve the meat downwards in slices.

Knuckle end of leg:
1. Starting at the wide end, carve in slices downwards to the bone.
2. To release the slices cut across the bone.
3. Turn the joint over and repeat on the other side.

Fillet end of leg:
Carve as lamb.

Blade:
1. Stand the joint with the crackling uppermost.
2. Lift off the crackling and divide into portions.
3. Slice the meat downwards to the blade bone which has a 'hump' in the middle.
4. Turn the whole joint over and slice at an oblique angle towards the widest part of the blade bone.

Carving lamb

Whole shoulder:
This tricky joint becomes easier to carve if you remove the blade bone.

1. Before cooking insert a long bladed knife and loosen the meat from all around the flat blade bone, working right back to the first joint.
2. Roast the shoulder in the normal way. When thoroughly cooked the blade bone will be loose. Grasp it with a paper towel and twist until it can be pulled out.
3. Wrap the knuckle with foil, hold the joint in your left hand and carve down in fairly thick slices until you reach the bone.
4. Turn the rest of the joint over, and, holding it by the knuckle, carve the rest of the meat.

Whole leg:
1. Place the joint on the dish with the round side uppermost. Insert the carving fork near the knuckle.
2. Make a cut in the centre right through to the bone. Make a second cut 5 mm/¼ inch away and remove the slice.
3. Continue slicing from either side of the first cut, angling the knife to obtain the longest slices possible, until all the meat has been cut from this side.
4. Turn the joint over, hold it firmly by the knuckle with your free hand and cut thin slices along the length of the leg.

Fillet end of leg:
1. Place on a dish so that the bone is upright in the centre of the joint.
2. Carve horizontally towards the bone, turning the joint from time to time.

Best end of neck:
This joint should always be either chined or chopped by the butcher.

1. If chined, simply remove the loose chine bone and carve the joint downwards between the ribs, dividing it into cutlets.
2. If 'chopped', carve between the chops.

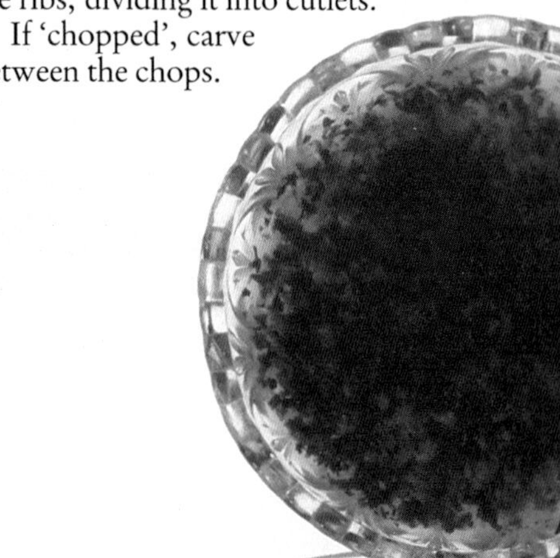

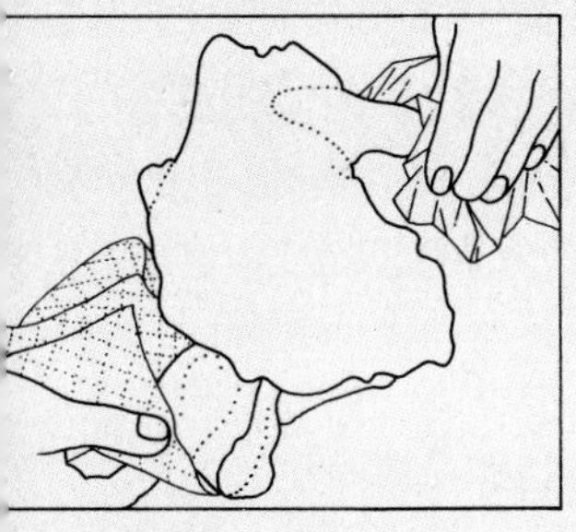
[R]emove lamb shoulder bone

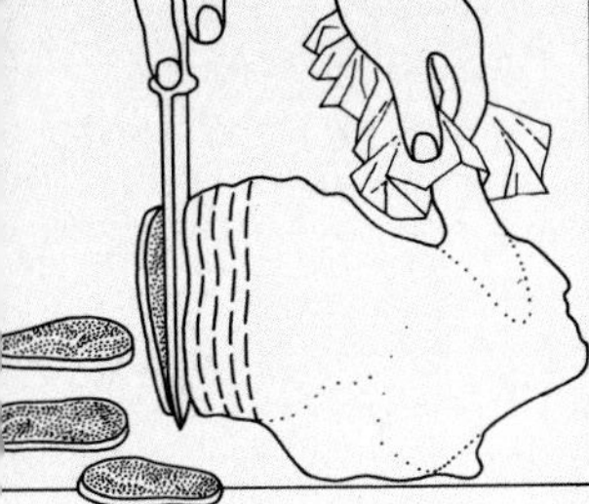
[C]arve in fairly thick slices

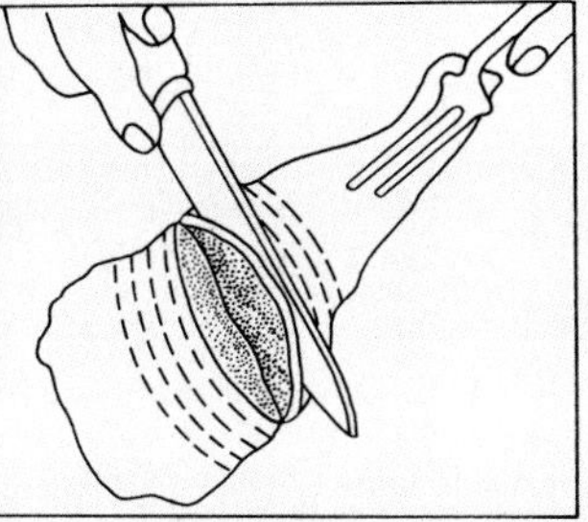
[C]arving whole leg of lamb

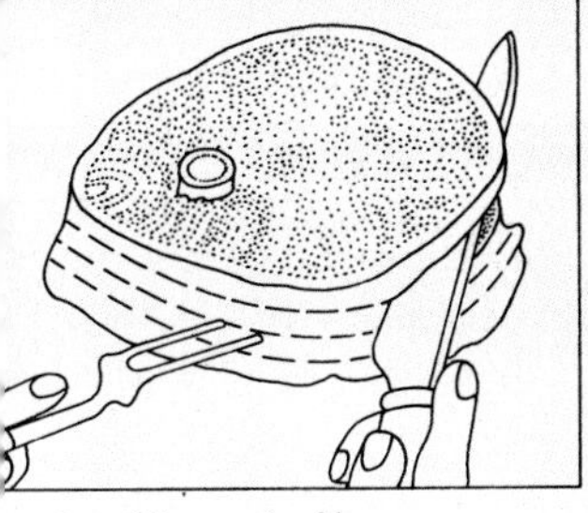
[C]arving fillet end of leg

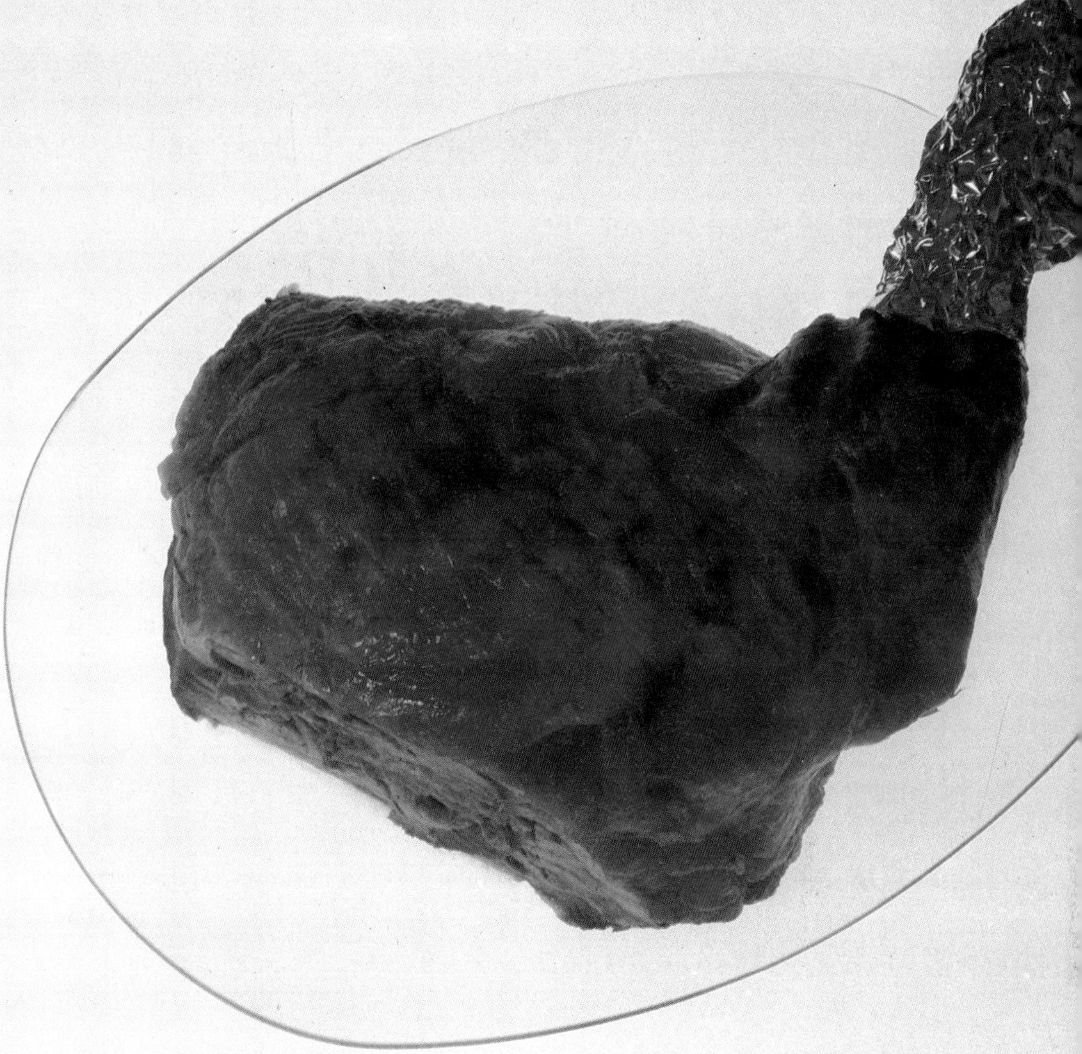

Carving bacon

Most small bacon joints are sold boneless and are very simple to carve. Two large joints that may pose problems are illustrated below.

Whole forehock (3–4 kg/7–9 lb):

1. Carve horizontally from the lean and meaty side of the joint. Cut about 4 slices 6 mm/¼ inch thick.
2. At the pointed end of the joint there may be a fatty piece. Cut it off.
3. Cut the fillet into slices until the bone is reached, carving vertically.
4. Continue carving, taking slices from both sides of the bone.
5. Keeping parallel to the bone, slice the meat from the knuckle.

Whole gammon (7¼–7½ kg/16–17 lb):

1. Working from the slipper area, carve off slices until the bone is reached. Cut off the knee cap.
2. Take slices from the corner of the meat. Remove the aitchbone.
3. Continue to carve the prime meat from the middle section into slices.
4. Turn the joint over so the underside is on top and continue carving.
5. Cut off slices of meat from the bone until the bone is reached on all sides.

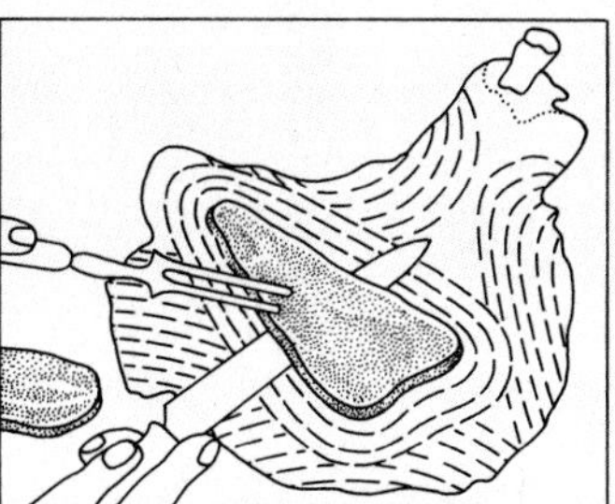
Carving whole forehock

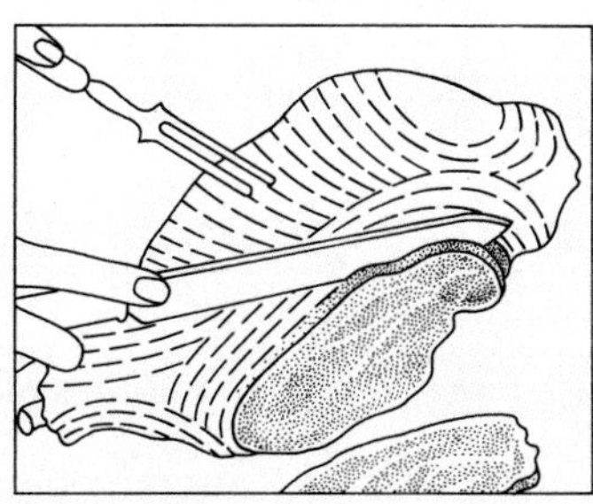
Carving whole gammon

POULTRY

Poultry adds welcome variety to both everyday and special occasion meals. Chicken and turkey in particular can be cooked in an infinite variety of ways to suit the time, convenience and creative mood of the cook. Both are now available all year round as oven-ready whole birds of varying weights and as cut portions, which are particularly useful when you want to give everyone a similar portion, such as a thigh or drumstick.

FRESH POULTRY

Fresh poultry is generally considered to have the best flavour and texture but is very perishable and must be cooked soon after purchase. Follow the label instructions, keep the bird refrigerated and use it within 2–3 days.

THAWING FROZEN POULTRY

Frozen poultry can be stored in a home freezer (−18°C, 0°F or below) for several months and this is a great convenience for the busy cook. Before cooking, however, it is important that all poultry is thoroughly thawed, otherwise it is difficult to cook through evenly, and undercooked poultry is a health hazard. When thawing whole poultry follow the label directions concerning the removal of the plastic bag and the giblets. Stand the bird on a rack with a tray beneath and cover loosely. Although slow thawing in a refrigerator is ideal it takes twice as long as thawing at room temperature, and large turkeys can seldom be accommodated in the refrigerator.

The following times for thawing at room temperature are a guide only as kitchen conditions vary considerably. To make sure the bird is completely thawed check that the legs move freely and that the body cavity is free of ice.

PREPARING POULTRY FOR COOKING

After the removal of the giblets and neck from the body cavities, oven-ready whole birds need very little preparation. If a few stubby feathers remain, grasp these between knife and thumb and pull them out. Rinse the bird inside and out under running cold water, drain, and pat the outside dry with paper towels.

CHECKING IF POULTRY IS COOKED

Pierce the thickest part of the thigh with a metal skewer and if the juices run clear the bir is ready to serve. If the juices are pink continu cooking for 15 minutes, then test again.

CARING FOR COOKED POULTRY

Cooked poultry is also very perishable. Eat it freshly cooked and hot, and never keep it warm and waiting for long periods. For eatin cold, cool the poultry as rapidly as possible b standing it in a cool, airy place, or by placing in a casserole in a sink of cold water. Refrigerate as soon as possible and use within days. Treat poultry stock and gravy in exactly the same way.

TURKEY COOKING GUIDE

Preheat the oven to 180°C, 350°F, Gas Mark

Oven ready stuffed weight	*Cooking time*
2¼ kg/5 lb	2½ hours
4½ kg/10 lb	3½ hours
6¾ kg/15 lb	4 hours
9 kg/20 lb	4½ hours

GIBLET STOCK

Rinse the neck, heart and gizzard in cold wat and place in a saucepan with any carcass trimmings and a sliced onion, carrot and celery stick. Add a bay leaf, 1 teaspoon salt, 6 peppercorns and enough cold water to cover. Bring to the boil, cover and simmer very gently for 1 hour. Strain and cool. When cold refrigerate and use for gravy, soup or sauces. This stock will keep for two days in the refrigerator. Boil for 5 minutes before using.

TURKEY LIVER AND BACON ROLLS

Wash the turkey liver and cut into rough 1 cm/½ inch pieces. Rind some rashers of smoked, streaky bacon, lay them flat and stretch out thinly with the blade of a knife. Cut the rashers into 10 cm/4 inch lengths, place a piece of liver at one end and roll up. Impale the rolls on a skewer and cook in the oven above the turkey for about 30 minutes, until crisp. Alternatively, grill, turning frequently, for 10 minutes.

Thawing and serving guide

Oven-ready pack	*Kitchen thawing guide (not in a refrigerator)*	*Approximate number of servings*
cut poultry portions	6–8 hours	allow 75 g–100 g/3–4 oz boneless meat or 175–225 g/6–8 oz meat on the bone, per portion
1½–1¾ kg/3–4 lb chicken	overnight	6–8
2¼ kg/5 lb turkey	15 hours	8–10
4½ kg/10 lb turkey	18 hours	12–14
6¾ kg/15 lb turkey	24 hours	18–20
9 kg/20 lb turkey	30 hours	26–30

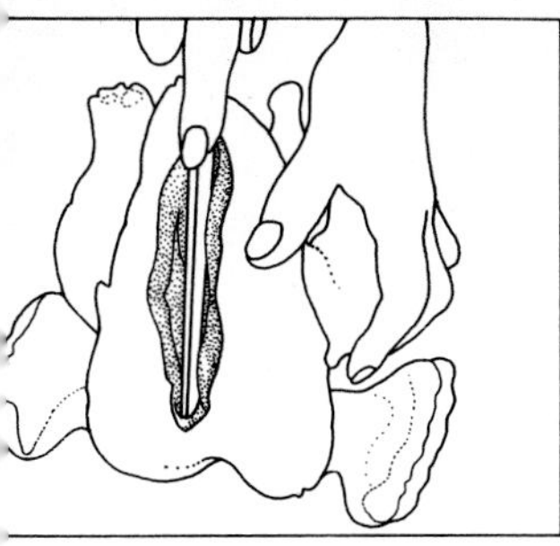

utting along the breastbone

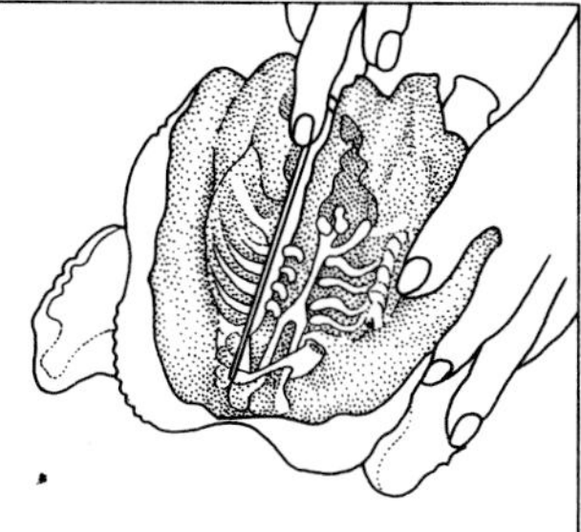

utting through the back

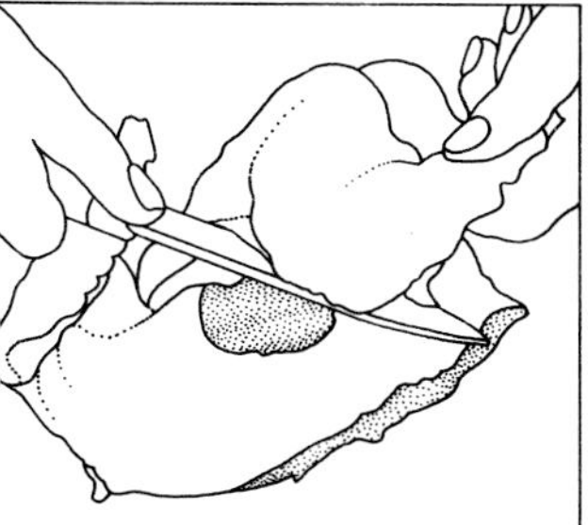

ft thigh and cut through

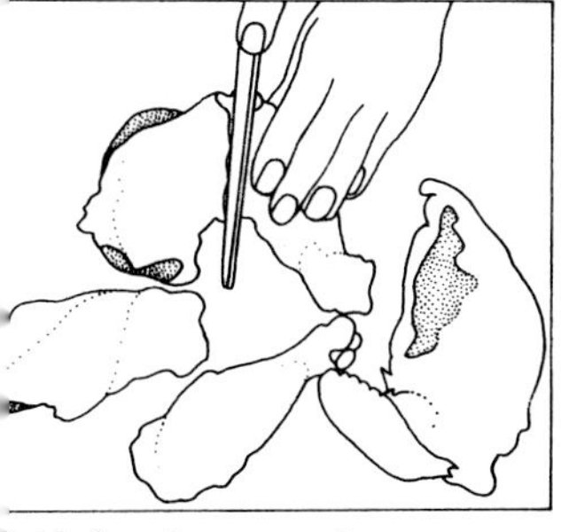

ivide legs into two pieces

PORTIONING A WHOLE CHICKEN

Although chicken portions are readily available it is often convenient and more economical to divide a whole bird at home. Small chickens are easily portioned with the aid of a chopping board, a sharp cook's knife and a heavy weight to tap the knife sharply through bony sections. Poultry scissors can be used instead.

There are various ways of cutting poultry but the one shown here is particularly simple.

For halves choose a 750 g/1½–1¾ lb bird.
For quarters choose a 1–1¼ kg/2–2½ lb bird.
For 6 portions choose a 1¼–1½ kg/2¾–3 lb bird.

1. Remove the giblets from the body and put the bird on a wooden chopping board. Chop off the wing tips, leg shanks and parson's nose. Use all these for making stock.
2. Place the bird with the parson's nose end towards you and cut closely along one side of the breast bone from end to end.
3. Open the bird out and cut through close to one side of the back from end to end. The backbone can then be removed entirely by cutting along close to the other side of the bone. The bird is now in 2 halves. Add the backbone to the stock.
4. To make quarter portions lay the halves on the board, cut side down. Raise one thigh with your left hand, ease the knife under it, angling it diagonally, and cut through to separate the breast and wing joint. Repeat with the other half.
5. To make 6 portions divide each leg into thigh and drumstick by cutting through the ball and socket joint.

CHICKEN BREASTS

One side of the breast of a small roasting chicken weighs from 150–225 g/5–8 oz and makes one portion. Breasts from larger birds divide into 2 fillets, one smaller than the other. You can cut the breast and wing portion from a whole chicken or buy ready cut, wingless breast portions.

Preparing chicken suprême

1. Lay the breast portion skin side down and with a sharp knife cut away the rib and wish bones. If the wing is attached cut this off at the ball and socket joint.
2. Turn the bird over, remove the skin and trim the breast into a neat shape. Refrigerate, wrapped, until ready to cook.

Preparing chicken escalopes

1. Complete steps 1 and 2 above. If large, divide the suprême into 2 fillets.
2. Lay the pieces between cling film or wetted double greaseproof paper. Beat gently with a rolling pin until evenly flattened to a thickness of about 1 cm/½ inch. Refrigerate, still wrapped, until ready to cook.

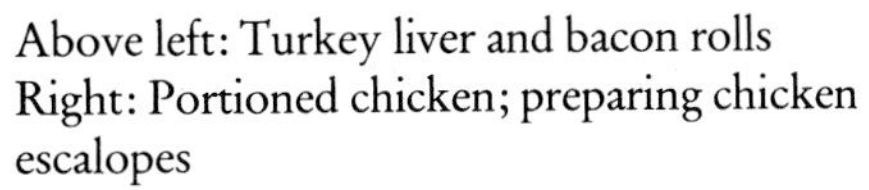

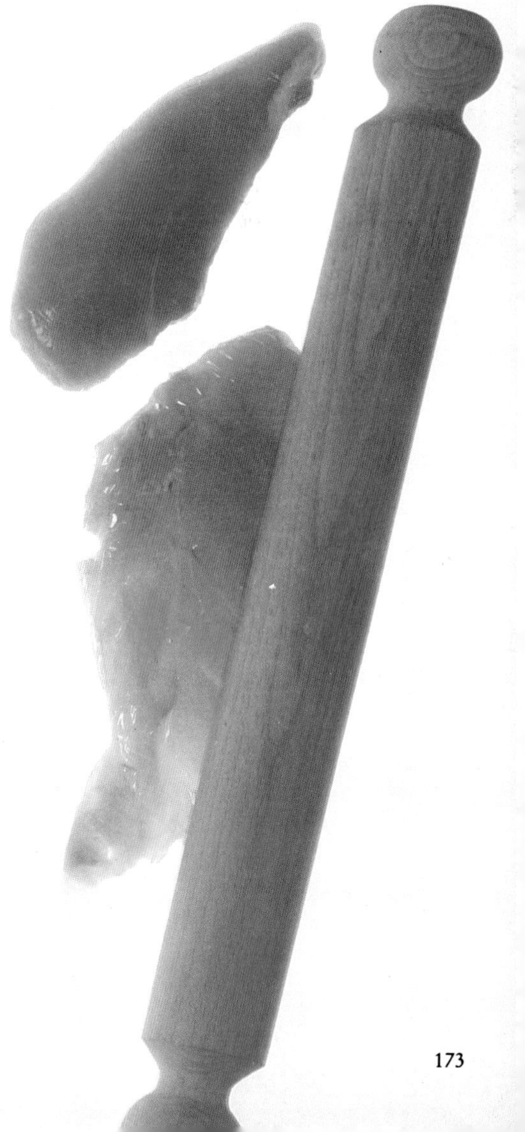

Above left: Turkey liver and bacon rolls
Right: Portioned chicken; preparing chicken escalopes

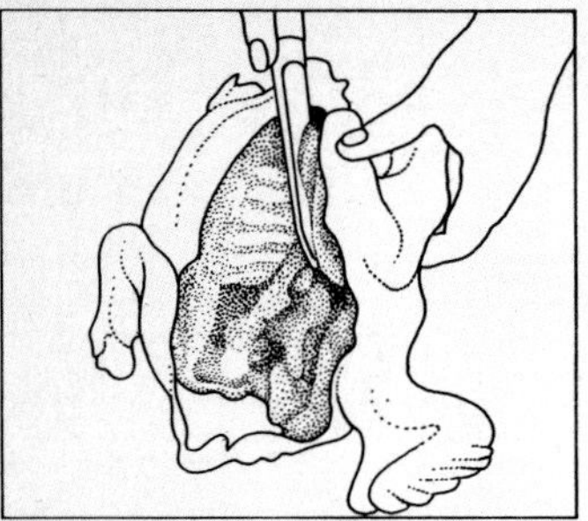

Work flesh from carcass

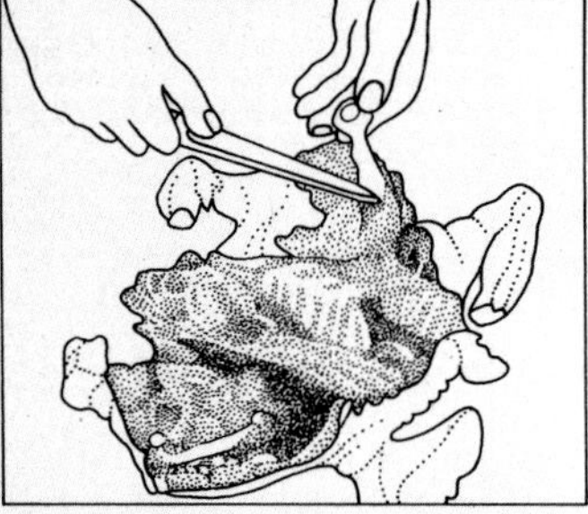

Scrape flesh from thigh bone

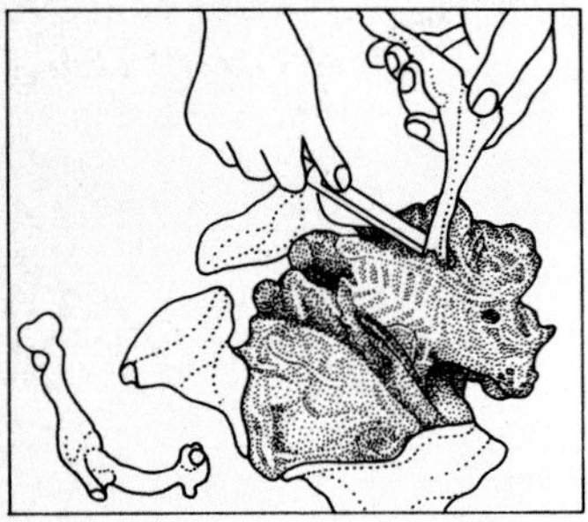

Loosen flesh from drumstick

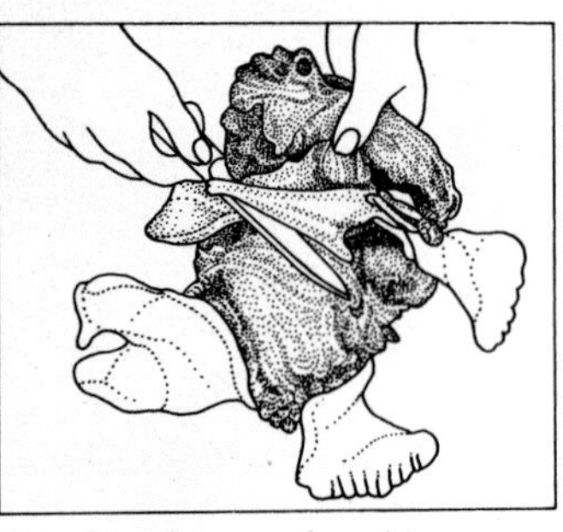

Cut along bone to free skin

BONING A CHICKEN OR TURKEY

When the bones are removed, a bird stuffed with a well-seasoned and savoury stuffing becomes an impressive hot or cold dish and one that can be carved easily and economically.

The simplest method, illustrated here, requires nothing more than a small sharp knife and, initially, a little patience. Try first with a chicken, then graduate to a small turkey, which has stronger leg sinews and these need to be removed along with the bones. Remember that the object is to keep the skin intact.

1. Remove the neck and giblets. Rinse the bird under running cold water, drain and pat dry with kitchen paper.
2. Cut off the leg shanks, the wings at the second joint, and the parson's nose.
3. Lay the bird breast side up on a board and cut through the skin along one side of the bone from neck to tail.
4. Keeping the knife pressed against the carcass, work the flesh away in short, clean cuts. Hold the skin and flesh with the left hand, peeling it away as the work progresses until the thigh joint is revealed. Repeat on the other side.
5. To bone the legs first cut through the ball and socket thigh joint and then loosen the flesh and scrape it away from the thigh bone.
6. Cut through the sinews around the tip of the drumstick and loosen the flesh, removing as many sinews as possible. Scrape the flesh away until the bone is free and can be pulled out. Repeat with the other leg.
7. Sever the ball and socket joint where the wing joins the body and scrape the flesh away from the wing bone until the bone can be pulled out. Repeat with the other wing.
8. Continue working the flesh away from the carcass on both sides of the bird until the backbone is reached. Carefully cut right along the backbone to free the skin, but take care to keep the skin intact. Lift out the carcass.
9. The bones and giblets can be used for stock immediately, or deep frozen until needed.

STUFFINGS

Good stuffings add flavour and texture as well as originality to an otherwise traditional roast bird. Make them moist and buttery and season them well.

Any extra stuffing can be rolled into balls and cooked separately, in a greased and covered dish, one shelf below the bird.

Quantities to allow:

225 g/8 oz stuffing for a 1½–1¾ kg/3–4 lb bird
450 g/1 lb stuffing for a 3½ kg/8 lb bird
750 g/1½ lb stuffing for a 5½ kg/12 lb bird
1 kg/2 lb stuffing for a 7¼ kg/16 lb bird

:low left: Country herb stuffing
:ft: Chestnut and sausage stuffing
:low: Apricot and hazelnut
:ffing

Chestnut and Sausage Stuffing

fakes about 750 g/1½ lb
reparation time: 20 minutes
'ooking time: 40 minutes

50 g/1 lb chestnuts
)0 ml/1½ pint chicken stock
5 g/1 oz chicken fat or butter
small onion, peeled and finely chopped
25 g/8 oz pork sausage meat
tablespoon chopped fresh parsley
lt
eshly ground black pepper

1. With a sharp knife make a small slit in each chestnut. Place them in a saucepan, cover with cold water, bring to the boil and simmer for 5 minutes.
2. Drain, peel off the shells and the inner brown skin. Returning the chestnuts to the saucepan, cover them with chicken stock and simmer for 30 minutes or until tender. Drain and chop roughly.
3. Melt the fat in a saucepan, add the onion and fry gently for 5 minutes until softened. Add the sausage meat, chestnuts, parsley, salt and pepper, and mix thoroughly.

Apricot and Hazelnut Stuffing

Aakes about 450 g/1 lb
'reparation time: 10 minutes,
lus 1 hour's soaking time

)0 g/4 oz dried apricots, soaked in cold water for 1 hour
)0 g/4 oz fresh white breadcrumbs
) g/2 oz hazelnuts, finely chopped
tablespoon chopped fresh parsley
) g/2 oz butter
small onion, peeled and finely chopped
nely grated rind and juice of 1 orange
egg, beaten
lt
eshly ground black pepper

1. Drain the apricots and chop them roughly.
2. Add the breadcrumbs, hazelnuts and parsley and mix well.
3. Melt the butter in a saucepan and fry the onion very gently until soft. Stir in the apricots and breadcrumbs mixture.
4. Add the orange rind and juice, the beaten egg and salt and pepper to taste. Mix thoroughly.

Country Herb Stuffing

akes about 450 g/1 lb
eparation time: 10 minutes

g/3 oz butter or bacon fat
nedium onion, peeled and finely chopped
0 g/4 oz smoked streaky bacon, rinded and chopped
5 g/6 oz dry white breadcrumbs
ely grated rind of 1 lemon
ablespoons chopped fresh parsley
2 teaspoons dried thyme
t
eshly ground black pepper
ittle milk to bind

1. Melt the fat in a frying pan and fry the onions and bacon together over a gentle heat for 5 minutes.
2. Add the breadcrumbs, stir, and cook for another minute.
3. Stir in the remaining ingredients, adding a little milk, as necessary, to bind the stuffing to a moist consistency.

PASTRIES

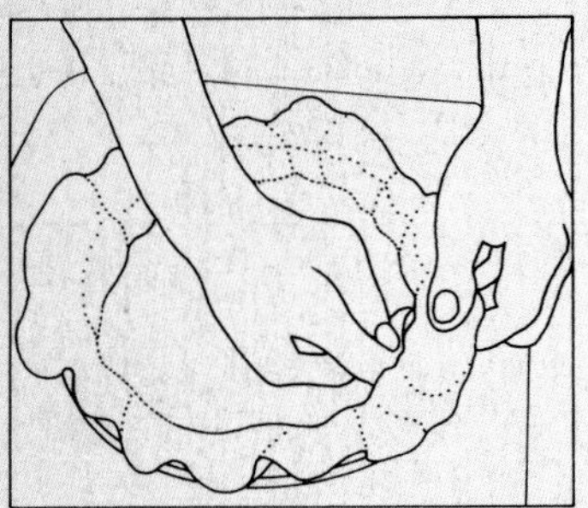

Lining a flan ring

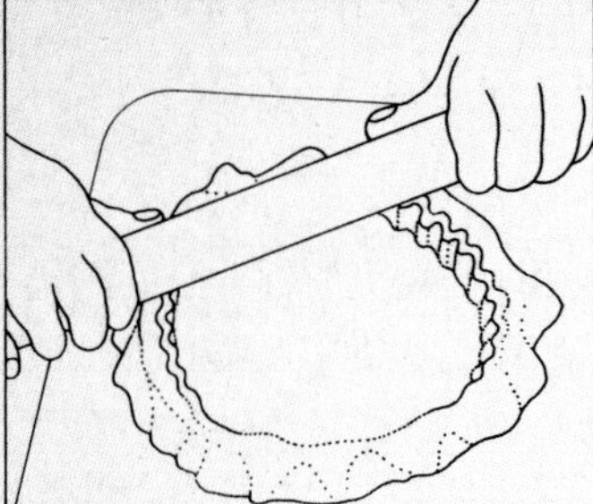

Rolling off excess pastry

There is an art in making good pastry which can easily be achieved by remembering a few basic rules, whether you are making everyday shortcrust or richer pastries for flans and French pâtisserie. As with most skills, practice makes perfect so it is worth persevering to master the art.

For all pastries you need cool working conditions, so begin early in the day before the kitchen gets hot and steamy. Formica kitchen surfaces are cool enough to use, or use marble or a wooden board specially for the purpose.

Handle the pastry as little as possible and use only fingertips when rubbing in fat.

Add iced cold water for mixing (except for choux and hot water crust) and always add it cautiously – too wet a mixture will shrink and lose shape when baked and is tough and hard to eat. Too little water causes cracking when rolling out which is difficult to handle, and results in a dry taste.

Roll the pastry out as lightly and as little as possible using only a little flour on the work surface.

Bake the pastry on the top shelf of a hot oven unless using a fan assisted oven when any shelf will do. Oven temperatures are given under the various recipes.

INGREDIENTS FOR PASTRY MAKING

The right ingredients play a large part in achieving good results. Plain flour is the best to use.

Butter, hard margarine and lard are the most commonly used fats, but proprietary vegetable shortenings (blended and whipped) and vegetable oils are often used today giving excellent results. Soft 'tub' margarines are not recommended for pastry making as they are not easy to handle.

For shortcrust pastry, a combination of half and half butter or hard margarine and lard (or vegetable shortening) produces the best results. For the richer pastries, it is best to keep to the fat specified in the recipe.

The quantity of water to add is approximately 1 teaspoon per 25 g/1 oz flour for shortcrust pastry, and 1 tablespoon per 25 g/1 oz flour for flaky pastry.

TO BAKE BLIND

If flans and tarts are to be filled with a cold or uncooked filling they are usually baked blind. This simply means baking the pastry without its filling.

To do this, line the flan or pie dish with the pastry and prick the base and sides with a fork so air can escape during baking. Place a piece of greaseproof paper in the pastry shell and fill with uncooked haricot beans, rice or stale bread crusts. Bake the pastry for 10 minutes until it has set. Remove the paper and beans from the pastry case and return it to the oven for a further 5 minutes to dry out.

Recipe note: when recipes state 100 g/4 oz shortcrust pastry it means shortcrust pastry made with 100 g/4 oz plain flour with the other ingredients in proportion.

Basic Shortcrust Pastry

reparation time: 10 minutes

00 g/4 oz plain flour
inch of salt
5 g/1 oz lard or shortening
5 g/1 oz hard margarine, cut into pieces
teaspoons water

ubbing fat into flour

This is probably the most popular pastry and is made by the rubbing-in method. It can be used for sweet and savoury dishes, such as fruit and meat pies, tarts, and sweet and savoury flans.

1. Sift the flour and salt together into a mixing bowl.
2. Rub the lard and margarine into the flour using fingertips. Continue for a few minutes until it resembles fine breadcrumbs.
3. Add the water, stirring with a round bladed knife.
4. Collect the dough together with one hand and lift it on to a floured surface. Knead lightly for a few seconds to give a firm dough.
5. The pastry can be used immediately but it is at its best after 10–15 minutes wrapped in foil or a plastic bag in the refrigerator.
6. When the pastry is required, roll it out on a floured board, turning it occasionally. Roll to a thickness of 3 mm/⅛ inch without pulling or stretching.
7. Use as required. Bake in a preheated oven at 200°C, 400°F, Gas Mark 6.

Flan Pastry

reparation time: 10 minutes

00 g/4 oz plain flour
inch of salt
5 g/3 oz butter or hard margarine and lard, cut into pieces
teaspoon caster sugar
egg, beaten

This is a slightly richer pastry made similarly to shortcrust. When sweetened, it is used for flan cases, small tartlets and other sweet pastries. Omit the sugar for savoury flans and tarts. This will line a 15 cm/6 inch flan ring.

1. Sift the flour and salt together into a mixing bowl and rub in the fat using fingertips. Continue for a few minutes until the mixture resembles fine breadcrumbs.
2. Stir in the sugar. Add the beaten egg, stirring until the mixture comes together.
3. Collect it together with one lightly floured hand and knead gently to give a firm dough. Roll out as for shortcrust pastry.
4. Bake in a preheated oven at 200°C, 400°F, Gas Mark 6.

'Fork mix' Shortcrust Pastry

reparation time: 5–10 minutes

½ tablespoons corn oil
tablespoon cold water
00 g/4 oz plain flour
inch of salt

This has a slightly different texture to the conventional pastry and is more suited to savoury dishes.

1. Put the oil and water in a large bowl and beat well together.
2. Sift the flour and salt together into a mixing bowl and gradually add to the oil and water mixture. Mix well to a dough using a fork.
3. Roll the dough out on a floured board or between non-stick paper, if it tends to be sticky.
4. Bake in a hot oven at 200°C, 400°F, Gas Mark 6.

Pâte Brisée

Preparation time: 15 minutes

150 g/5 oz plain flour
pinch of salt
100 g/4 oz chilled butter, cut into 1 cm/½ inch pieces
1 teaspoon sugar
5 teaspoons water

This is a very rich shortcrust pastry, producing a crunchy, buttery crust. It can be used for sweet and savoury dishes.

1. Sift the flour and salt together into a mixing bowl. Rub the fat into the flour between fingertips until the size of oatmeal flakes, rather than breadcrumbs.
2. Stir in the sugar and add the water.
3. Bind together with one hand and lift out on to a lightly floured board or table top. With the heel of the hand press the pastry away from you to a length of 15 cm/6 inches. This blends the fat in completely.
4. Gather the dough together into a ball, sprinkle with flour and place it in a polythene bag or cling film and place in the refrigerator for about 1 hour.
5. To use, roll the pastry out on a lightly floured surface. (It may require softening up by working it with hands in order to roll out without cracking.) The thickness of the pastry should be 3 mm/⅛ inch.
6. Bake in a preheated oven at 200°C, 400°F, Gas Mark 6.

Pâte Sucrée (French Flan Pastry)

Preparation time: 15 minutes

100 g/4 oz plain flour
pinch of salt
50 g/2 oz butter at normal room temperature
50 g/2 oz caster sugar
2 egg yolks

This is a rich pastry made on the pastry board or on a marble slab, rather than in a mixing bowl. It is particularly suitable for French patisserie; thin, crisp and melting in texture. It does not need baking beans when baked blind. This will line a 15 cm/6 inch flan ring.

1. Sift the flour and salt together on to the work top, or pastry board, and make a well in the centre.
2. Place the butter and sugar in the centre and using fingertips work the butter and sugar together.
3. Add the egg yolks to the butter mixture and work these into the mixture. Gradually draw in the flour and knead lightly until smooth.
4. Wrap the dough in a polythene bag or in cling film and chill in the refrigerator for 1 hour.
5. Use to line a 15 cm/6 inch flan ring and either roll out the mixture with a floured rolling pin, or mould the pastry into a flan ring with fingers.
6. Bake in a moderately hot oven at 190°C, 375°F, Gas Mark 5.

LAYERED PASTRIES

These are traditional farmhouse pastries. Use a combination of half and half lard and butter or hard margarine for best results. The fat for flaky pastry must be of the same consistency as the dough with which it is to be combined, so the fat is worked with a knife on a plate beforehand. For rough puff pastry, the fat should be firm so that it retains its shape when mixed with the flour. All layered pastries require 'resting' in the refrigerator for 10–15 minutes between rollings. Cover with greaseproof paper to prevent the surface becoming hard. Remember to roll very lightly and not to stretch the dough during shaping.

Rough Puff Pastry

Preparation time: 20 minutes, plus resting time

225 g/8 oz plain flour
pinch of salt
175 g/6 oz firm butter or hard margarine and lard mixed, cut into 2 cm/¾ inch cubes
squeeze of lemon juice

This pastry gives a similar result to flaky pastry but the flakes are not as even, so when appearance and even rising are important flaky pastry should be used.

1. Sift the flour and salt into a mixing bowl.
2. Add the fat to the flour and stir gently taking care not to break up the pieces. Stir with a palette knife, binding the mixture together with the water and lemon juice, to produce a stiff dough. Do not knead.
3. Turn the dough on to a floured board and roll into a strip 30 cm × 10 cm/12 × 4 inches.
4. Fold the bottom third of pastry up and the top third down, then give the pastry a half turn so the folds are at the sides. Seal the pastry edges with a rolling pin.
5. Repeat the process, rolling and folding the pastry four times in all.
6. Leave to 'rest', wrapped in foil or greaseproof paper, in the refrigerator for at least 30 minutes before using. Roll out and use as required.
7. Bake in a hot oven at 220°C, 425°F, Gas Mark 7.

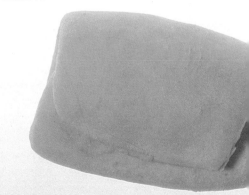

Flaky Pastry

reparation time: 30 minutes,
lus resting time

25 g/8 oz plain flour
inch of salt
75 g/6 oz butter or hard
 margarine and lard
tablespoons cold water
queeze of lemon juice (optional)
eaten egg, to glaze

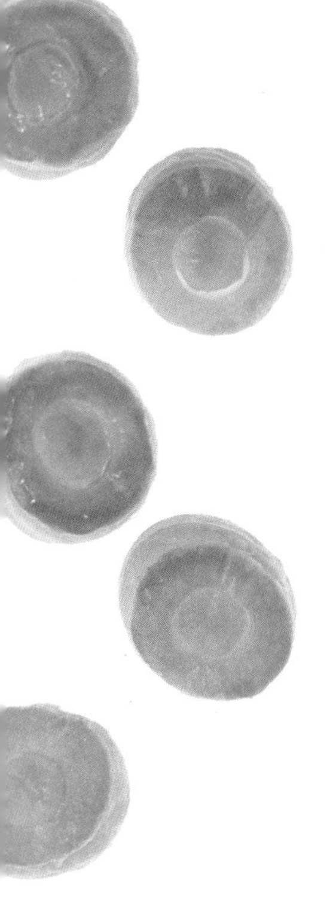

1. Sift the flour and salt together into a mixing bowl.
2. Soften the fat by working it with a knife on a plate. Divide the fat into 4 equal portions.
3. Rub one quarter of the softened fat into the flour. Mix to a soft dough with water and lemon juice.
4. On a floured board, roll out the dough to an oblong 30 × 7½ cm/12 × 3 inches.
5. Take another quarter of the fat, divide it into 1 cm/½ inch pieces and dot them over the top two thirds of the pastry.
6. Fold the bottom third of pastry up and the top third of the pastry down, so that the blank third is now sandwiched between 2 fat-dotted layers. Seal the pastry edges with a rolling pin.
7. Flour the rolling area and re-roll the pastry as before. Repeat the process until all the fat is used up, resting the pastry in the refrigerator between rollings.
8. Wrap the pastry in foil and leave in refrigerator for 30 minutes before using. This makes it easier to handle.
9. Roll the pastry out lightly on a floured board to a thickness of 5 mm/¼ inch. Brush with beaten egg before baking for a shiny golden finish.
10. Bake in a preheated oven at 220°C, 425°F, Gas Mark 7.

To make vol-au-vents

1. Roll out the pastry to 5 mm/¼ inch thickness and cut out 5 cm/2 inch rounds using a plain cutter. Place the rounds on a wetted baking sheet and brush with beaten egg. Using a 3 cm/1¼ inch plain cutter, mark a circle in the centre of each but do not cut right through. Chill for 10–15 minutes.
2. Bake above the centre of a preheated oven at 220°C, 425°F, Gas Mark 7 for 10–15 minutes until well risen and golden brown.
3. Remove the centres and either use the vol-au-vents hot, or cool them on a wire tray. Spoon out any soft pastry with a teaspoon. Fill the cases, replace the tops and serve.

When making vol-au-vents for a party, it is best to reheat the pastry cases in the oven and then fill them with hot fillings rather than reheat filled cases.

FILLINGS:

Each filling is sufficient to fill 20–24 vol-au-vents.

Mushroom Vol-au-vents

Make up 150 ml/¼ pint white coating sauce and add 50 g/2 oz fried chopped mushrooms, salt and pepper and a dash of Worcestershire sauce.

Prawn Vol-au-vents

Fry 100 g/4 oz shelled prawns and add to 150 ml/¼ pint white coating sauce with a little lemon juice, and salt and pepper.

Ham and Egg Vol-au-vents

Chop 100 g/4 oz cooked ham and add to 150 ml/¼ pint white coating sauce with, salt and pepper and 1 chopped hard-boiled egg.

To make palmiers

Roll out the pastry thinly into a long strip. Brush with water and sprinkle with sugar. Fold each end into 3, then fold over making 8 layers. Cut into 1cm/½ inch slices, chill, then cook in a preheated oven at 230°C, 450°F, Gas Mark 8 until beginning to colour. Turn them over and bake until golden.

Quick Flaky Pastry

reparation time: 10 minutes,
lus 30 minutes in the refrigerator

75 g/6 oz hard margarine,
 chilled
25 g/8 oz plain flour
inch of salt
tablespoons cold water

A very good result can be achieved by this quick method of making flaky pastry whereby all the chilled margarine is grated into the flour.

1. Wrap the margarine in foil and place it in the frozen food compartment of the refrigerator for 30 minutes, as it needs to be very firm for grating.
2. Sift the flour and salt into a mixing bowl then, using the coarse side of a grater, grate the chilled margarine into the flour, holding it in the foil as you grate.
3. Using a palette knife, mix the fat into the flour, then bind it together with the water.
4. Lift the dough on to a floured board, knead lightly, then wrap in foil and place in the refrigerator for at least 30 minutes before using.
5. Roll out to a thickness of 5mm/¼ inch and use as required.
6. Bake in a preheated oven at 220°C, 425°F, Gas Mark 7.

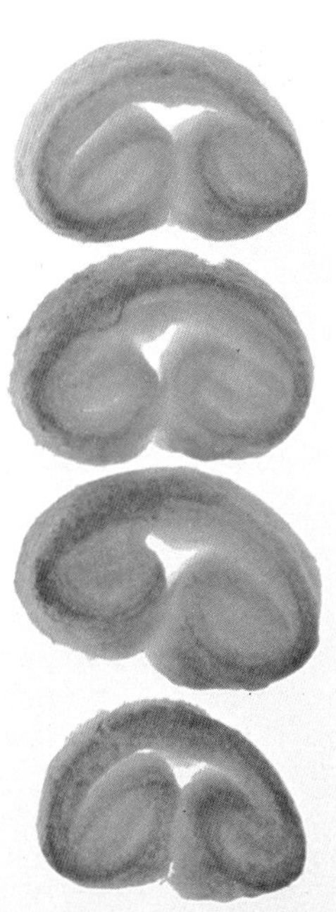

Hot Water Crust Pastry

Preparation time: 10–15 minutes

450 g/1 lb plain flour
2 teaspoons salt
100 g/4 oz lard
200 ml/7 fl oz milk and water mixed

Chicken and veal filling:
100 g/4 oz lean ham, cubed
175 g/6 oz pie veal, cubed
225 g/8 oz cooked chicken or game, cut into small pieces
300 g/11 oz sausage meat
salt
freshly ground black pepper
1 egg, beaten, to glaze
150 ml/¼ pint jellied stock

Hot water crust pastry is made with boiling water which makes it possible to mould it into a raised pie which holds its shape during baking and when it is cold. If you do not have the special metal mould you can use a small cake tin. This pastry is used for game pies, veal and ham pies and is particularly suitable for special occasion picnics or buffet parties.

1. Sift the flour and salt into a large mixing bowl.
2. Place the fat and liquid in a saucepan and heat gently until the fat has melted, then bring to the boil.
3. Remove the saucepan from the heat and pour the liquid into a well in the dry ingredients. Work quickly using a wooden spoon to form a soft dough.
4. Turn out on to a floured board and knead until smooth. Use as required.
5. It is important to keep the dough covered with a cloth or plate when not actually being used to prevent it hardening.

To shape a raised pie
1. Lightly grease the mould or a 15 cm/6 inch cake tin.
2. Take three-quarters of the pastry, leaving the remaining quarter covered, and roll it out to line the sides and bottom of the mould or cake tin.
3. Mix the meats and seasoning for the filling together and fill the pie.
4. Roll the remaining pastry out to make a lid. Damp the inner top edge of the pie wall and press the lid into place. Press the edges well together forming a rim. Flute the edges. Make a hole in the centre and decorate the top with pastry leaves made from trimmings. Glaze the top with beaten egg.
5. Bake in the centre of a preheated oven at 220°C, 425°F, Gas Mark 7 for 15–20 minutes then reduce to a moderate heat 180°C, 350°F Gas Mark 4 for a further 1½ hours.
6. If you have used a loose-bottomed cake tin or metal pie mould remove the pie from the tin after 1½ hours cooking, glaze the sides with beaten egg and cook for a further 30 minutes to brown the sides of the pastry.
7. Heat the jellied stock, allow to cool slightly, then fill the pie up with it through the hole in the top. Leave the pie to get cold before serving sliced with salads.

Suet Crust Pastry

Preparation time: 10 minutes

225 g/8 oz self-raising flour
½ teaspoon salt
100 g/4 oz shredded beef suet
8 tablespoons cold water

Sweet filling:
675 g/1½ lb prepared fruit
50–75 g/2–3 oz sugar

Savoury filling:
550 g/1¼ lb stewing steak, cubed
salt
freshly ground black pepper
3 tablespoons beef stock

This pastry can be used for both sweet and savoury dishes. It can be steamed, boiled or baked. Self-raising flour is used here to produce a light result.

1. Sift the flour and salt into a mixing bowl and stir in the suet. Add enough cold water to give a light, elastic dough and knead lightly until smooth.
2. Roll the dough out on a floured board to a thickness of 5 mm/¼ inch.
3. Grease a 1.2 litre/2 pint pudding basin and prepare a steamer.
4. Roll out the pastry to a large circle, cut out a quarter.
5. Fold the remaining pastry into three, place inside the greased basin and unfold carefully. Fill with the prepared mixture. Damp the edges of pastry with water.
6. Gather the rest of the pastry into a ball. Roll it out into a circle to fit the top of the basin and place on top of the filling, sealing the edges well.
7. Cover the basin with greased, greaseproof paper with a pleat in centre to allow for expansion. Top with foil or a pudding cloth and secure with string. Make a handle out of string, to make lifting the pudding in and out of saucepan or steamer easier. Steam for 3–4 hours, topping up with water when necessary.

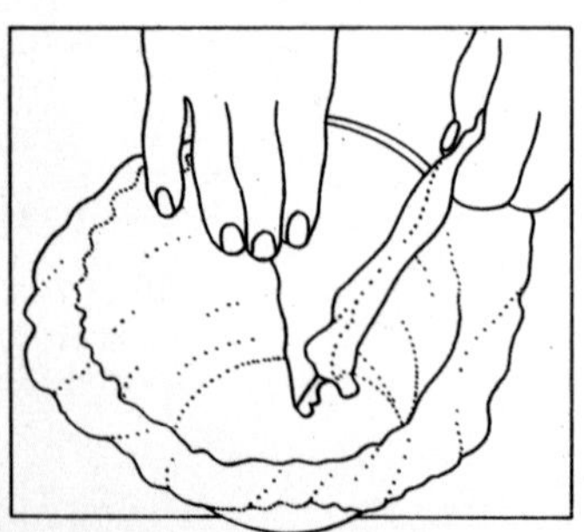
Lining a basin with pastry

From bottom to top: Suet crust pastry with sweet filling; Hot water crust pastry with chicken and veal filling; Choux pastry buns; Aigrettes frying

Choux Pastry

'reparation time: 15 minutes

·0 g/2 oz butter or margarine
50 ml/¼ pint water
·5 g/2½ oz plain flour, sifted
: eggs

:clairs:
50 ml/¼ pint double cream, lightly whipped
·0 g/2 oz plain chocolate, melted

'rofiterôles:
50 ml/8 fl oz double cream, lightly whipped

auce:
00 g/4 oz plain chocolate
tablespoons golden syrup

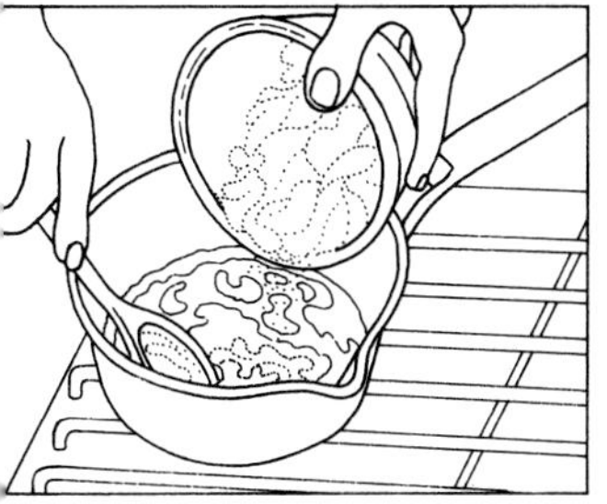
·dding the flour

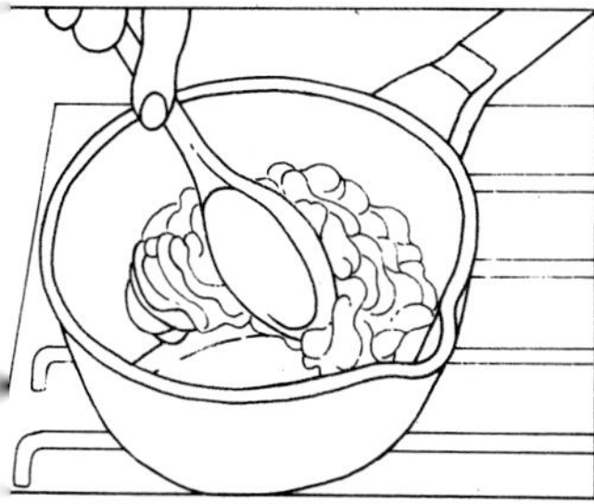
·eating until smooth

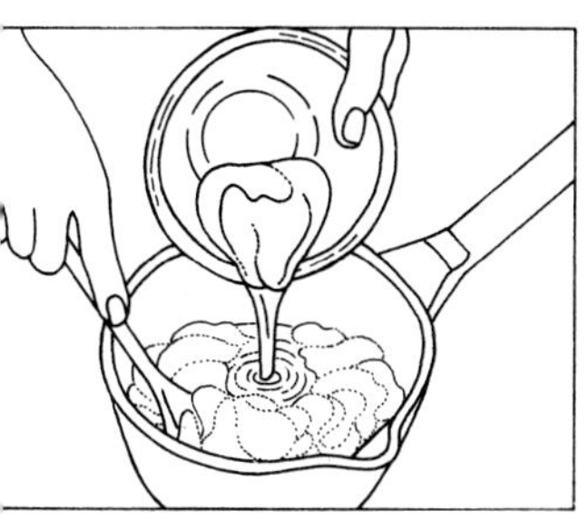
·eating in the eggs

This pastry is used for making profiteroles, éclairs and aigrettes (cheese-flavoured choux pastry). For best results it is important to follow the instructions carefully.

1. Place the fat and water in a saucepan and heat very gently until the fat has melted but before the liquid reaches boiling point.
2. Bring to the boil and quickly tip in all the flour at once. Reduce the heat and beat the paste briskly with a wooden spoon until it is smooth and forms a ball in the centre.
3. Remove the saucepan from the heat and allow to cool slightly. Beat in the eggs one at a time, beating until the mixture is smooth and glossy, and soft enough to pipe.

For aigrettes
Quickly beat in 50 g/2 oz grated mature Cheddar cheese after incorporating the eggs. Deep-fry the pastry in teaspoonfuls and in batches. Keep them warm, and serve as a cocktail savoury.

For éclairs, profiteroles and choux buns
1. Put the mixture into a forcing bag, with a plain round pipe of 1 cm/½ inch diameter. Pipe into fingers (for éclairs) 10 cm/4 inches long on a baking tray lined with non-stick paper, keeping the lengths even and cutting the paste off with a wet knife against the edge of the pipe.
2. For profiteroles and choux buns, pipe in rounds of 5 cm/2 inch diameter. Allow room between the shapes for expansion when cooking.
3. Bake just above the centre of a fairly hot oven at 200°C, 400°F, Gas Mark 6 for 25–30 minutes until well risen and crisp.
4. Slit down the sides with a sharp pointed knife to allow the steam to escape, and leave on a wire tray to cool.
5. Fill the éclairs with whipped cream and dip the tops in melted chocolate.
6. For profiteroles, make the chocolate sauce by melting the chocolate in a basin over a pan of hot water. Blend in the golden syrup. Fill the profiteroles with whipped cream, place on a serving dish and pour over the hot sauce.

VARIATIONS:

The savoury choux buns may be filled with the following fillings, or pâté mixtures:

Cream together 100 g/4 oz full fat soft cheese and 50 g/2 oz softened butter and 1 crushed garlic clove. Season with salt and pepper.

Cream together 100 g/4 oz full fat soft cheese, 50 g/2 oz softened butter and 2 teaspoons tomato purée and season with salt and pepper.

Cream together 225 g/8 oz butter and 2 teaspoons mushroom or anchovy essence. Add pepper to taste.

BREADS

Whether it is the fresh smell of bread baking or the actual kneading of the dough, there is something very satisfying about making your own bread.

PRINCIPLES OF BREAD MAKING

Bread is not difficult to make providing you remember that yeast is a living organism and requires gentle warmth, food and moisture to encourage growth. It obtains food from the flour, and moisture from the liquid used to bind the mixture. In these conditions, the yeast grows giving off carbon dioxide which gives the characteristic spongy texture of bread. The aroma of fresh bread is produced by the growing yeast.

Yeast is not always used as the raising agent in bread making; bicarbonate of soda and baking powder are used for tea breads and soda breads.

BASIC INGREDIENTS

The basic ingredients used for all breads are flour, yeast, salt and water.

Flour

For best results, it is advisable to use a strong plain flour. This has a higher proportion of protein, called gluten, which gives a large volume and better texture than ordinary plain flour. Speciality flours which can also be used are:

Wholemeal – 100% wheat
Wheatmeal – 81% wheat
Stoneground – wholemeal or wheatmeal
Rye flour – for continental rye bread

Yeast

Fresh yeast: will keep for up to one week in a sealed container in the refrigerator, so only small quantities need be bought at a time. It is creamy coloured and crumbly in texture and has a characteristic smell of wine. It tends to deteriorate in the freezer if stored for longer than 1 month.

It is available in health food shops and bakers' shops.

Dried yeast: can be bought in a supermarket and some chemists, and stored in its container for up to 6 months in a cool dry place. It is sold in the form of small, fawn–coloured hard granules.

Salt

All bread doughs require salt for flavour. Too much inhibits the growth of the yeast. 2 teaspoons salt to 450 g/1 lb flour is the right proportion.

Liquid (water or milk)

Use tepid liquid which feels just warm when tested with a finger. Hotter liquid will kill off the yeast, so the bread will not rise.

From the top: fresh yeast; activated yeast; yeast dough; kneaded dough; risen dough; shaped and proved dough; finished breads
Centre: dried yeast

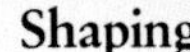

neading yeast dough

BREAD MAKING PROCESS

Warming
For yeast mixtures the flour and liquid should be warm.

Activating the yeast
Fresh: crumble the yeast into a basin and add a little of the warmed liquid and blend to a cream. Pour in the rest of the liquid.
Dried: take 150 ml/¼ pint of the liquid given in the recipe, warm it to blood heat and dissolve 1 level teaspoon sugar in it. Pour the liquid into a cup and sprinkle on the yeast, whisking with a fork. Leave to stand in a warm place for 10 – 15 minutes until the surface is covered with bubbles and the granules have dissolved. Use the mixture as directed in the specific recipe.

When substituting dried yeast for fresh, use half the amount: 15 g/½ oz dried yeast is equivalent to 25 g/1 oz fresh yeast.

Mixing the dough
Add the liquid (whether water, milk, beaten eggs or melted fat) all at once to the dry ingredients and mix with a round bladed knife. The dough should be of a soft consistency.

Kneading
Turn the dough out on to a floured board and knead using both hands, turning the dough as you work. Kneading strengthens and develops the gluten and spreads the yeast evenly throughout the mixture. Allow 10 minutes kneading for 1½ kg/3 lb flour, after which the dough should be elastic and not sticky.

Rising
Place the kneaded dough in an oiled plastic bag or lidded container and leave to rise. It will take: 24 hours in the refrigerator; 12 hours in a cold room or larder; 2 hours at room temperature; or 45 minutes in a warm kitchen, (above the cooker).

Shaping
Turn the risen dough out on to a floured board and knead for 2–3 minutes to break down any other bubbles. Mould into the required shape or make into bread rolls allowing 40 g/1½ oz dough per roll. Place in greased tins or on baking sheets. Glaze with beaten eggs or salted water before proving.

Proving
Place the filled tins or baking sheets into a large, oiled plastic bag and leave to rise until the dough is doubled in size and springs back when lightly pressed with a finger. This will take anything between 15 and 50 minutes depending on where you put it (see rising), and obviously rolls will prove more quickly than a loaf of bread.

Baking
Bread is baked in a very hot oven at 230°C, 450°F, Gas Mark 8. Cooked bread should be well risen and golden brown. It should sound hollow when tapped underneath with the knuckles.

CAKES

METHODS OF CAKE-MAKING

Depending on the quantities of sugar, fat and eggs, and the methods used, cakes are classified as rich, plain and sponge.

Rich cakes contain equal quantities of fat and sugar and are made by the creaming method, when the fat and sugar are creamed together. Victoria sandwich, Madeira, queen cakes and rich fruit cakes are made by this method.

Plain cakes contain up to half fat to flour and sugar, and are made by the rubbing-in method, when the fat is rubbed into the flour as for pastry. Light fruit cakes, rock buns and raspberry buns are made by this method.

Sponge cakes contain no fat but a high proportion of eggs and sugar, and are made by the whisking method, when the eggs and sugar are whisked together until thick and the flour is folded in. They must be eaten on the day they are made as they do not contain fat so do not store well.

Gingerbreads are made by the melting method, when the treacle or syrup is heated in a saucepan, and then poured on to the dry ingredients.

INGREDIENTS

Flour

Self-raising flour is normally used for most cakes but plain flour is used for sponges and rich fruit cakes.

Fats

Butter has an excellent flavour so is ideal for cake making, but margarine is a good substitute. If using a hard margarine, allow it t stand at room temperature for 1–2 hours before using for creaming. Soft margarines car be used direct from the refrigerator and only require 1–2 minutes of beating with an electric mixer.

Sugar

Caster sugar is best to use for creaming and whisking. Granulated sugar can be used for plain cakes.

Raising agents

Self-raising flour contains its own raising agen Plain flour and baking powder or plain flour and a combination of bicarbonate of soda and cream of tartar can be used instead.

CAKE TINS

Use good strong cake tins. Some tins have a loose bottom or a device for loosening the cake from the tin, which are useful.

Paper cases and aluminium foil cases: these may be used instead of tins. If you do not have the right size tin for a cake, you can shape your own using 4 layers of aluminium foil.

Preparation of tins

Brush the tins over with melted fat or oil. They may be dredged with flour as an additional precaution. Rich cake tins also require lining with oiled greaseproof paper or non-stick paper.

To line a deep tin

Cut a piece of greaseproof paper long enough to go round the inside of the tin, and 5 cm/2 inches higher than the edge. Cut two pieces to fit the bottom of the tin. Fold up the bottom edge of the long strip about 2.5 cm/1 inch, creasing it well and snip the folded piece at intervals with a pair of scissors: this enables the band of paper to fit a round, square or oblong base. Brush the paper with oil and place the base paper in position, then the side strip, and finally the second base paper over snipped edge of band.

BAKING CAKES

Preheat the oven prior to making cakes.

To test whether a cake is cooked

Small cakes should be well risen, golden brow and firm to touch. For large fruit cakes, insert hot skewer or knitting needle in the centre of the cake. It should come out perfectly clean. Any mixture sticking to it means the cake needs longer cooking.

For sponge cakes, press the centre of the cake lightly with a finger. The cake, if cooked, should be spongy and have no impression fror the finger mark.

Cooling

Allow cakes to cool slightly in their tins then turn out on to a cooling rack.

Storing

Store cakes in an air-tight lidded container. Large fruit cakes should be wrapped in aluminium foil before putting in a tin.

Never store cakes and biscuits in the same tin; the biscuits absorb moisture from the cake and lose their crispness.

BISCUITS

Biscuits are made by the same method as cake using varying proportions of ingredients, and are simply rolled and cut out before baking.

AKE-MAKING FAULTS

oblem	Why the cake failed			
	Rubbed in and creamed	*Scones*	*Melting method (e.g. gingerbread)*	*Whisked*
lose xture	Too much liquid Insufficient creaming of fat and sugar Over stirring of flour Curdling of creamed mixture	Insufficient raising agent Too heavy handling of dough Not enough liquid Oven too cool	Too high a proportion of treacle or syrup	Eggs and sugar not beaten enough Flour stirred in, instead of folded using a metal spoon
neven xture	Over-stirring or uneven mixing		Insufficient beating-in of raising agent	
ry and umbly xture	Baked for too long in too slow oven Too much raising agent		Insufficient liquid	
racking	Too hot an oven Too stiff a mixture Too small a tin Baked on too high a shelf in oven	Insufficient kneading or badly done Badly handled when transferred to baking sheet	Baked in too high a shelf in oven Too hot an oven	
ruit sinking	Damp fruit–fruit if washed must be dried in a low oven spread out on trays Sticky glacé cherries–wash off syrup and toss in flour Too soft a mixture – it must be quite stiff to hold flour Using self-raising flour instead of plain flour			
ake that inks	Too soft a mixture Too much sugar Too much raising agent Too cool an oven so centre of cake doesn't rise Too hot an oven when cake is removed before it is cooked Too short a cooking time		Too much raising agent	
ry fruit ake	Baking at too high a temperature Too stiff a mixture		Too much raising agent	
urnt fruit n outside	Too high a temperature Greaseproof paper should be placed over surface if browning too quickly			
Jnder-ooked on op, burned nderneath		Baking sheet too large for oven, no circulation of air. There needs to be a gap of 5 cm/2 inches between sides of shelf and baking sheet		

INDEX

A

B

C

D

E

T

V

W

Y

ACKNOWLEDGEMENTS

Photography: Gina Harris

Photographic styling:
Carolyn Russell
Endpaper photography:
Robert Golden

The publishers would like to thank the following companies for their help in sponsoring photography: **British Poultry Meat Association** representing Britain's chicken producers; **New Zealand Lamb Information Bureau; Record Foods** (pasta); **White Fish Authority**

The publishers would like to thank the following companies for the loan of accessories for photography:
p.19, 67 **Craftsmens Potter,** Marshall St., London W.1.
p.39 **The Copper Shop**, Neal St., London W.C.2.
p.118, 119, 126, 144, 148, 149, 150, 151 **David Mellor**, Sloane Square, S.W.1.
p. 163, 164, 165, 170–1, 174–7, 182, 184–5 **Pyrex Ltd.**